IMAGES
of America

BURLINGTON

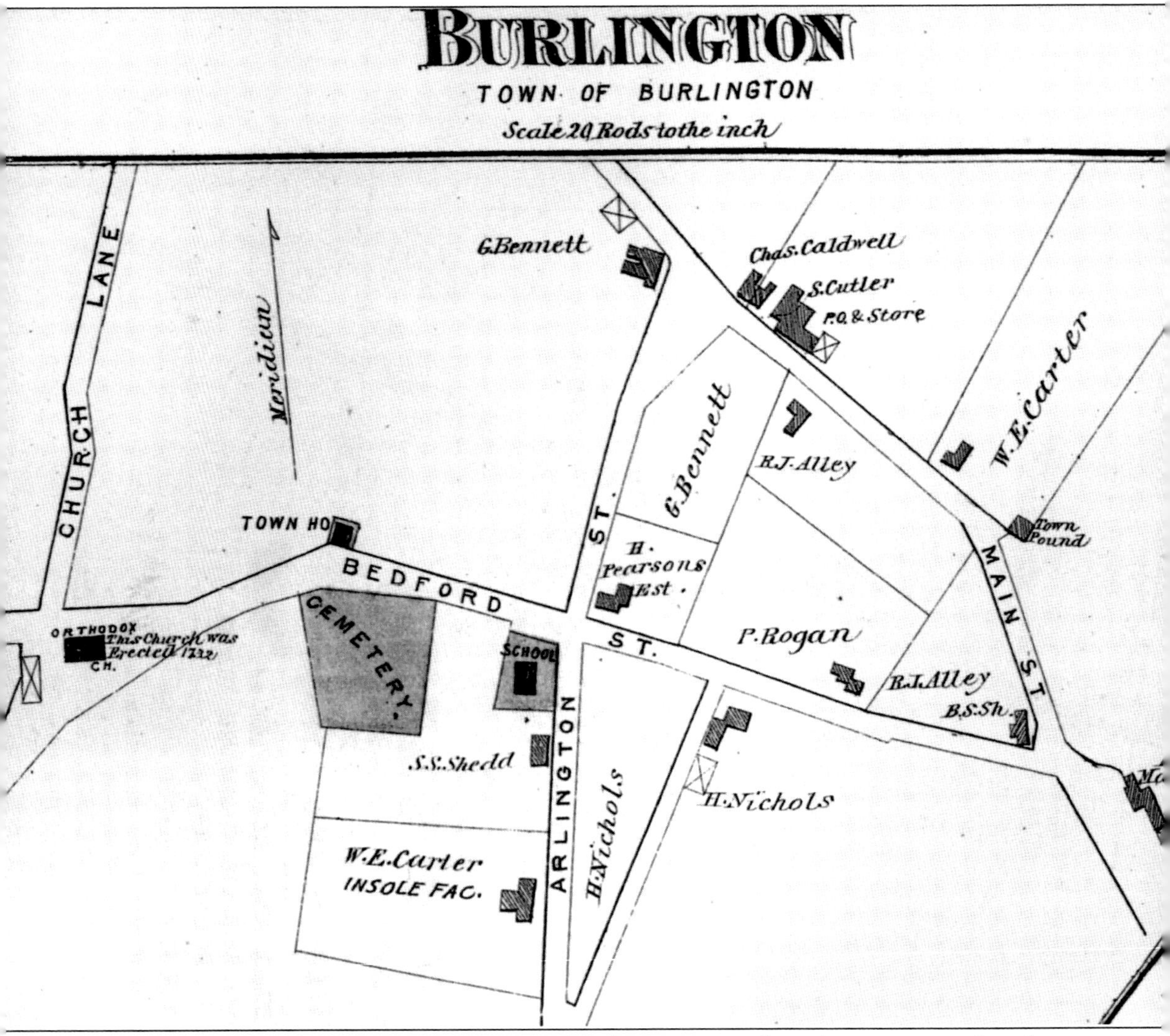

This map of Burlington's common in 1875 shows private lots, businesses, and a thriving Massachusetts farm community. The source is *County Atlas of Middlesex*, published by J.B. Beers and Company of New York in 1875. The large-format book was compiled from annual surveys. (Courtesy of R.J. Costa.)

IMAGES
of America

BURLINGTON

Robert J. Costa

ARCADIA
PUBLISHING

ISBN 978-0-7385-0902-0

Published by Arcadia Publishing
Charleston, South Carolina

Printed in the United States of America

Library of Congress Catalog Card Number: 2001090993

For all general information contact Arcadia Publishing at:
Telephone 843-853-2070
Fax 843-853-0044
E-mail sales@arcadiapublishing.com
For customer service and orders:
Toll-Free 1-888-313-2665

Visit us on the Internet at www.arcadiapublishing.com

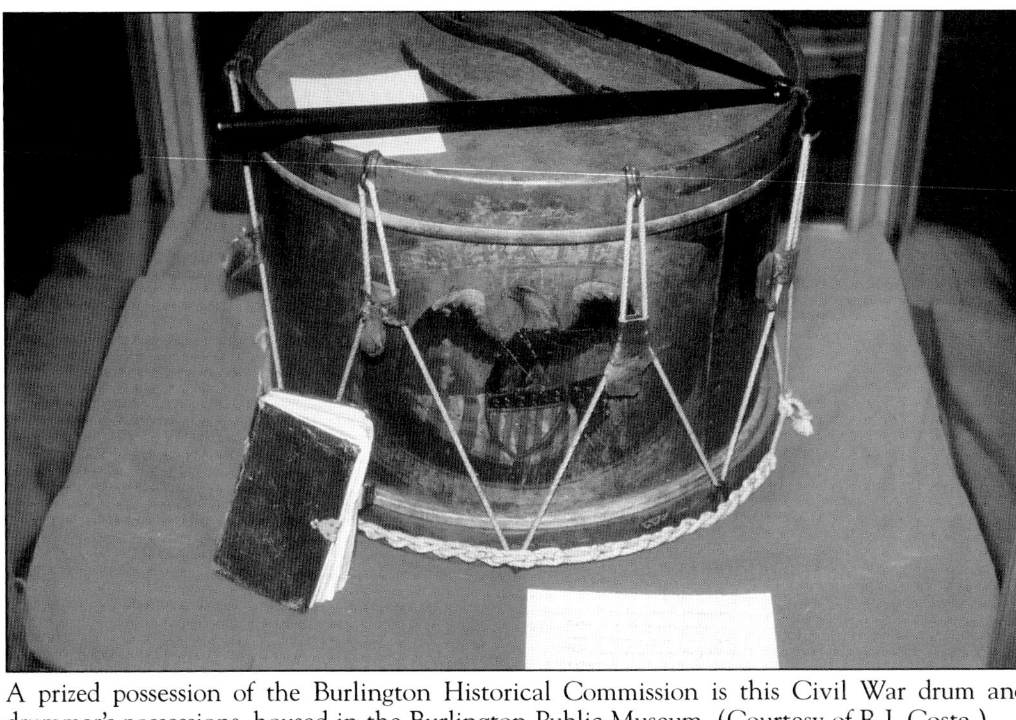

A prized possession of the Burlington Historical Commission is this Civil War drum and drummer's possessions, housed in the Burlington Public Museum. (Courtesy of R.J. Costa.)

Contents

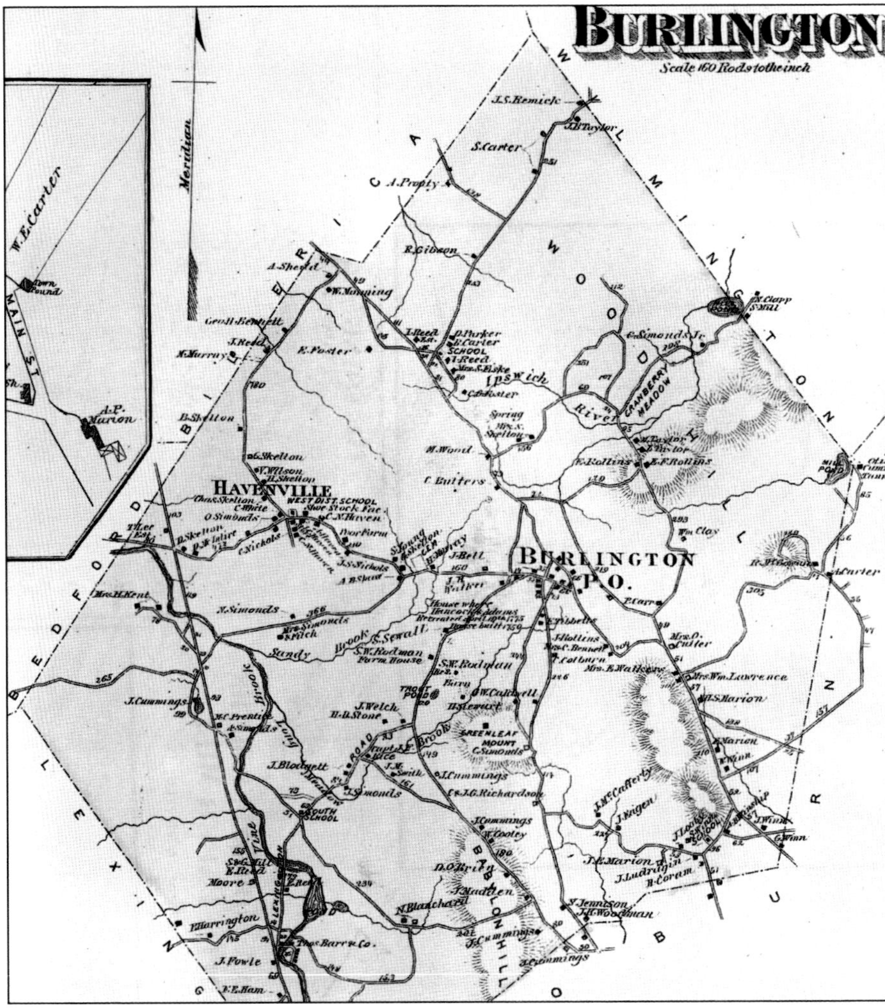

Acknowledgments

This book would not have been possible without the extensive collection of photographs acquired and preserved by longtime town historian John "Ed" Fogelberg. The collection is now housed in the Burlington Town Archives, carefully and expertly administered by town archivist Lisa Plato, whose assistance has been invaluable in the creation of this work. Thanks also go to the Burlington Historical Commission for the use of its collection and its support of this project. The text was created using, in part, research done by Lisa Plato and John Goff in his 1998 publication *The Historic Preservation Survey of Burlington*. Local historian Lotta Rice Dunham's 1951 *History of Burlington*, edited by current resident Rob Zahora, was also a helpful guide. I would also like to thank my children, Kristen and Lauren, and my wife, Jan, for their support throughout this project.

Images from the Burlington Archives consist of photographs taken from the Burlington Historical Commission Collection, the Fogelberg Collection, and the Crawford Collection. Permission to reproduce or republish images must be provided by the institution noted in the credit line.

Introduction

The town of Burlington, incorporated on February 28, 1799, has a rich and varied history that reflects American history from its Colonial roots, to Revolutionary War days, to the nation's rich agricultural and architectural heritage.

In 1641, Increase Winn was born in a dwelling that stood on the site of the present-day John Winn house, located on the corner of Winn and Wyman Streets. The Winn family played notable roles in the town's and state's history through the early 20th century. Another early family of merit and distinction throughout three centuries is the Wyman family. In 1666–1667, brothers Francis and John Wyman established one of the earliest farms in this area. The Wymans and Winns both served their town in the opening events of the American Revolution and through the quest for incorporation.

During the first days of the American Revolution, residents of the Burlington area played host to a series of little-known but historically significant events. In 1775, Burlington was a distinct but not separate part of the town of Woburn. Considered the Second Precinct of Woburn from 1730 to 1799, Burlington was incorporated as a town on February 28, 1799. On April 18 and 19, 1775, John Hancock and Samuel Adams made two visits to the Second Precinct while on their way from the Provincial Congress. On April 19, 1775, local legend holds that Sylvanus Wood, a farmer and militiaman of the Second Precinct of Woburn, held British soldiers captive on the farm of local minuteman Capt. James Reed. It has also been documented that Dea. Samuel Walker hid the valuable contents of the Harvard College library in the squash house on the family farm.

In the 19th century, Burlington was known for its agricultural excellence, developing large farms, including the Walker, Wyman, Skelton, McIntire, and Reed farms. The Reed Ham Works established a wide market for its specialty (smoked hams), and Grand View Farm was a thriving dairy business by *c.* 1900. Burlington was known for its expansive and festive agricultural fairs held yearly on Burlington's town common, celebrating the town's major contributions to agricultural excellence. Through the generous gift of Marshall Simonds, who died in 1905, Burlington received acres of land for use as a public park and funds for a new town hall and high school as Burlington entered its third century.

In 1999, the town celebrated its bicentennial with a yearlong series of activities and events that included the publication of *History of Burlington 1641–1950*, by Dunham and Zahora, and the republication of the town history book *Burlington: Part of a Greater Chronicle*, by Ed Fogelberg, with an afterword by Joan Miles. Through the work of the schools and townspeople, a commemorative photograph booklet was produced and many projects were created. The Burlington Historical Commission promoted a historic house architectural and historical study, which resulted in the publication of a historic house survey that sheds new light on old myths. After years of neglect and disinterest regarding local history and local historical landmarks, a new interest has emerged in the town that seeks to preserve and add to the historical record.

The photographic series that forms the basis of this book comes from the generous gift collection of longtime Burlington writer, educator, and historian Ed Fogelberg. In 2000, Fogelberg moved from Burlington to Arizona and donated his large collection of photographs and prints to the town. The collection is housed in the Burlington Archives room and represents a vivid portrait of daily life in this small agricultural town in eastern Massachusetts. There are photographs of distinctive houses that no longer stand, public buildings long lost, celebrations, and daily life. The Burlington Historical Commission has also received many donations from private individuals. All these images have contributed to a better understanding of the town's rich past.

One

Celebrations and Disasters

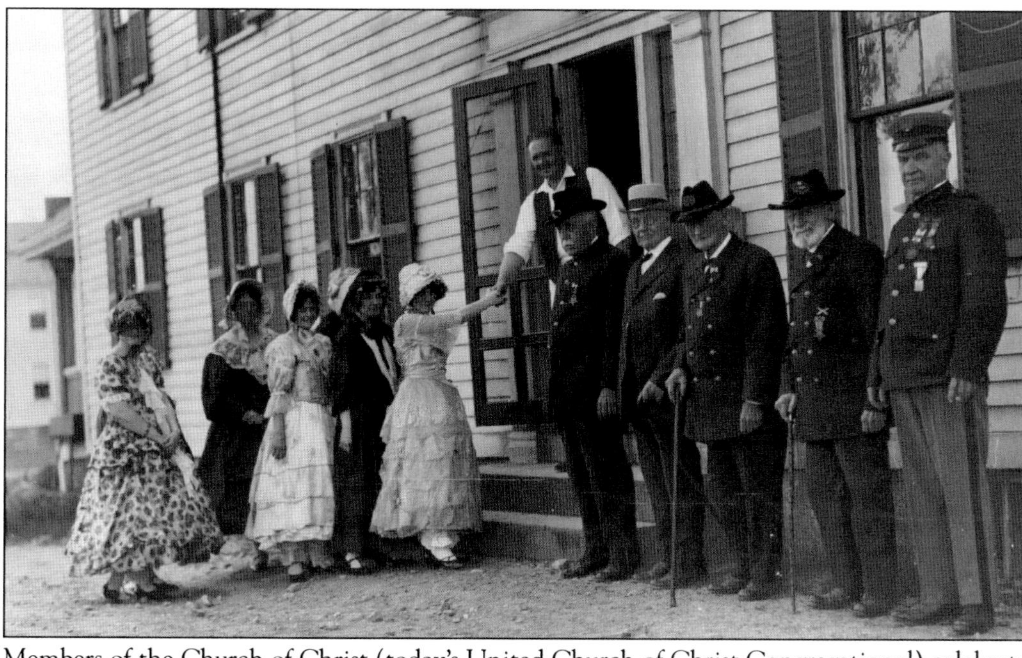

Members of the Church of Christ (today's United Church of Christ Congregational) celebrate the bicentennial of the "raising" of the Second Parish Meetinghouse. The photograph was taken in 1932 in front of the Marion Tavern. The women in the picture arrived by stagecoach. Shown, from left to right, are Mabel Keating, Mrs. Ralph MacDonald, Evelyn Foster Blake, Helen MacIntire Bussey (only bonnet showing), Lucy McCarthy Fiske, Alice Foster, Gove Sleeper (innkeeper), ? Wyler (GAR), Otis Simonds (son of Marshall Simonds), William F. Cook (GAR), Frank Smith (GAR), and ? Maloney. (Courtesy of the Burlington Archives, No. 34.)

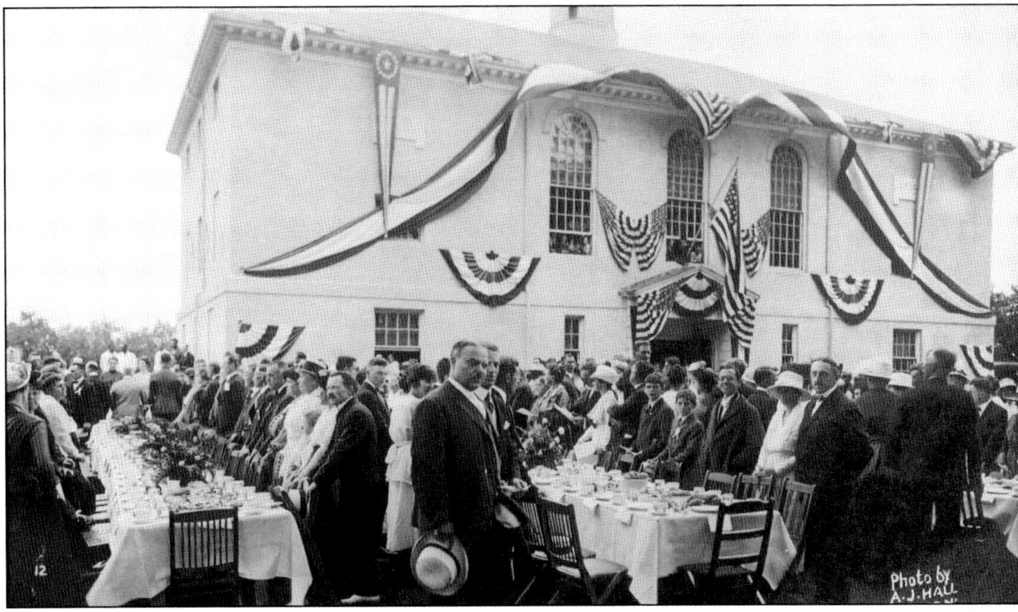

Townspeople pose at the banquet tables in front of the second town hall during the Welcome Home Jubilee on July 12, 1919. The jubilee was held to celebrate the return of Burlington troops from the battlefields of World War I. Aside from the townwide banquet, the day featured band concerts, athletic competitions, and patriotic speeches. Each veteran was awarded a bronze medal that was engraved with the town seal. (Courtesy of the Burlington Archives, No. 414.)

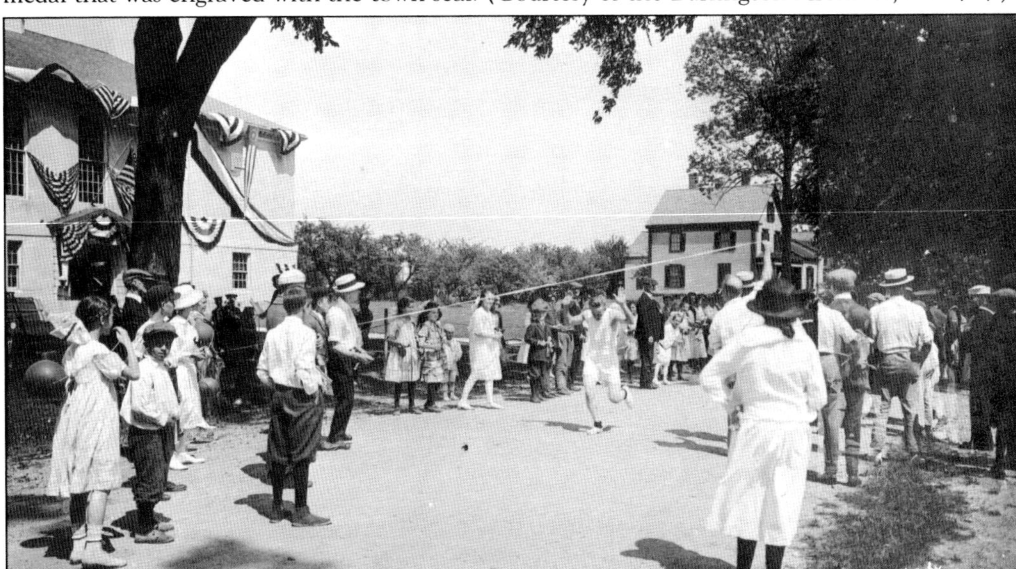

Gathered in front of Burlington's second town hall on Center Street, children and adults watch the conclusion of a road race during the Welcome Home Jubilee of 1919. Notice the house and orchards of the Blodgett farm, now the location of the Colonial Building at 35 Center Street. The house was built by Albert Wood sometime before 1851 and was once the home of William E. Carter, who ran a shoe heel factory on Cambridge Street. The second town hall was built in 1915. It was demolished in 1969 to make room for the new police station. (Courtesy of the Burlington Archives, No. 413.)

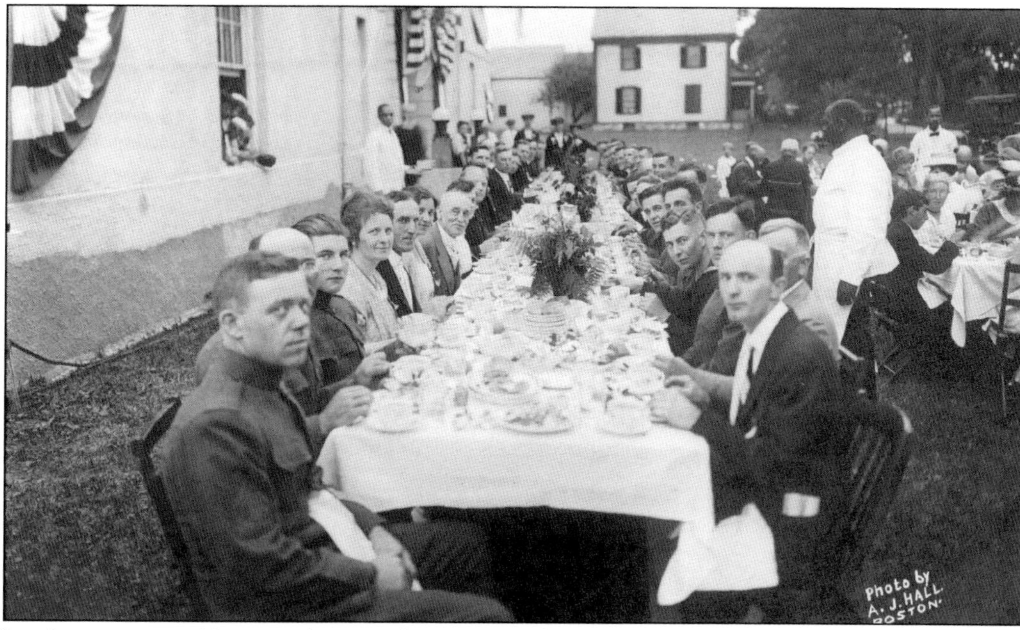

In this scene, soldiers, sailors, and townspeople pose at the head banquet table during the Welcome Home Jubilee, held in honor of Burlington's veterans of World War I. This photograph shows the stucco front and foundation of Burlington's second town hall, with the Blodgett house in the distance. (Courtesy of the Burlington Archives, No. 408.)

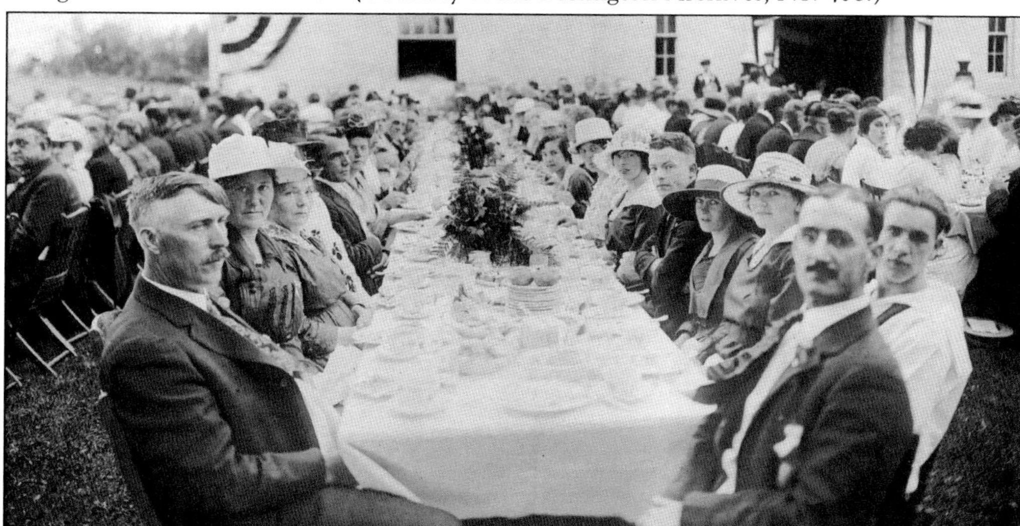

Based on information from the town archives, the man at the right in front is Samuel F. Sewall (1875–1937). Various members of the Sewall family played prominent roles in Massachusetts and Burlington history for over three centuries. From a family of ministers, politicians, and activists, Samuel F. Sewall was a great-grandson of Rev. Samuel Sewall and was a nephew of suffragette and local historian Martha Elizabeth Sewall Curtis. Sewall was a founding member of the Burlington Grange in 1915. This organization was noted for its community work. The Burlington Grange raised money for the needy and donated one-third the cost of Burlington's first fire truck as well as other charitable and civic work. (Courtesy of the Burlington Archives, No. 410.)

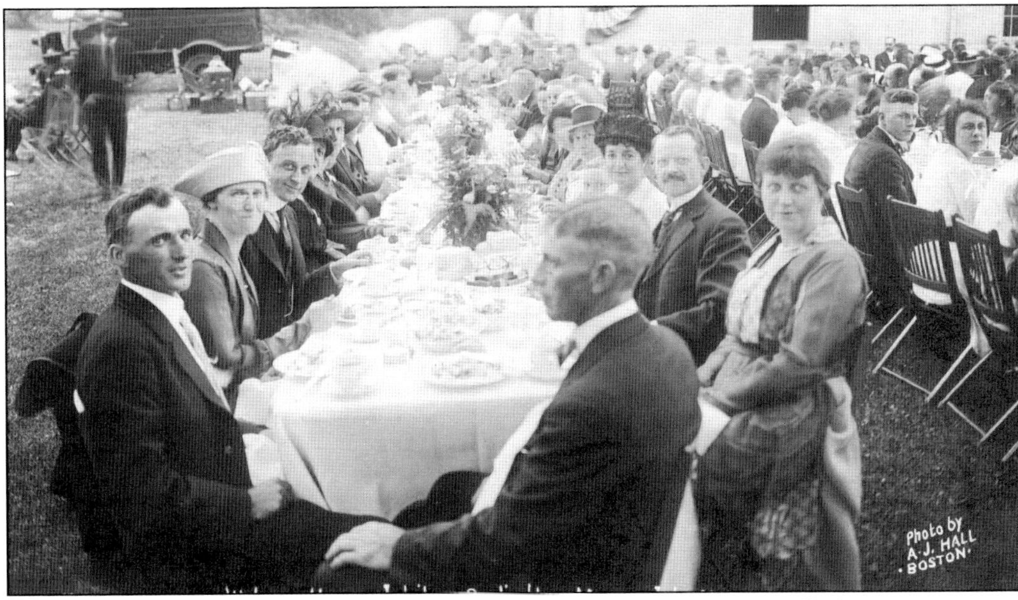

In this scene of the townwide celebration that welcomed Burlington's World War I veterans home, the man seated to the left in the front is Selwyn Harrison Graham. The Graham family has a long and distinguished history in the town of Burlington. Born in 1889, Selwyn Graham ran for the office of town clerk in 1912. He won the election and served for 22 years. His wife, Maud Smith Graham, was elected town clerk in 1935 and resigned due to illness in 1969. The Grahams occupied that office for 56 years. Selwyn Graham also served on the committee for Burlington's first high school as well as the board of assessors, school committee, and cemetery committee. (Courtesy of the Burlington Archives, No. 412.)

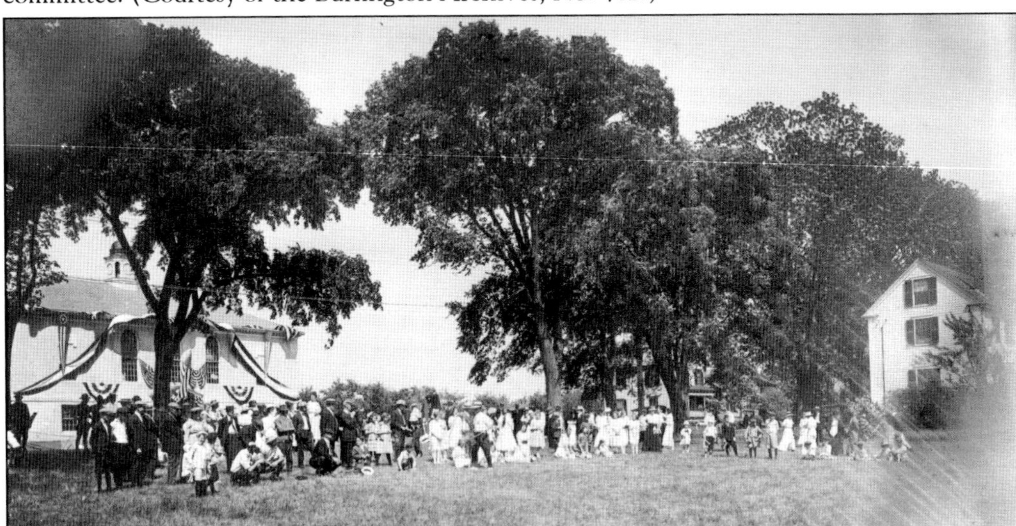

Children and adults watch activities on the town common during the Welcome Home Jubilee of 1919. Notice the stately elm trees that graced the common as well as many other areas of the town at the turn of the century. The second town hall is in the background, and the Blodgett house is visible behind the elms on the right. The house to the right of the trees is the Church of Christ parsonage. Many of the elm trees of Burlington were destroyed by the Hurricane of 1938. (Courtesy of the Burlington Archives, No. 401.)

The Burlington town seal was used as the central design in the Welcome Home Jubilee celebration booklet. It shows the seal surrounded by the U.S. coat of arms and the flags of various countries of the world. The Burlington town seal features the Sewall Mansion as the focal point, with important town dates around the inner and outer circles. In 1642, Burlington was part of the town of Woburn. In 1730, the northern portion of Woburn became a separate parish of Woburn. On February 28, 1799, the area became the town of Burlington. (Courtesy of the Burlington Archives, No. 416.)

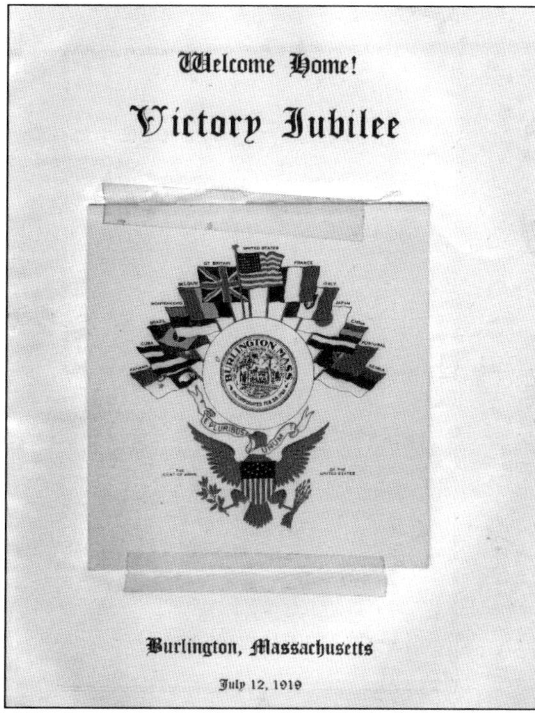

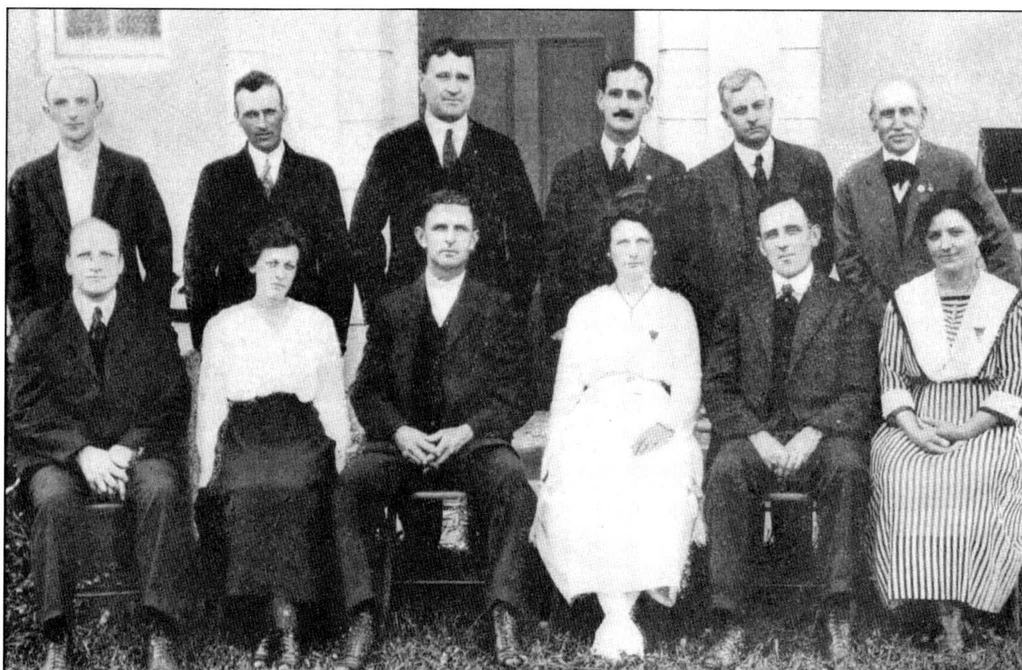

This image shows the Welcome Home Jubilee Committee. From left to right are the following: (front row) Rev. Richard T. Broeg, Mrs. Richard T. Broeg, Arthur W. Nichols, Mary F. Pollack, Joseph M. McDowell, and Mrs. Joseph M. McDowell; (back row) John F. Tessier, Selwyn H. Graham, Ira Decker, Samuel F. Sewall, Charles E. Giff, and John J. McDowell. (Courtesy of the Burlington Archives, No. 132.)

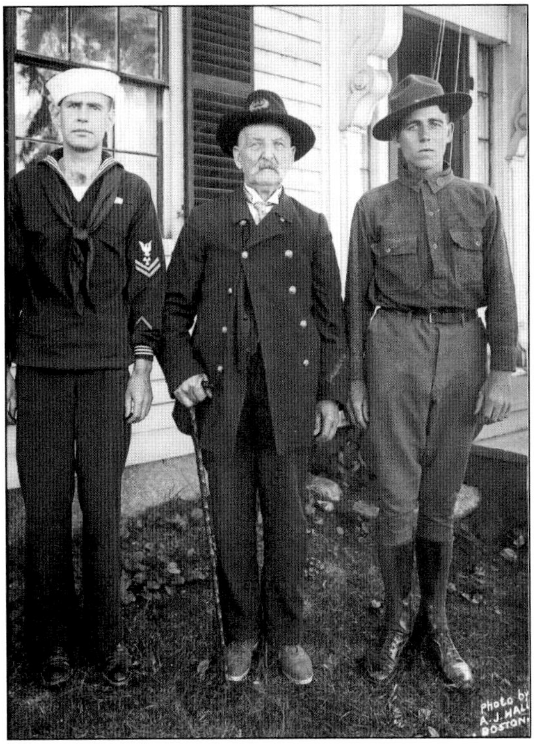

Veterans from two wars, the Civil War and World War I, pose in front of the Marion Tavern on July 12, 1919, during the Welcome Home Jubilee. The man in the center (unidentified) was the only surviving member of the Grand Army of the Republic (GAR) from the area. Eighty-five men from Burlington enlisted in the Civil War. Thirty Burlington men saw action on the battlefields of World War I. (Courtesy of the Burlington Archives, No. 504.)

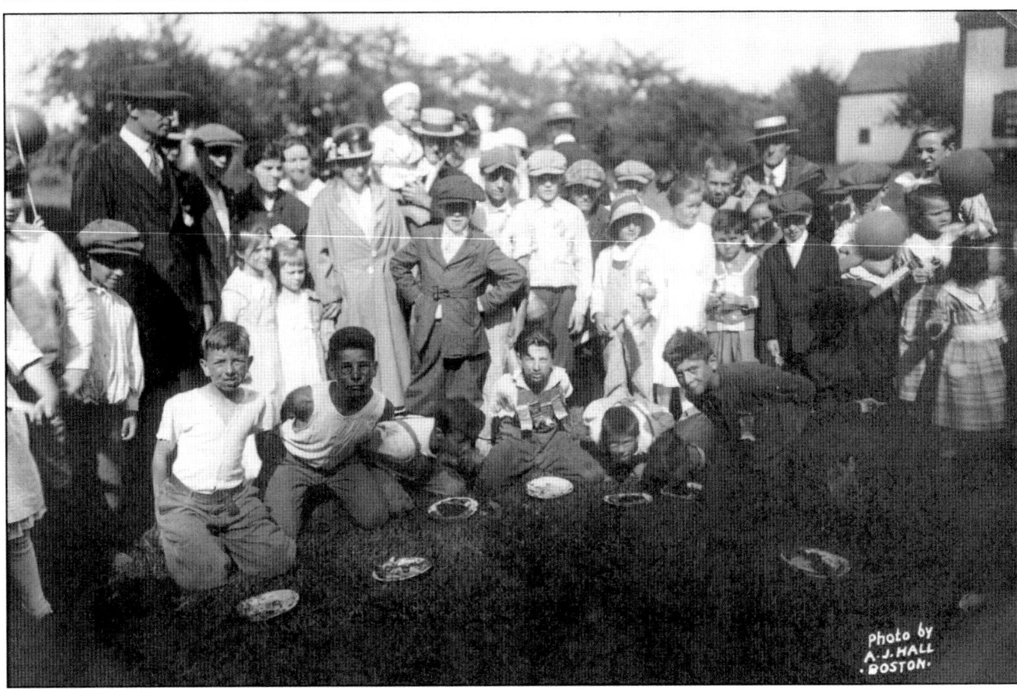

Young and old gather on the town common to enjoy the festivities during the jubilee that was held in honor of Burlington's servicemen upon their return from World War I. The contestants shown here seem to have enjoyed the competition, in this case a pie-eating contest. (Courtesy of the Burlington Archives, No. 32.)

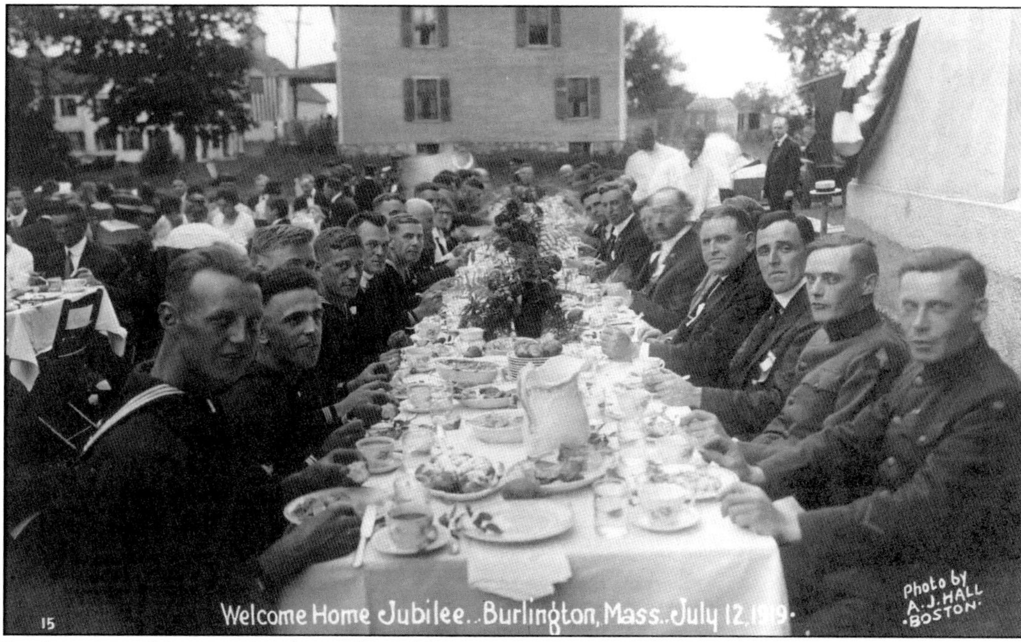

Burlington soldiers and sailors of World War I prepare to feast at a banquet held in their honor during the Welcome Home Jubilee. The head table was located in front of the second town hall and to the side of the Captain John Wood Tavern. The tavern, located where today's fire department is, played a key role in many local events before it was demolished in 1957. The Gleason-Bennett-Simonds house and barn is in the upper left corner of the photograph. (Courtesy of the Burlington Archives, No. 499.)

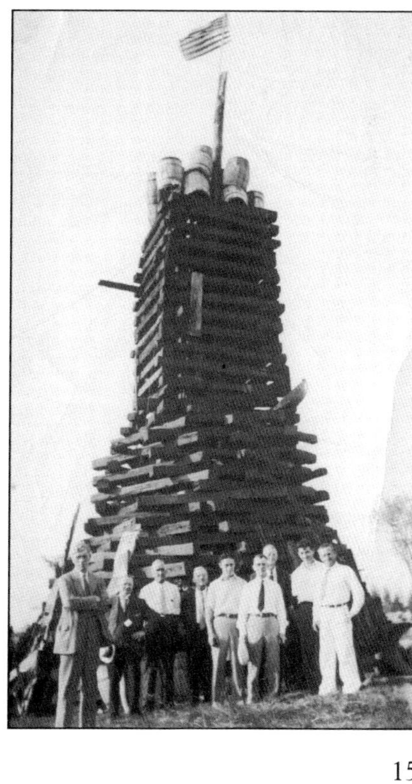

Members of the Burlington Men's Civic Club pose in front of a large bonfire structure on the top of the hill at Simonds Park. The 40- to 50-foot bonfires were sponsored by the civic club and held on the night before the Fourth of July. The Burlington Men's Civic Club was organized in 1937 to promote "civic betterment." The club supported the building of Burlington's first high school and sponsored the Fourth of July fireworks, a strawberry festival, and the Burlington Agricultural Fair. (Courtesy of the Burlington Archives, No. 30.)

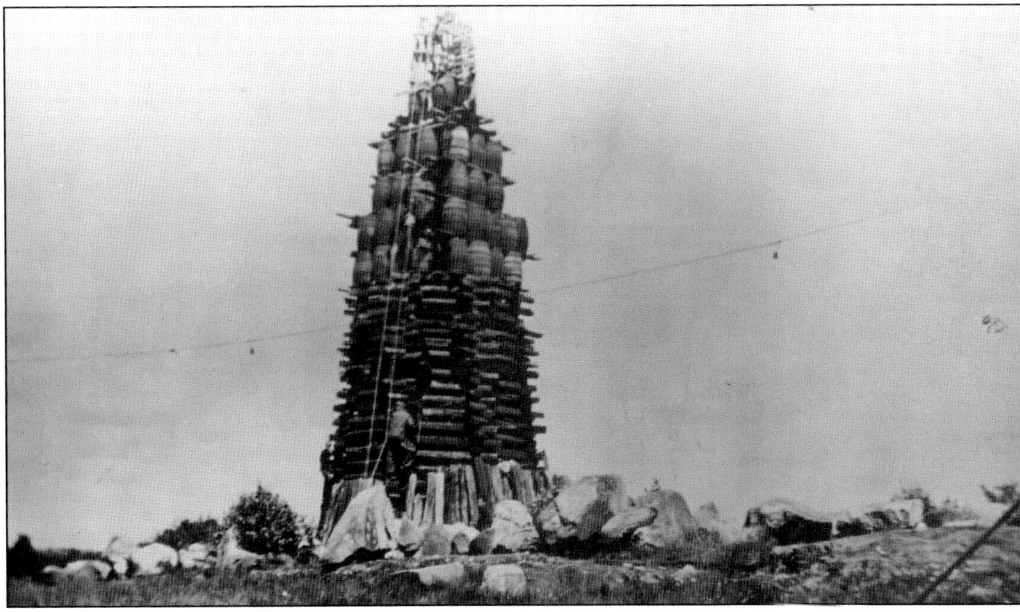

Final preparations for the Fourth of July bonfire take place on the top of the hill at Simonds Park sometime in the 1930s. Loren Blenkhorn was in charge of collecting materials, and Stewart Oldford was in charge of construction. Many Burlington citizens helped out, including the volunteer fire department. The last bonfire was held in 1940. (Courtesy of the Burlington Archives, No. 445.)

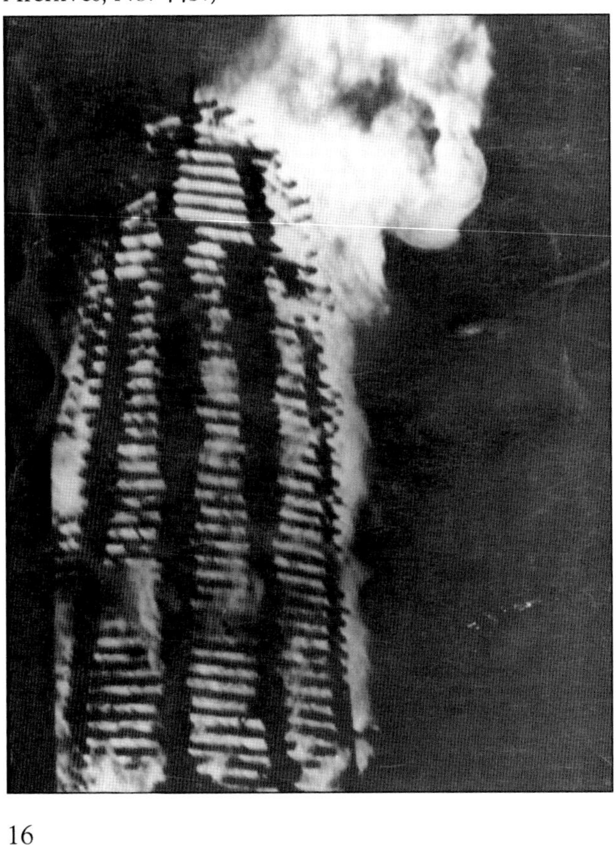

Shown is one of the 40- to 50-foot bonfires sponsored by the Burlington Men's Civic Club. Bonfires like this one and fireworks attracted about 10,000 people to the town. Town historian Ed Fogelberg recalled that one such blaze nearly caused a fire in the Second Parish Meetinghouse (today's United Church of Christ Congregational) when some of the large barrels atop the structure fell and rolled down the hill toward the church. By 1940, the bonfires became history. (Courtesy of the Burlington Archives, No. 446.)

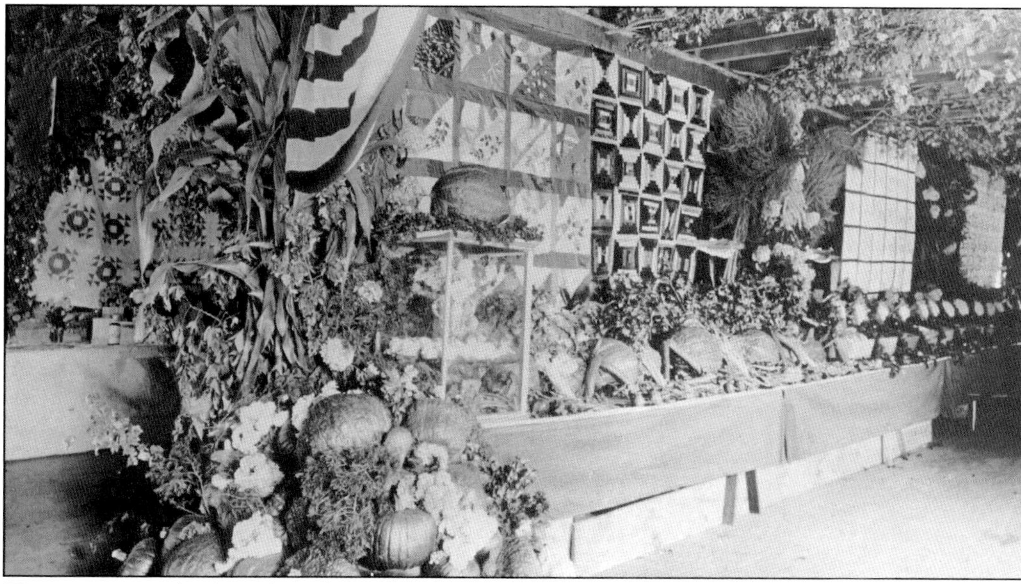

This attractive display of produce and needlework at the Burlington Agricultural Fair, *c.* 1900, rivals anything seen at the Topsfield Fair today and showcases the agricultural heritage of the town. As early as 1868, Burlington hosted a town fair that promoted excellence in agriculture. The Burlington Agricultural Society and later the Burlington Grange ran large, festive, well-attended fairs that attracted governors, mayors, congress members, as well as thousands of visitors. (Courtesy of the Burlington Archives, No. 31.)

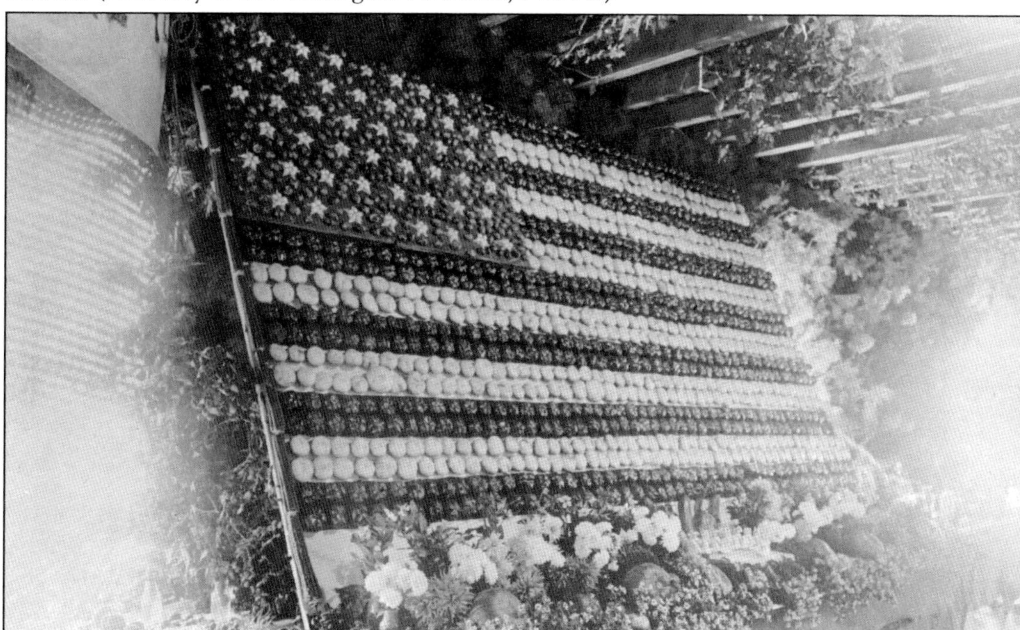

This patriotic display of produce and flowers, *c.* 1900, was one attractive feature of the annual Burlington Agricultural Fair. Held in and around the town hall and the town common area, the fair consisted of exhibits of domestic arts, vegetables, farm equipment, animals, flowers, and historical displays. Games, contests, speeches, and band concerts rounded out the program. (Courtesy of the Burlington Archives, No. 278.)

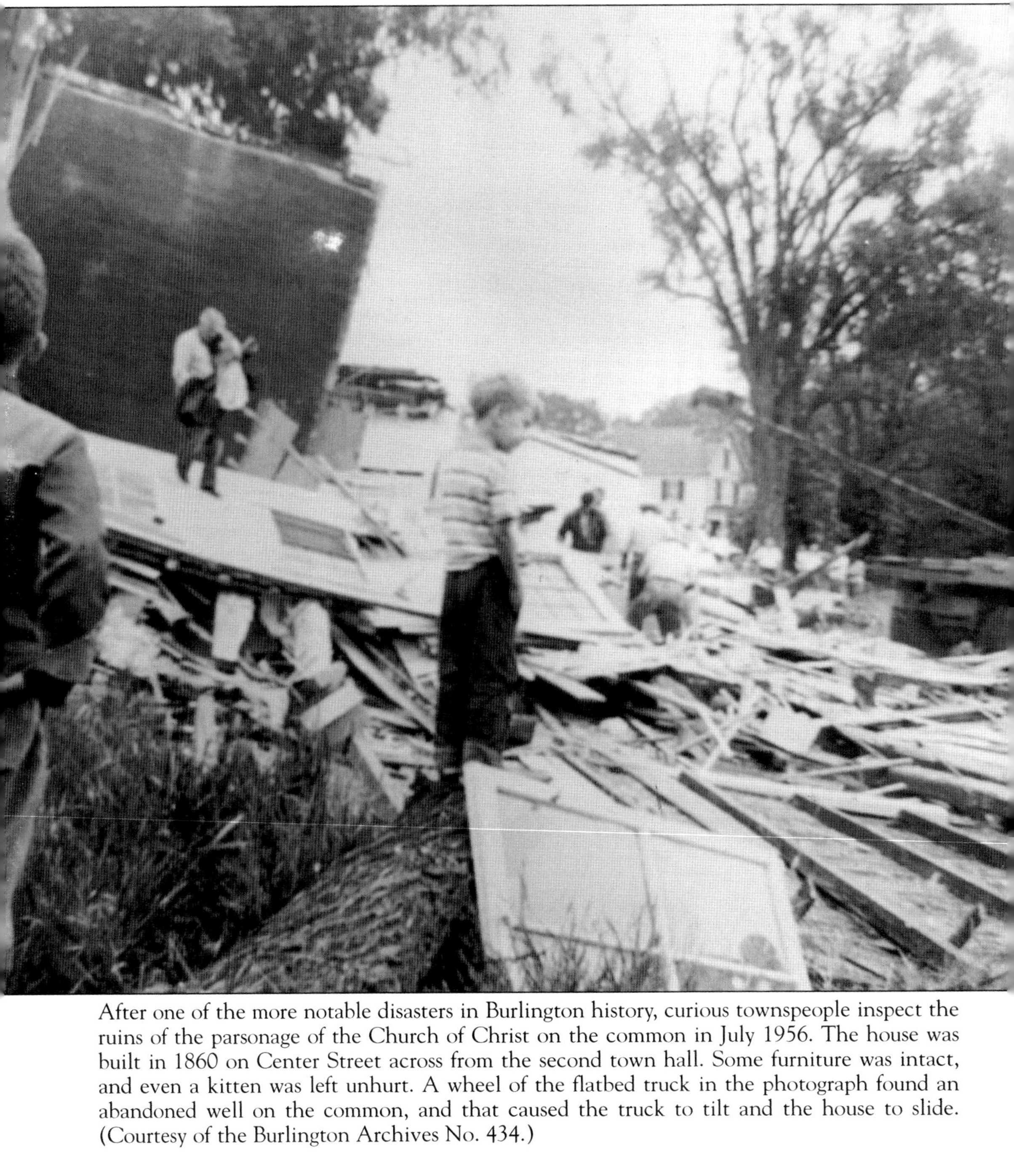

After one of the more notable disasters in Burlington history, curious townspeople inspect the ruins of the parsonage of the Church of Christ on the common in July 1956. The house was built in 1860 on Center Street across from the second town hall. Some furniture was intact, and even a kitten was left unhurt. A wheel of the flatbed truck in the photograph found an abandoned well on the common, and that caused the truck to tilt and the house to slide. (Courtesy of the Burlington Archives No. 434.)

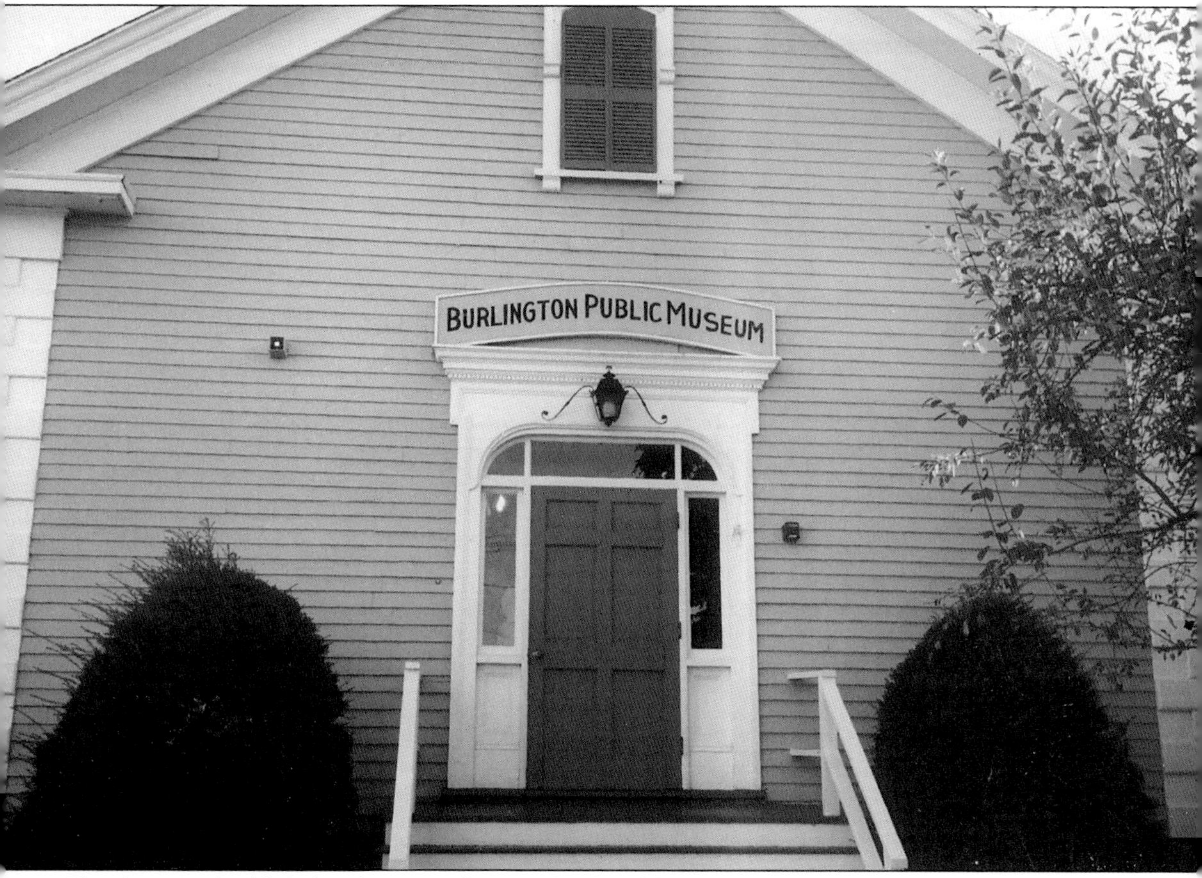

This historic building has been used as a school, a library, a police station, and currently as the Burlington Public Museum. It was built in 1855 and called the Center School. When the Union School opened in 1898, it became obsolete and was reborn as the town's library until c. 1967. For nine years, it was the home of the police station. It was nearly destroyed by fire on August 25, 1970, after local youths threw an explosive into the building in retaliation for police crackdowns on juveniles. (Courtesy of the Burlington Archives, No. 485).

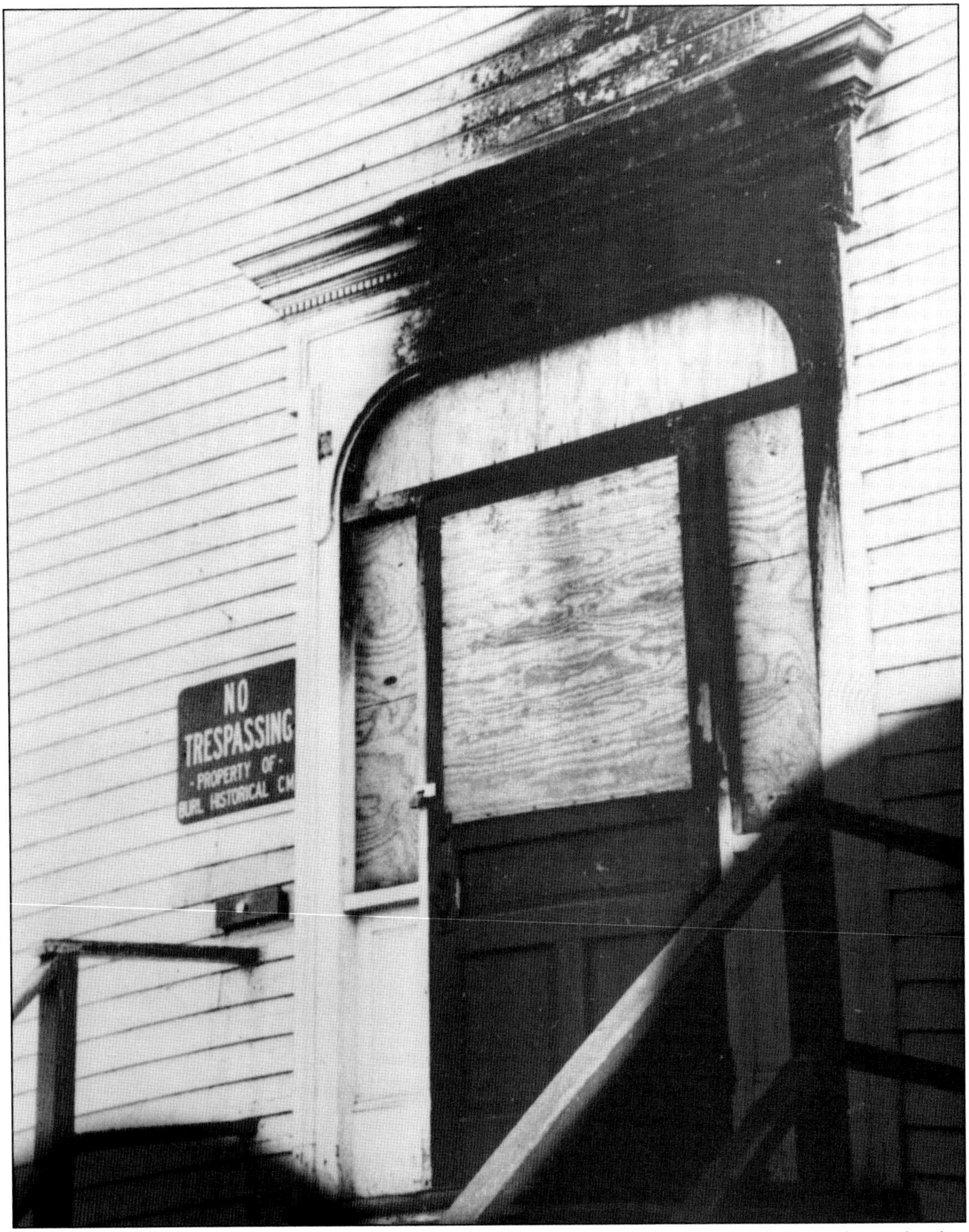

The police department had taken over the old library building on the corner of Cambridge and Bedford Streets as a temporary headquarters in 1967, while awaiting the construction of the new police station. Sometime shortly before midnight on August 25, 1970, a fire bomb was thrown through one of the windows facing the garage lot, and flames quickly spread through the front of the building. The blast destroyed much of the interior of the structure and disrupted all police communications. The building was renovated and now houses the Burlington Public Museum, which was dedicated on April 19, 1975. The crime was never solved. (Courtesy of the Burlington Archives, No. 482.)

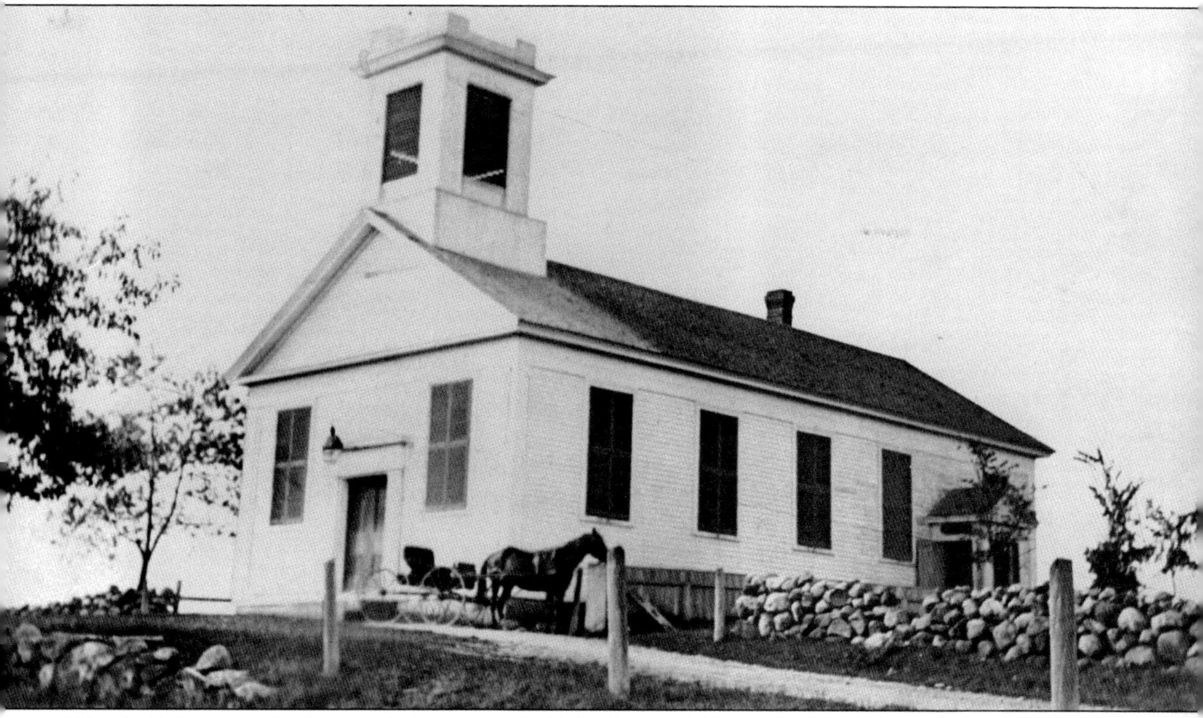

This building was Burlington's first town hall, built in 1844 on the land that is now occupied by the Simonds Park Little League field. The construction of the building was authorized by town meeting on December 18, 1843, and was enlarged and repaired in 1879. Many records of the town's early history were housed in this structure. The town house became the center of activity for political and townwide social events sometime after 1879. On the second floor was a large ballroom that was used for many dances and gatherings. In May 1902, the town house burned to the ground, and many historical items and records were lost. (Courtesy of the Burlington Archives, No. 28.)

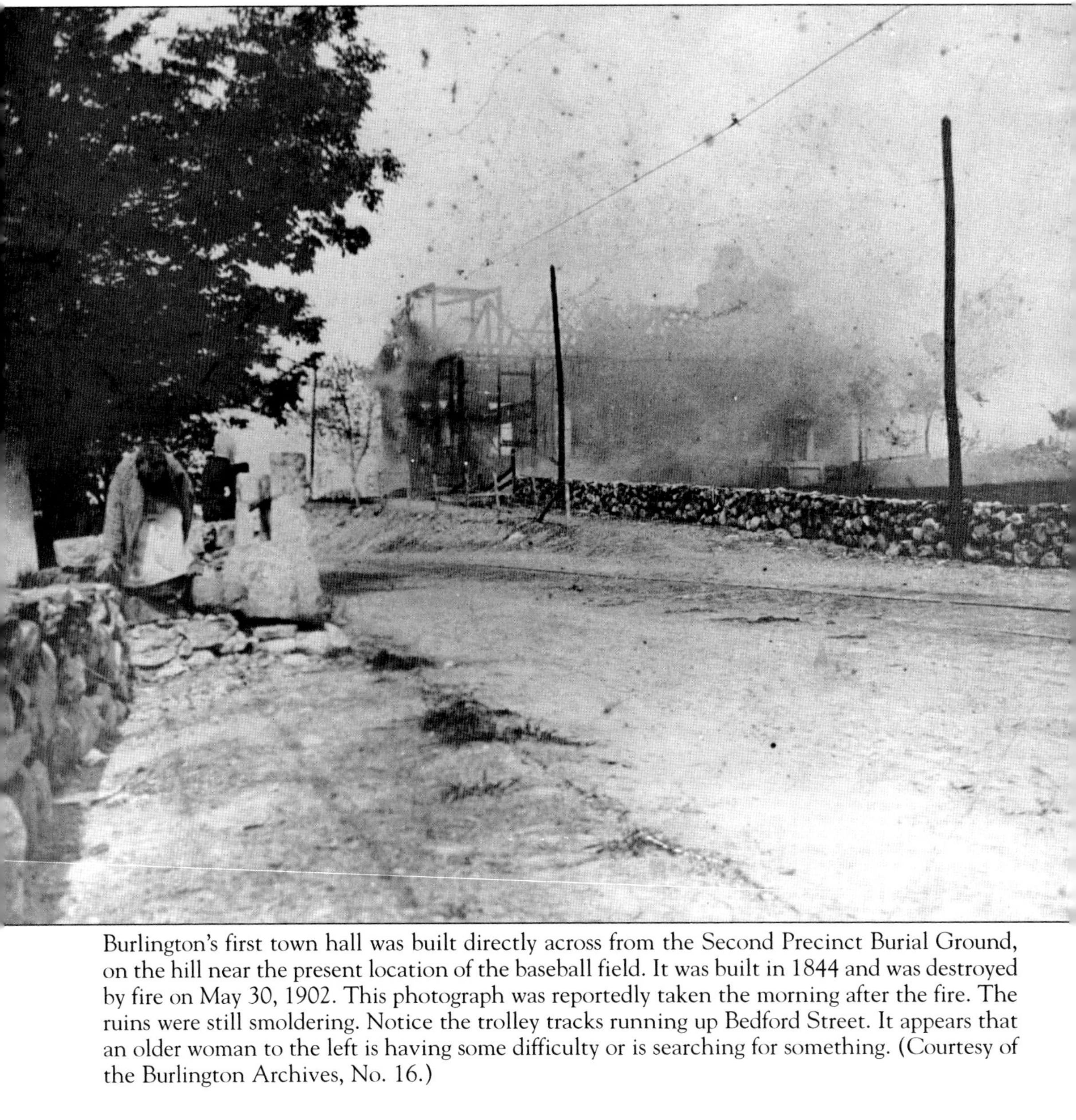

Burlington's first town hall was built directly across from the Second Precinct Burial Ground, on the hill near the present location of the baseball field. It was built in 1844 and was destroyed by fire on May 30, 1902. This photograph was reportedly taken the morning after the fire. The ruins were still smoldering. Notice the trolley tracks running up Bedford Street. It appears that an older woman to the left is having some difficulty or is searching for something. (Courtesy of the Burlington Archives, No. 16.)

Two

April 19, 1775: Revolution

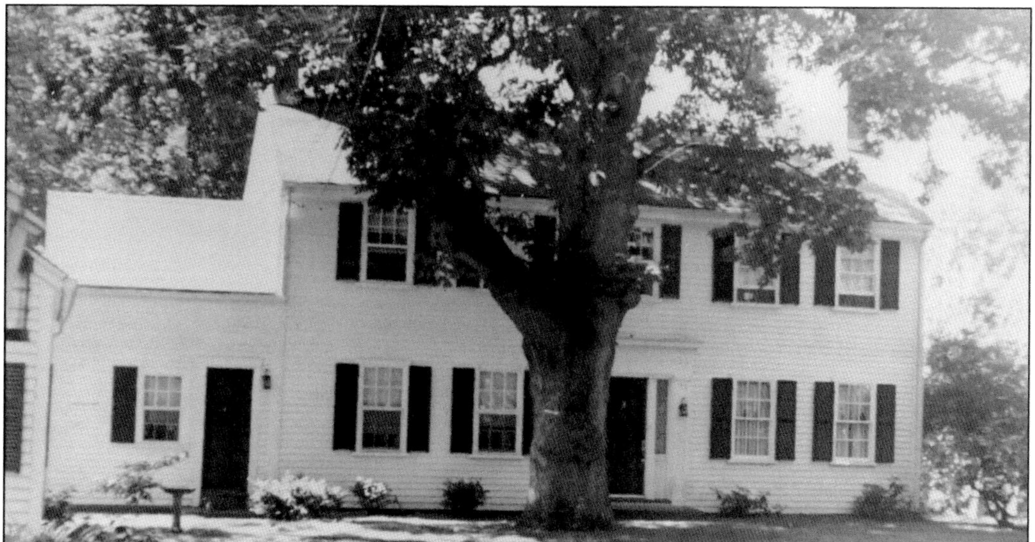

During the 18th century, this site was the location of a house built by Captain Burton, possibly a Revolutionary War patriot and merchant. Located off County Road, which was then a major pathway in the area, Captain Burton allegedly relied on smuggling restricted trade goods for a portion of his income. Years after Burton left the area, other owners of the house discovered a well-hidden room in the center of the house, possibly used to conceal illegal goods. Legend has it that the large oak tree in the center of the photograph was used as a meeting place for the Third Company of militiamen from Woburn's Second Parish (Burlington) on April 19, 1775, as they marched to Lexington and Concord. The present structure was built c. 1830 and is located at 3 Winona Road. The tree was twice struck by lightening—once in 1900 and again in the 1980s, when it was removed. (Courtesy of the Burlington Archives, No. 491.)

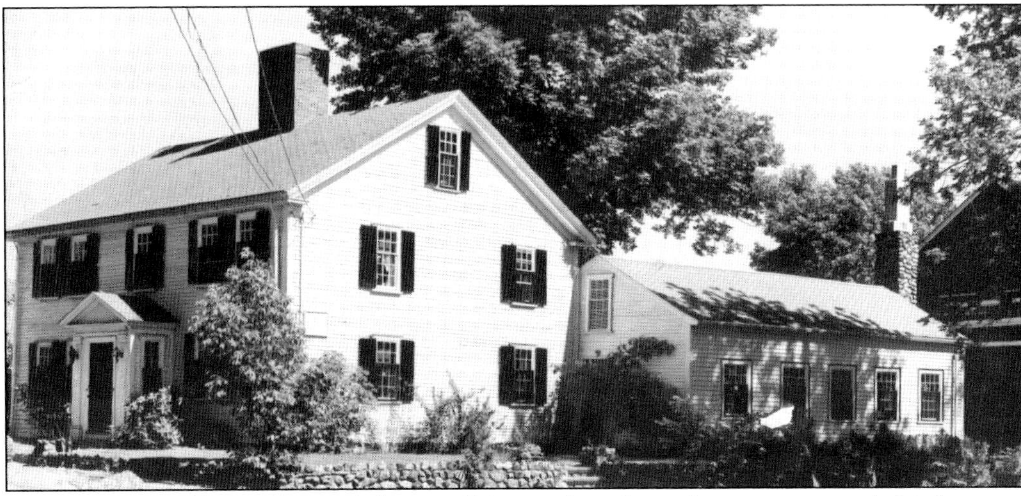

Capt. Joshua Walker—who, with his son John, is thought to have constructed this house at 9 Bedford Street—was the commander of the militia company from Woburn's Second Precinct during the American Revolution. Born in 1728, Walker was a veteran of the French and Indian War and led the Third Company of minutemen from Woburn's Second Precinct to Lexington and Concord on April 19, 1775. Although the company reached Lexington after the opening battle of the Revolution, the men saw action in the ambush of the British troops at the "Bloody Angle" in Lincoln and in later engagements of the American Revolution. (Courtesy of the Burlington Archive, No. 386.)

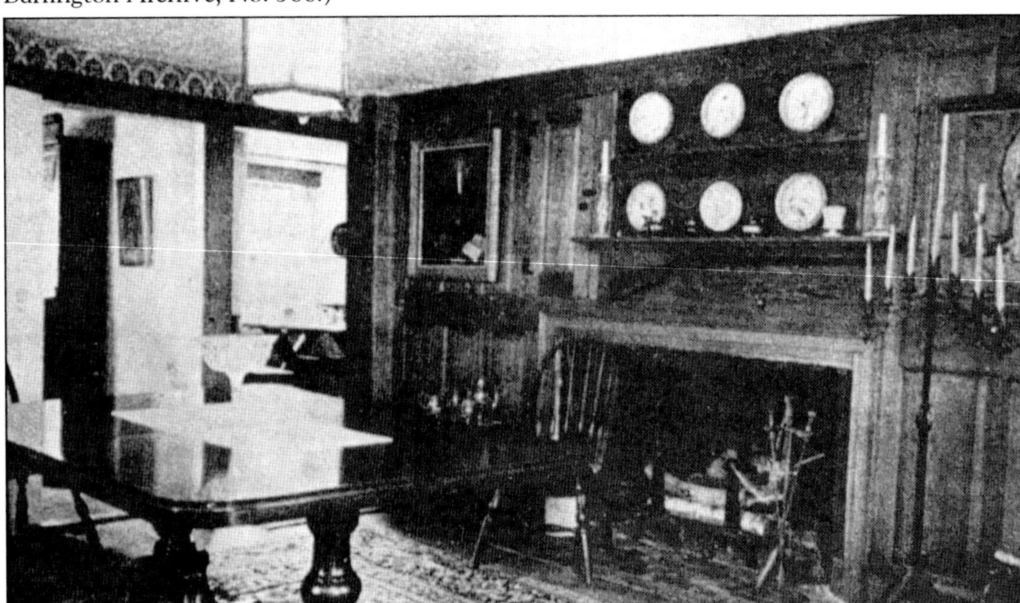

The Walker house is a Colonial-style structure with an attached barn and an outbuilding. The house was probably built between 1770 and 1780 by both John Walker and his father, Joshua. The Walker family played a notable role in Burlington history from 1642 to the incorporation of Burlington in 1799. In 1798, John Walker was appointed major general by President John Adams during an undeclared war with France. It was in this house that James Walker was born to Gen. John Walker and Lucy Johnson in 1793. James Walker was a noted educator, religious reformer, and Harvard College president (1853–1860). (Courtesy of the Burlington Archives.)

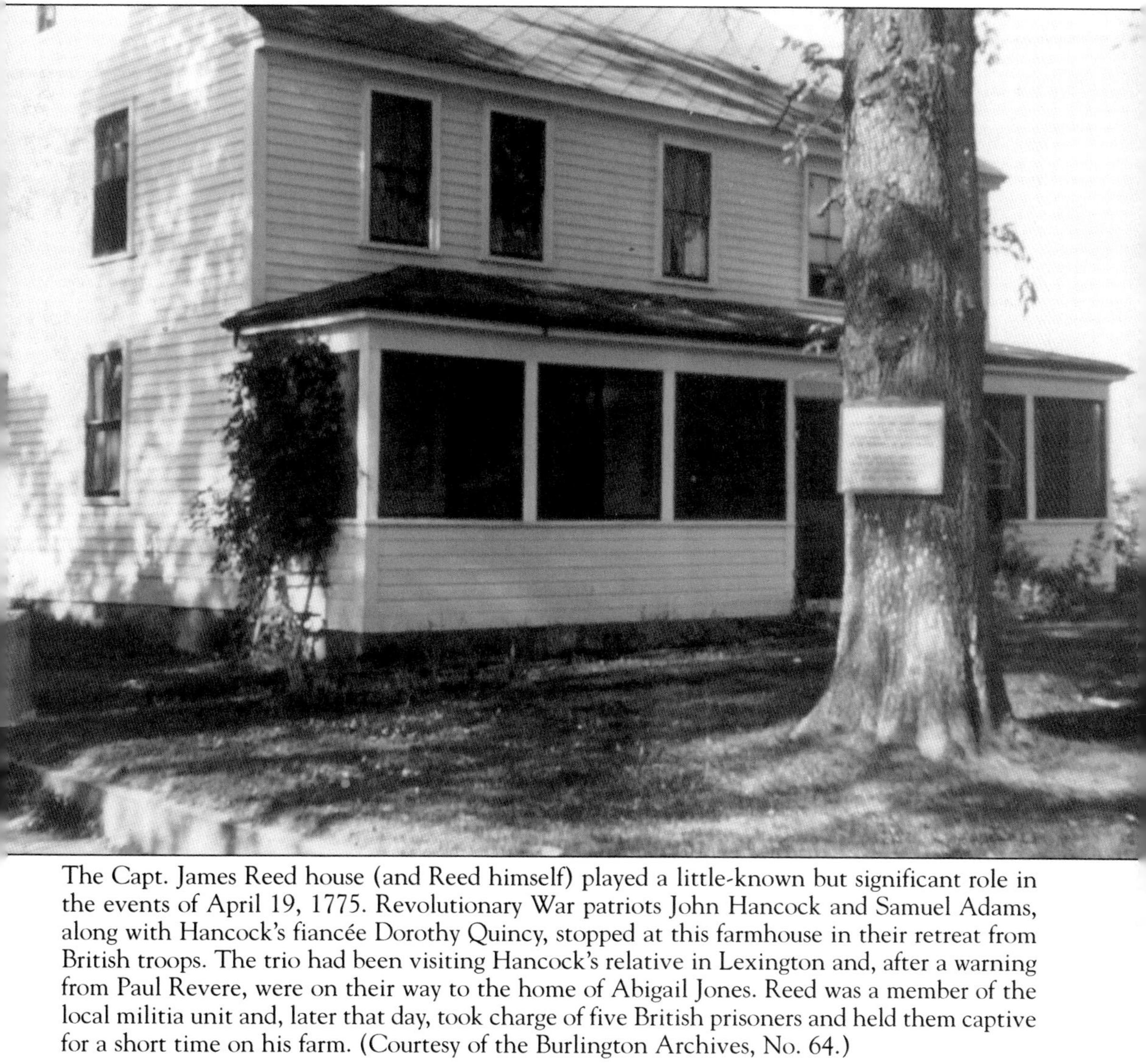

The Capt. James Reed house (and Reed himself) played a little-known but significant role in the events of April 19, 1775. Revolutionary War patriots John Hancock and Samuel Adams, along with Hancock's fiancée Dorothy Quincy, stopped at this farmhouse in their retreat from British troops. The trio had been visiting Hancock's relative in Lexington and, after a warning from Paul Revere, were on their way to the home of Abigail Jones. Reed was a member of the local militia unit and, later that day, took charge of five British prisoners and held them captive for a short time on his farm. (Courtesy of the Burlington Archives, No. 64.)

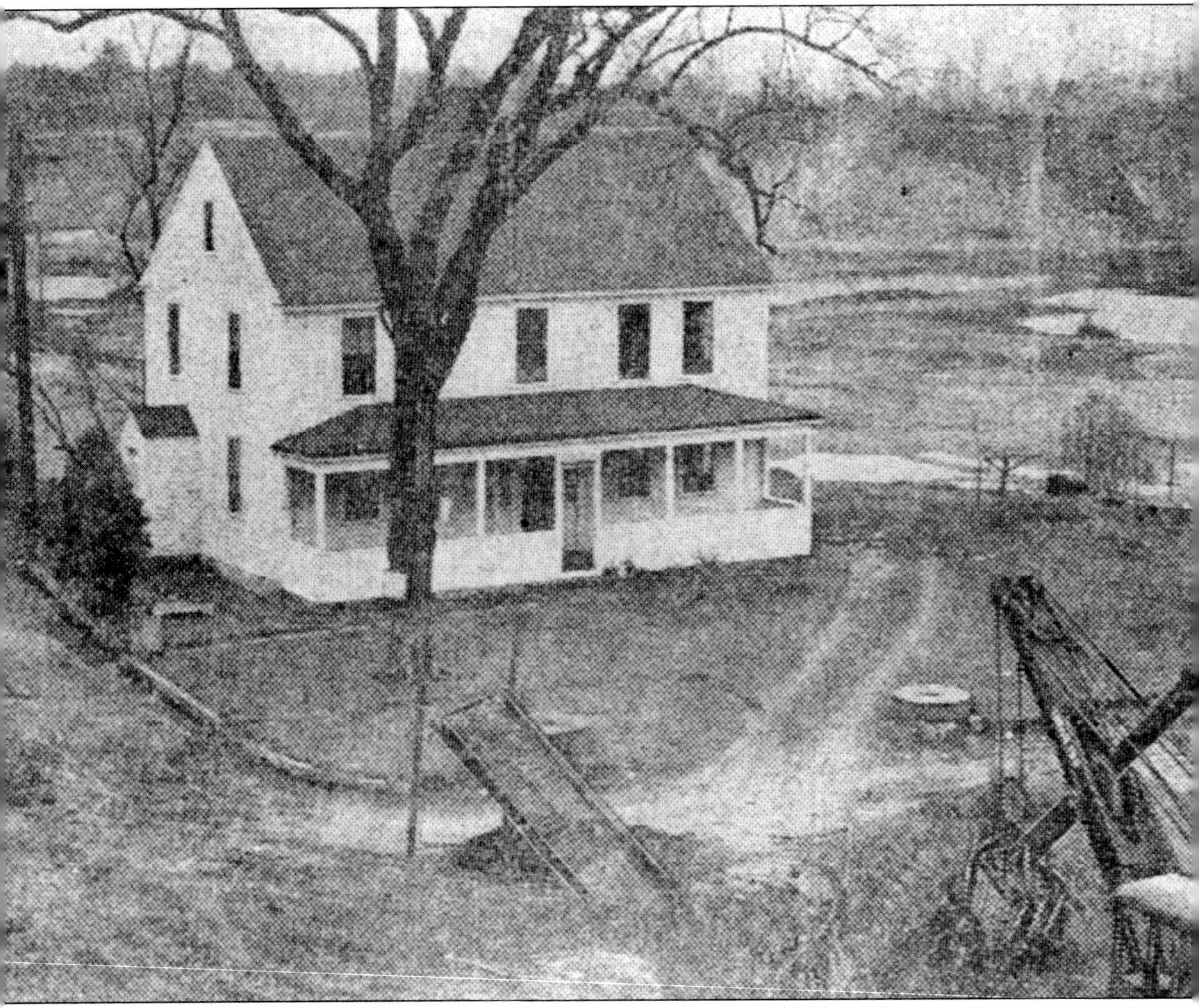

According to town archive sources, this house was built in 1740 by Swithin Reed, father of Capt. James Reed. It was located at the southern end of today's Lexington Street where the Burlington Mall parking lot is now located. The Reed family operated gristmills, sawmills, and cider mills during the 18th century using Vine Brook as a power source. This image shows the historic structure standing alone and neglected. Notice the large millstone directly in front of the earth-moving equipment. The house was moved to make way for Route 128 in the 1950s, fell into disrepair, and was destroyed by fire. (Courtesy of the Burlington Archives, No. 338.)

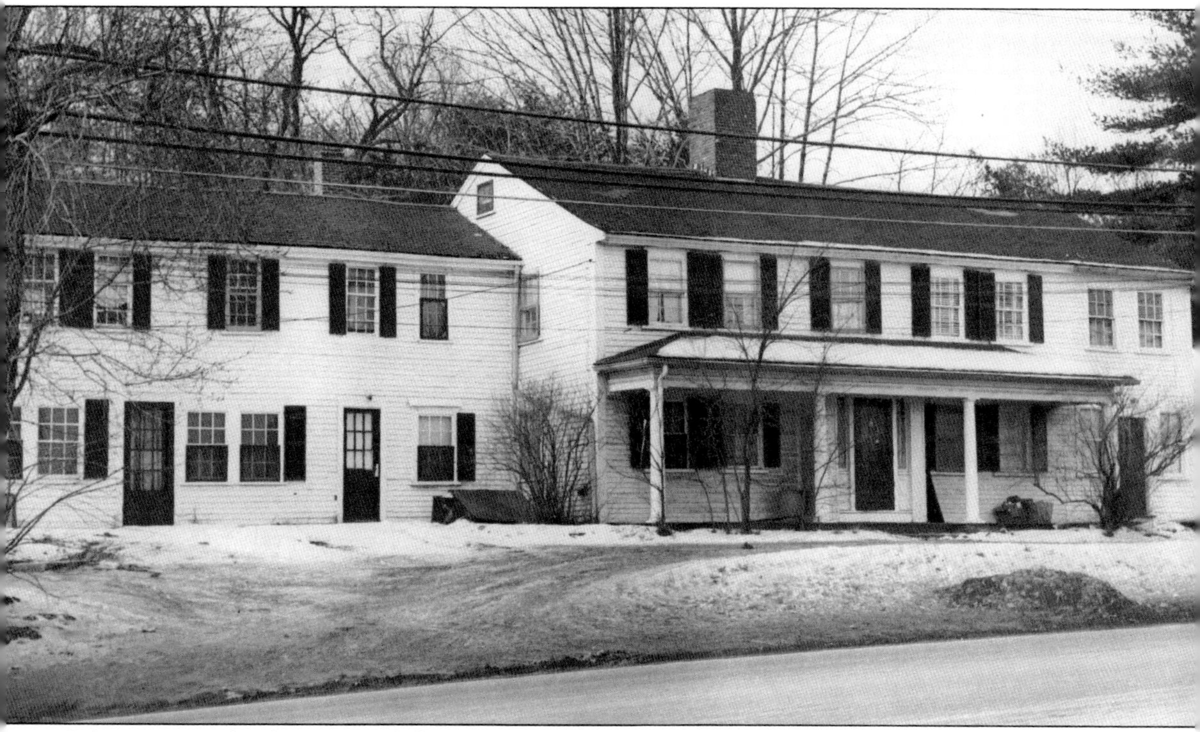

Sylvanus Wood, who acquired this property in 1810, was an eyewitness to the events on the Lexington battle green on April 19, 1775. Hearing the Lexington alarm bell ring shortly before dawn, he joined Capt. John Parker and the Lexington minutemen on the town green and witnessed the event that would lead to American freedom from the British. Later on that day, he is said to have captured one of the first prisoners of the conflict and was awarded a small pension by Congress for the rest of his life. The house in the photograph was located across from Dale's Pharmacy and was part of his farm. The house was destroyed by fire and was razed by the town in June 1985. (Courtesy of the Burlington Archives, No. 74.)

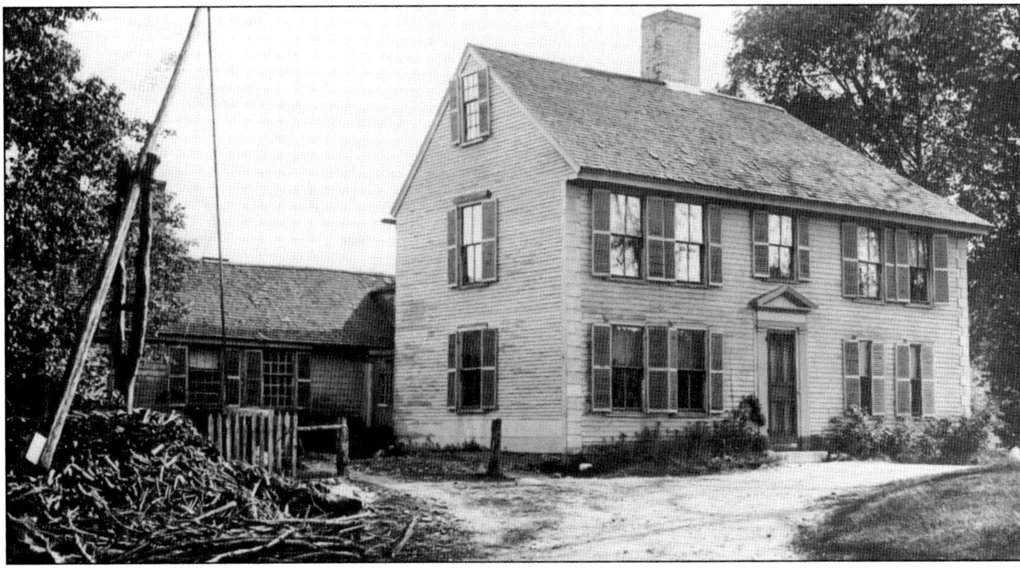

It was to this house that John Hancock and Samuel Adams stopped to visit and seek refuge from British soldiers on April 19, 1775. As the local legend goes, Hancock and Adams were about to dine on a large salmon, in the company of Abigail Jones and Rev. John Marrett, when a messenger warned the group of the British approach. Led by the minister and an African American slave, Cuff, the company was safely guided to the remote farmhouse of Amos Wyman. This view shows the left-hand side of the L-shaped mansion. (Courtesy of the Burlington Archives, No. 49.)

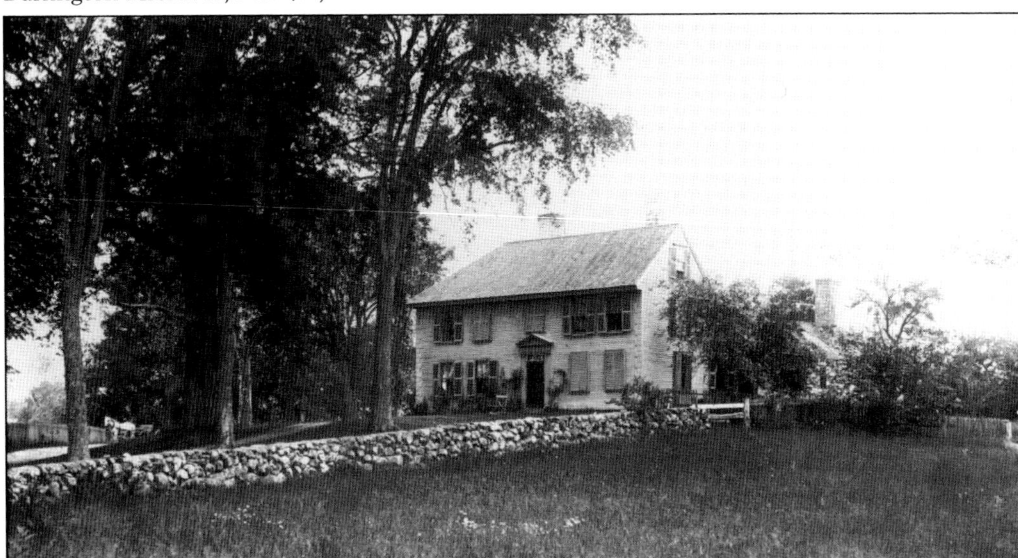

The Johnson-Jones-Sewall house (better known as the Sewall House) was built prior to 1733 by Benjamin Johnson, whose family donated land to the Second Parish of Woburn in order to erect a meetinghouse and to set aside land for a burial ground in 1769. The ownership of the house was passed to Rev. Thomas Jones in 1751 and to Rev. John Marrett by 1774. The 16-room, L-shaped mansion became the parsonage of the Second Parish congregation in 1751 and remained in use as a parsonage until 1844. This view of the historic structure was taken from Lexington Street. (Courtesy of the Society for the Preservation of New England Antiquities.)

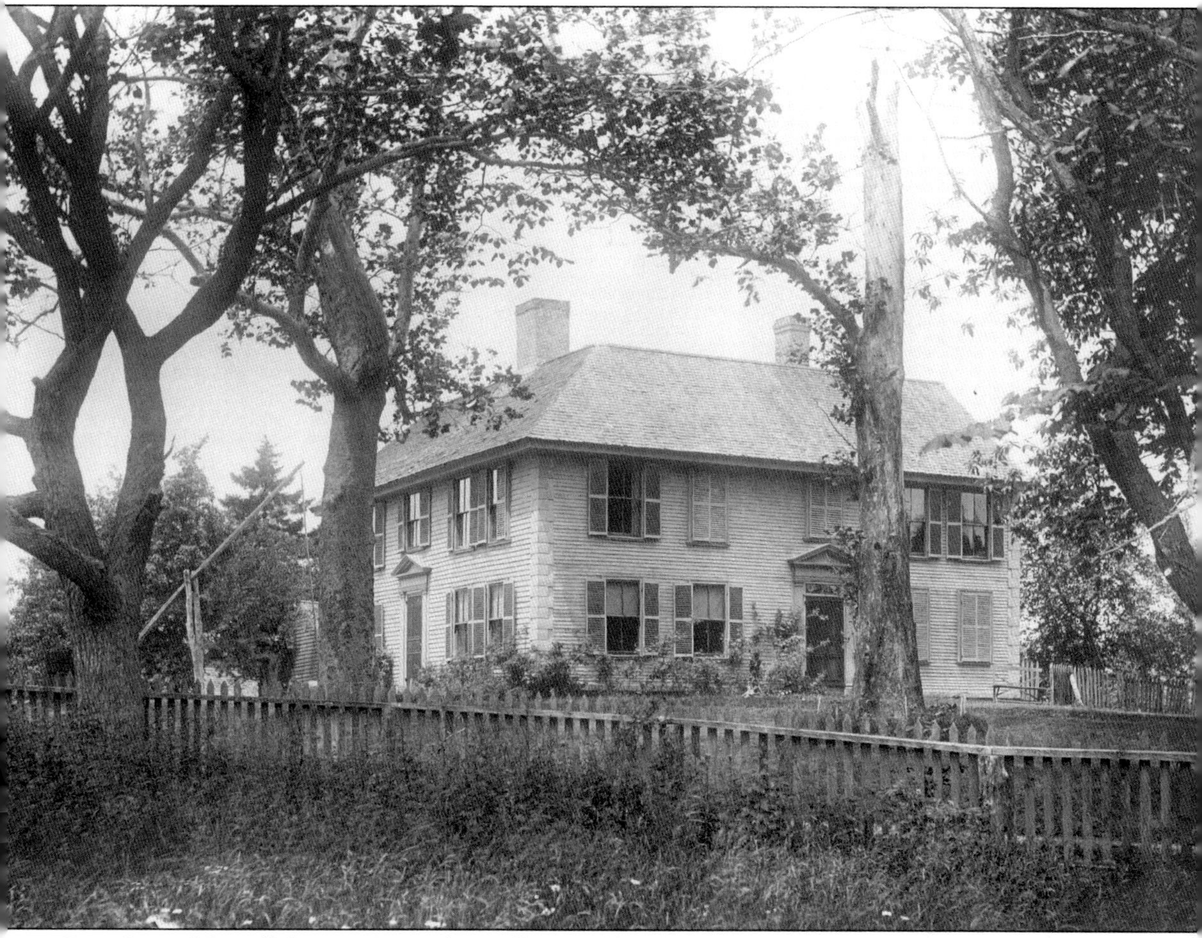

Rev. Samuel Sewall, his son Samuel Sewall Jr., and his daughter Martha Elizabeth Sewall Curtis all occupied the house at various times for most of the 19th century. All of the Sewalls shared a great love and interest in history and writing. The house became the repository for a great collection of documents and artifacts pertaining to the history of the area from the earliest settlement. On April 23, 1897, a tragic fire destroyed the 16-room landmark, and a great deal of knowledge of local history was lost. A second house was built on the site; it burned to the ground in 1916. The site can be found where a modern home stands now, on a knoll between Old Colony Road and Hancock Avenue on Lexington Street. The historical structure that bore witness to so many significant events was chosen as the central motif of Burlington's official seal. (Courtesy of the Society for the Preservation of New England Antiquities.)

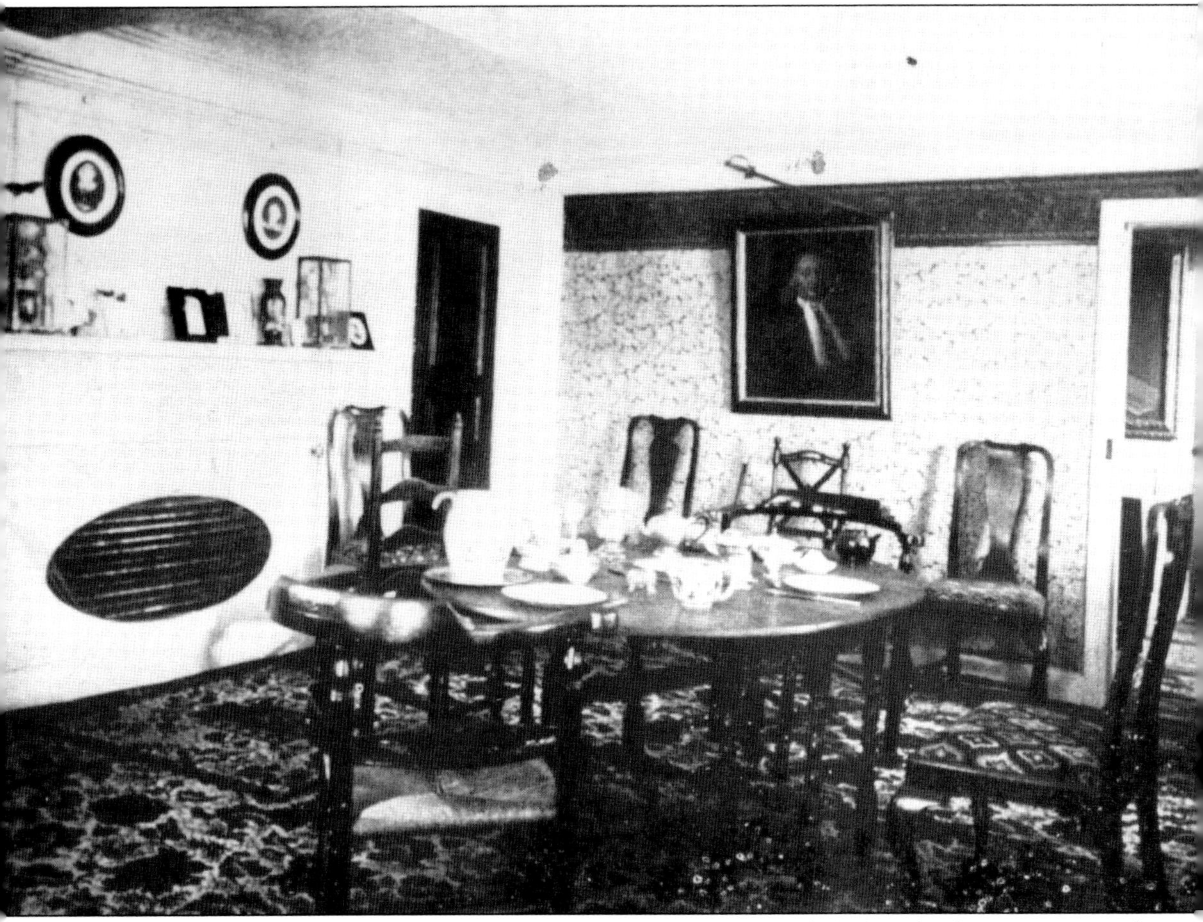

The "best room" of the Sewall House is shown in the years shortly before the fire. A portrait of Chief Justice Samuel Sewall of Salem witchcraft fame hangs on the wall. Rev. Samuel Sewall, who came to the Burlington church in 1814, was a direct descendant of the chief justice. Also pictured is the sword of Rev. John Marrett and the cane of Samuel Sewall. The table, chairs, and china are said to be the ones used when John Hancock and Samuel Adams visited on April 19, 1775, and were served the famous salmon meal. The house was built prior to 1733 by Benjamin Johnson and became the home of Samuel Sewall and his family throughout the 19th century. It was the home of Burlington clergy for more than 100 years. On April 23, 1897, a fire destroyed the historic mansion. (Courtesy of the Burlington Archives, No. 50.)

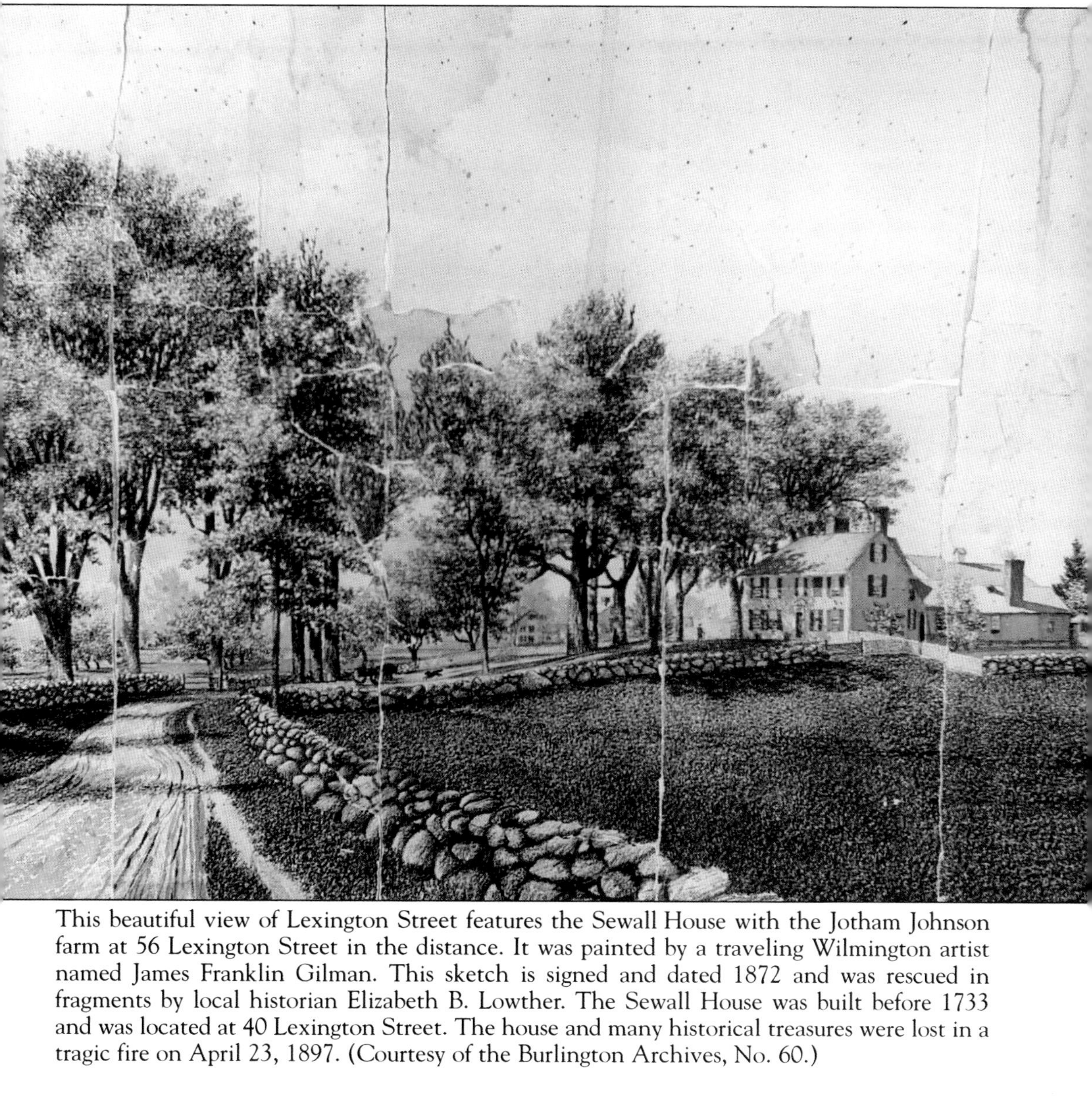

This beautiful view of Lexington Street features the Sewall House with the Jotham Johnson farm at 56 Lexington Street in the distance. It was painted by a traveling Wilmington artist named James Franklin Gilman. This sketch is signed and dated 1872 and was rescued in fragments by local historian Elizabeth B. Lowther. The Sewall House was built before 1733 and was located at 40 Lexington Street. The house and many historical treasures were lost in a tragic fire on April 23, 1897. (Courtesy of the Burlington Archives, No. 60.)

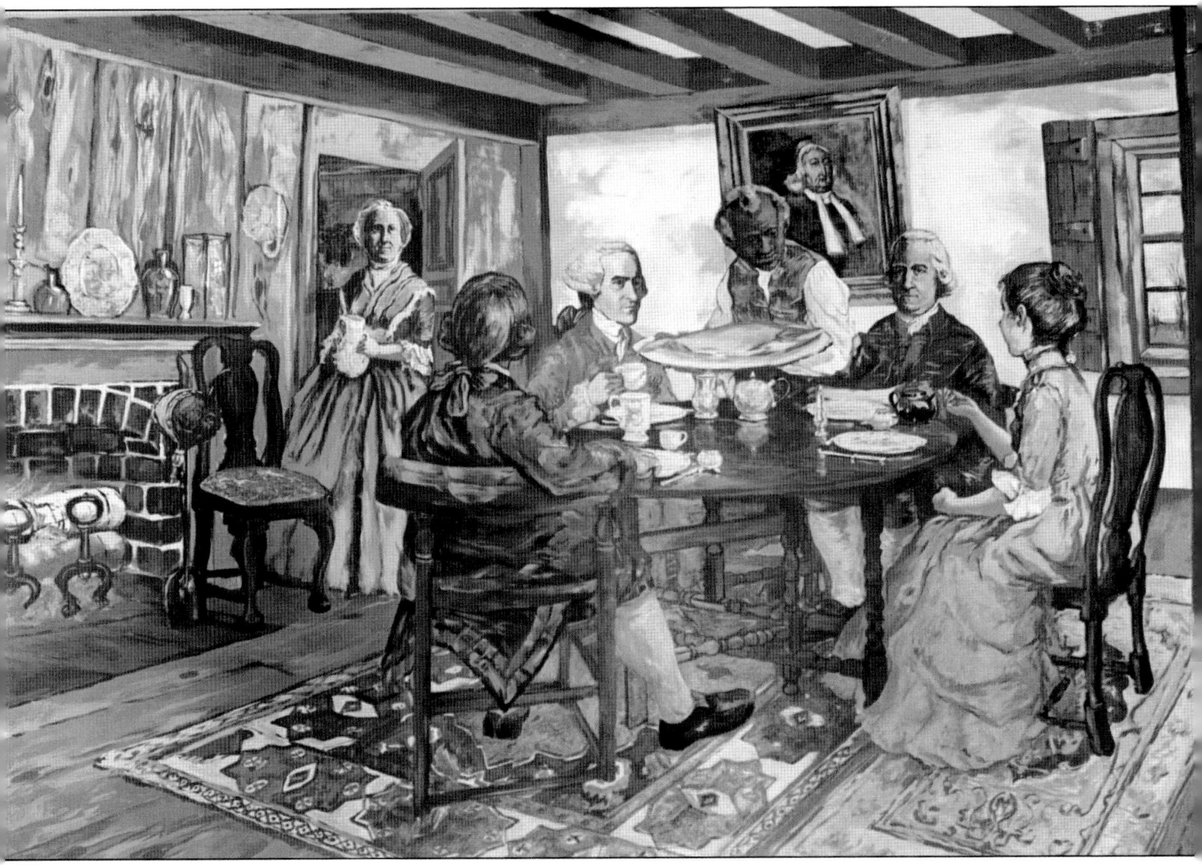

This mural depicts the salmon lunch at the home of Abigail Jones on April 19, 1775. Standing in the doorway is Abigail Jones, widow of Rev. Thomas Jones. Seated with his back to the viewer is Rev. John Marrett, who was the minister of the town from 1774 to 1813. John Hancock, wealthy merchant and patriot, is seated next to Marrett. Serving the salmon is Cuff, the African American slave of the Jones family. Samuel Adams, revolutionary firebrand and later governor of the commonwealth, is seated beside Dorothy Quincy, Hancock's fiancée. Hancock and Adams left the meal on the table when a messenger gave false information about the approach of British Regulars and the group fled to the farmhouse of Amos Wyman. The mural was done in 1974 by two local artists—Donald Gorvett and Jeffrey Weaver—for the 175th anniversary of the town. It covers one wall in the foyer of the Burlington Public Museum. (Courtesy of the Burlington Archives, No. 470.)

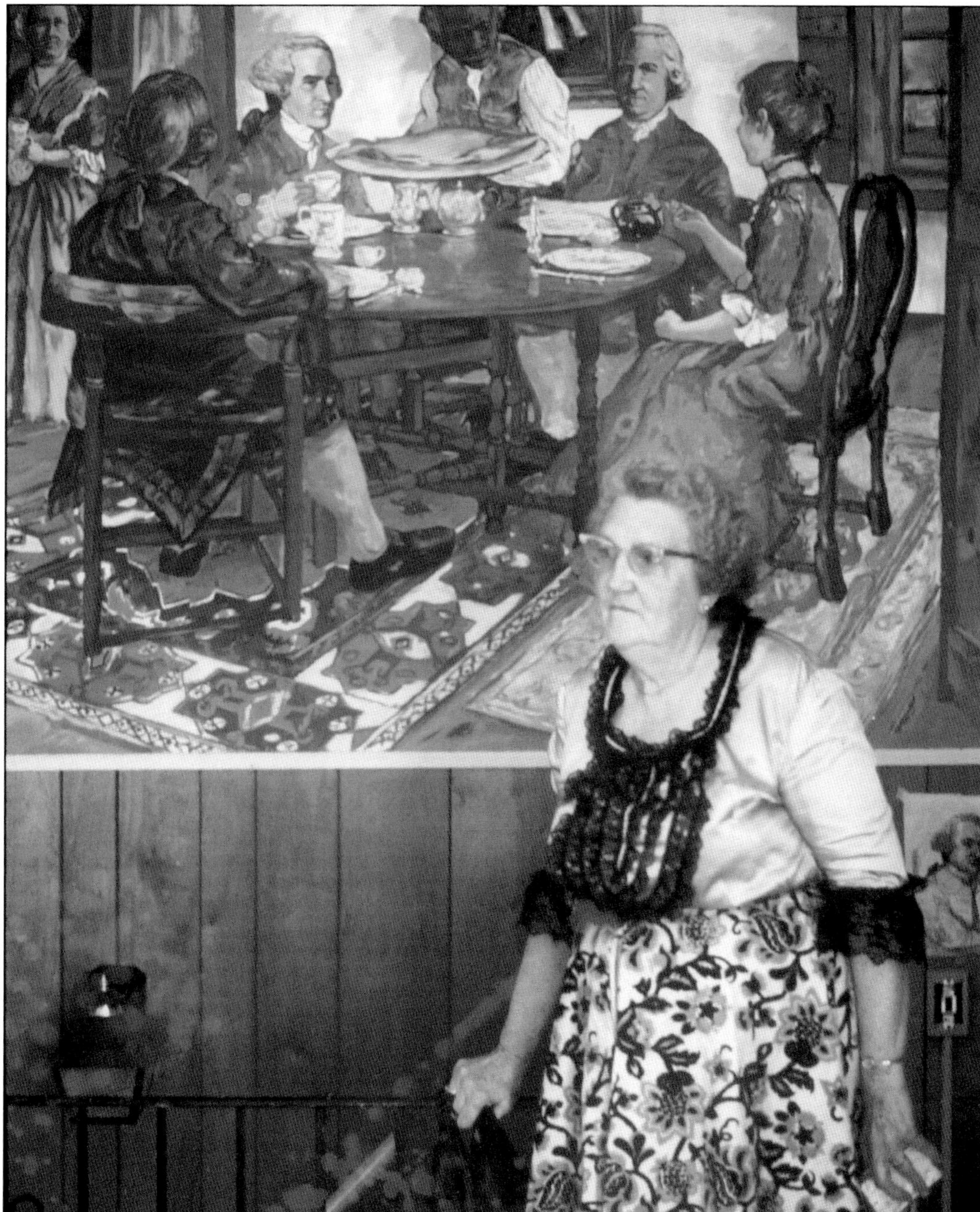

Mary Elizabeth Bennett Lowther, community activist and local historian, stands before the mural in the Burlington Public Museum. "Lib" was born into Burlington history on August 23, 1902, in an upstairs room of the historic Wood Tavern. The tavern was located where the fire station is today and was a town social and political spot. Lowther was connected to two historically prominent Burlington families, the Bennetts and the Sewalls. Her great love was history, and she made many notable achievements, such as helping to prevent the destruction of the West School, working toward creating a town museum, promoting a historic district, and publishing a town history. (Courtesy of the Burlington Archives, No. 487.)

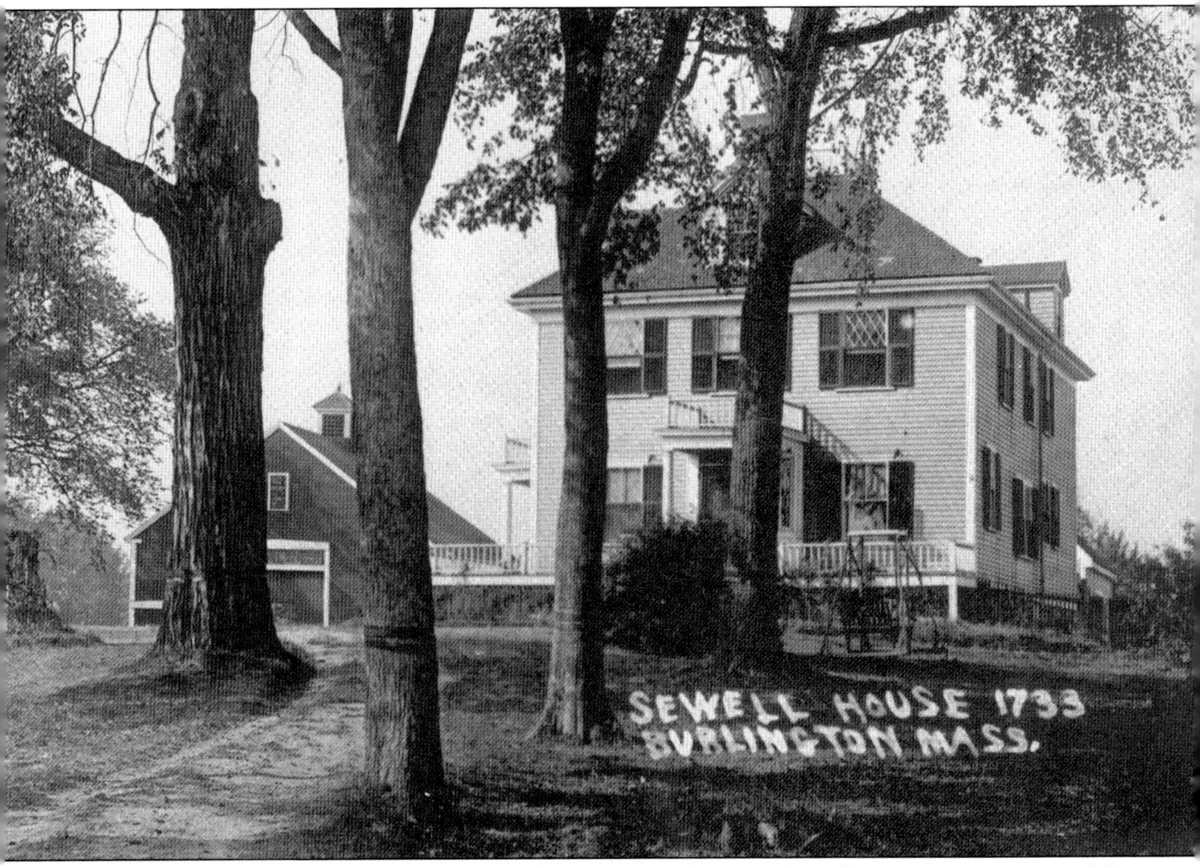

In the year of the disastrous fire that destroyed the historic Sewall House, ownership of the property passed to Samuel Sewall Jr.'s daughter Martha Elizabeth Sewall Curtis, and a new house was constructed. The original barn survived the fire and was part of the property. A fire destroyed the second Sewall House and the 18th-century barn in 1918. (Courtesy of the Burlington Archives, No. 394.)

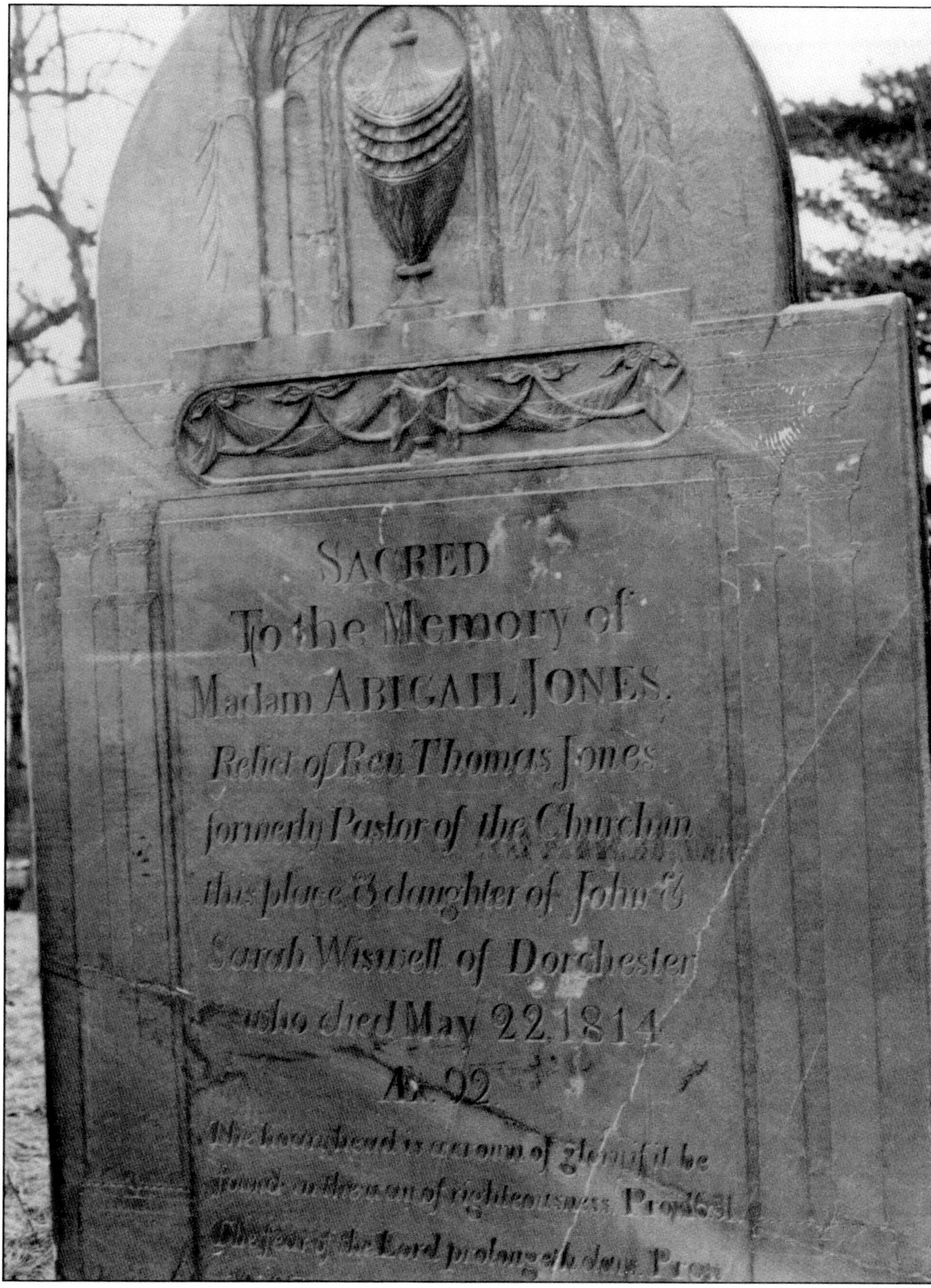

Abigail Wiswall Jones, a notable woman in Burlington history, was born in Dorchester and came to Woburn's Second Parish Church with her husband, Rev. Thomas Jones, in 1751. At the time of the Revolution, Abigail Jones lived in the Benjamin Johnson house, at 40 Lexington Street. She was the hostess at the salmon lunch served to distinguished guests John Hancock and Samuel Adams on April 19, 1775. A venerable Abigail Jones was also present on March 18, 1799, in Capt. John Wood's social hall to celebrate the incorporation of the town of Burlington. Her gravestone is in the Second Precinct Burial Ground, across from Simonds Park. (Courtesy of the Burlington Archives, No. 449.)

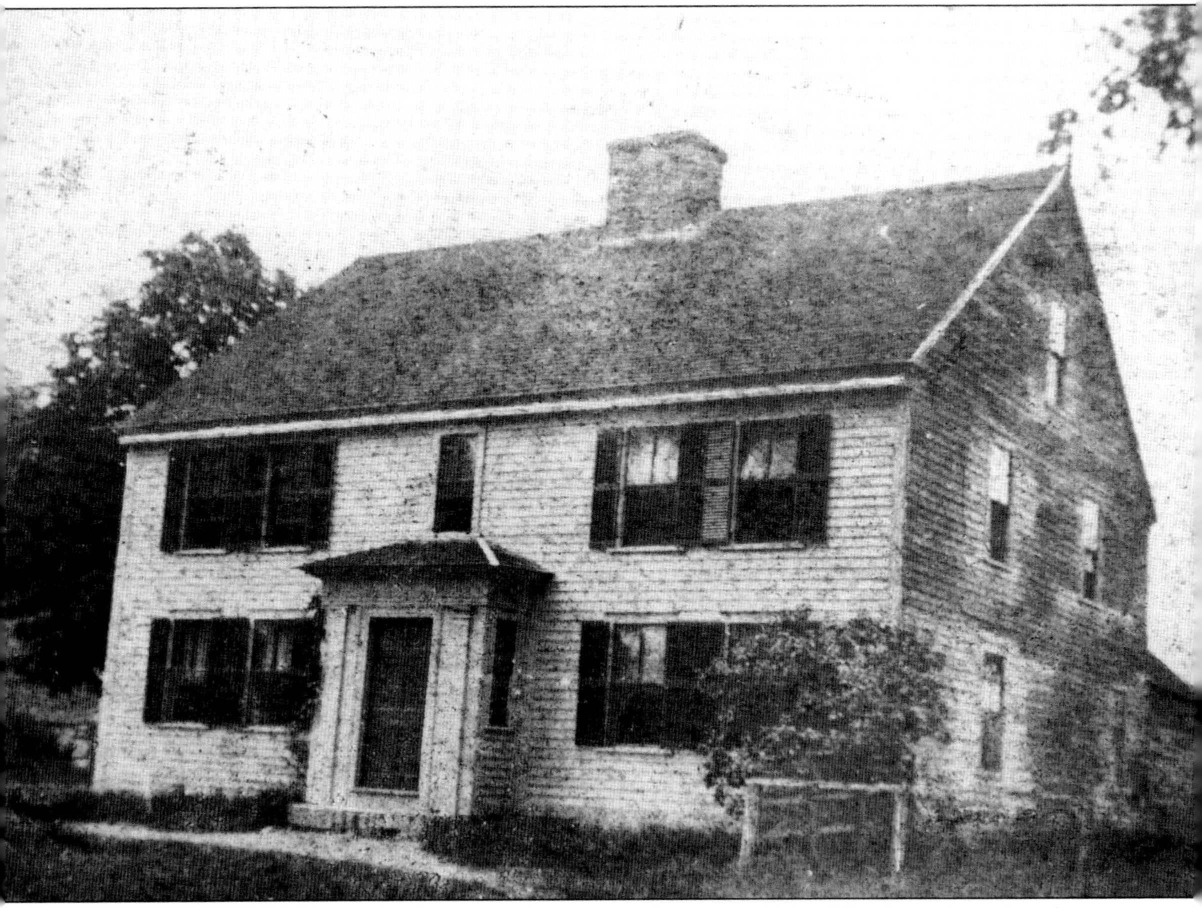

Capt. John Wood built this house in the center of town in 1764. Wood was born in what was then Woburn's Second Parish in 1740. At age 16, he enlisted in the militia and fought in the French and Indian War. He later fought in the American Revolution, serving under the command of Col. Loammi Baldwin from Woburn. The Wood Tavern had a close connection to the history of Burlington, for it was here on March 18, 1799, that the new town of Burlington celebrated its incorporation with a townwide banquet in the upstairs social hall. After a succession of owners, the town purchased the property in 1957 and tore the building down. By 1959, a new fire station stood on the site. (Courtesy of the Burlington Archives, No. 51.)

Three

SCHOOLS AND SCHOOLHOUSES

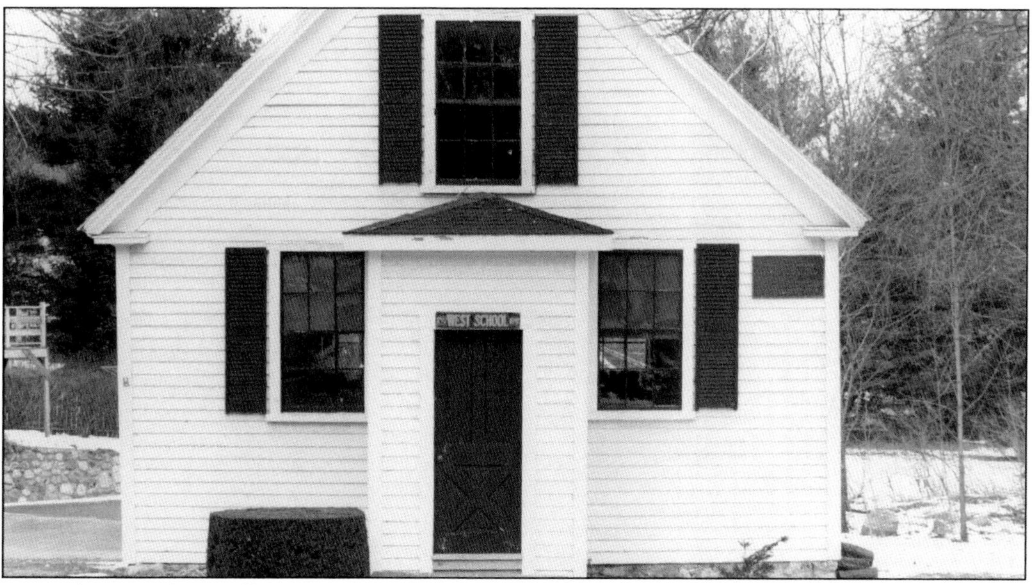

According to John Goff's *Historic Preservation Survey of Burlington*, the West School is historically significant as a rare, Federal-period one-room schoolhouse. Originally built in the area of Simonds Park in 1794, it was called the Center School. Sometime between 1830 and 1840, the building was moved to the Havenville section of Burlington, which was then a separate village with a leather shop, post office, and small residences. The birth of the Burlington Historical Society occurred over the struggle to preserve this building in 1964. Then used as a garage, the building was one of four constructed in various parts of Burlington (Woburn's Second Parish) in 1794. Targeted for demolition in the 1960s, the school was saved by a group of historically minded citizens. Today it is a town museum operated by the Burlington Historical Commission. (Courtesy of the Burlington Archives, No. 2.)

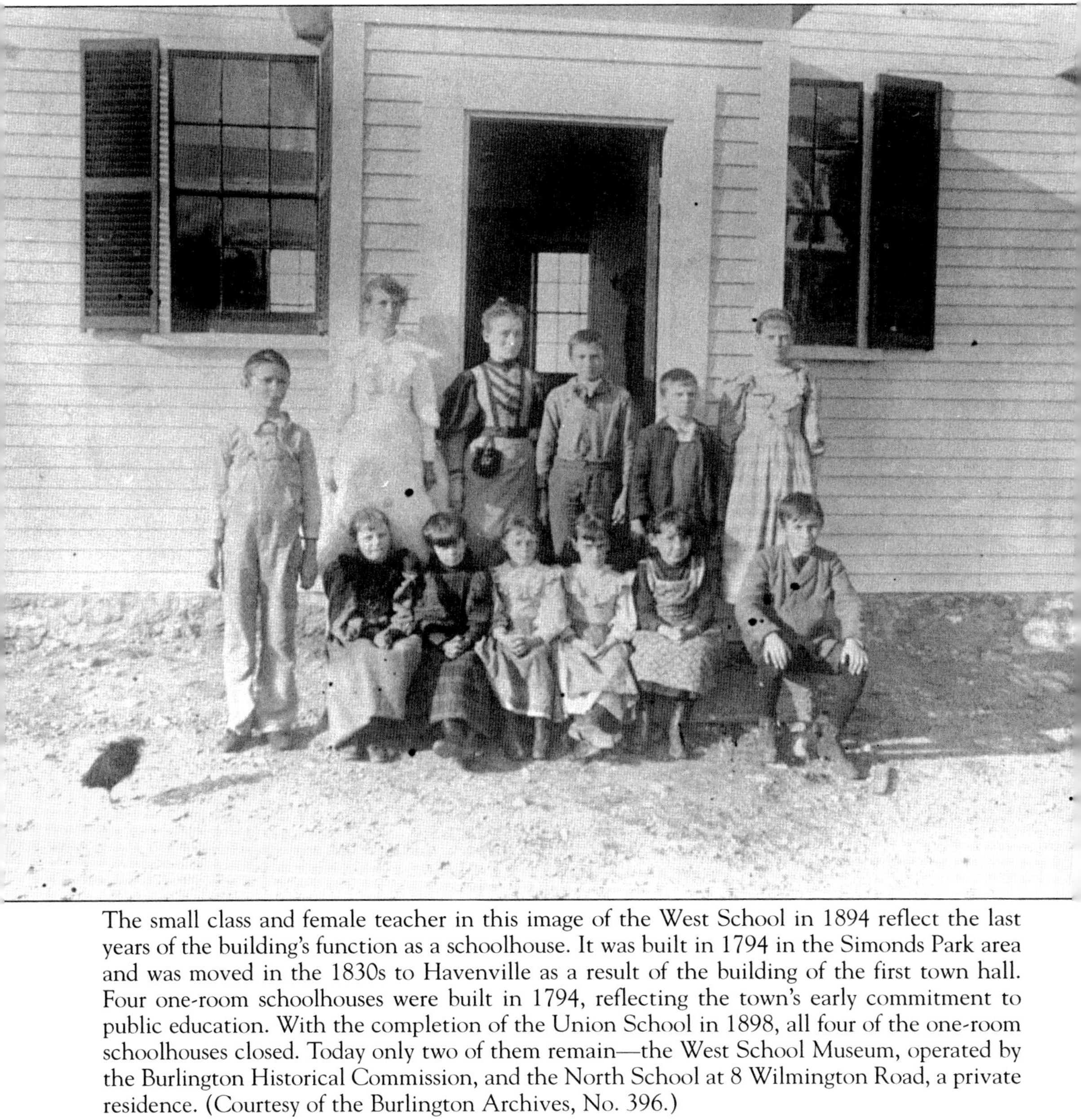

The small class and female teacher in this image of the West School in 1894 reflect the last years of the building's function as a schoolhouse. It was built in 1794 in the Simonds Park area and was moved in the 1830s to Havenville as a result of the building of the first town hall. Four one-room schoolhouses were built in 1794, reflecting the town's early commitment to public education. With the completion of the Union School in 1898, all four of the one-room schoolhouses closed. Today only two of them remain—the West School Museum, operated by the Burlington Historical Commission, and the North School at 8 Wilmington Road, a private residence. (Courtesy of the Burlington Archives, No. 396.)

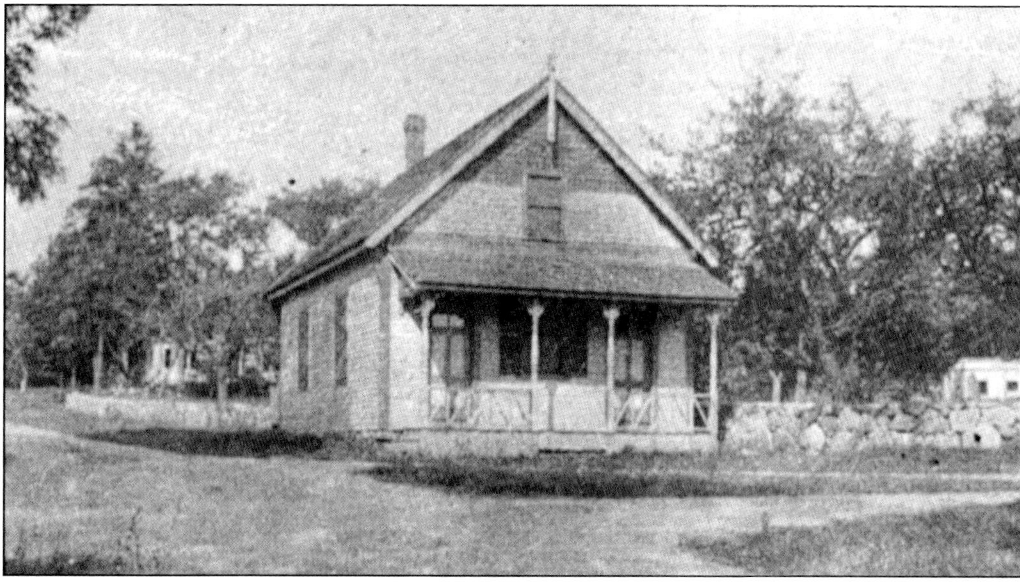

The North School, or the Lt. Jesse Dean District Schoolhouse, was originally on property that belonged to the Reed family. Lieutenant Reed was a member of Capt. John Wood's militia company from 1775 to 1783. After the Revolution, a boundary dispute with the town led Isaiah Reed to move the building to the Wilmington Road line, where it is located today. It is now a private residence. (Courtesy of the Burlington Archives, No. 489.)

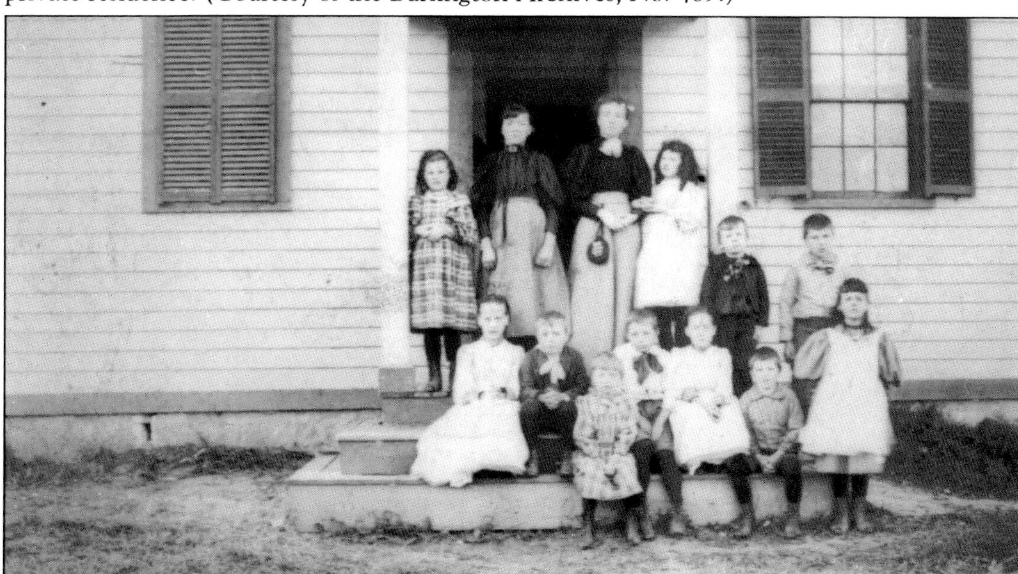

According to the Burlington Archives, this building is the East School, or the Lt. Joseph Winn District School. Teacher Cora McIntire (1869–1935) is shown standing in the doorway with her students c. 1900. McIntire taught from 1891 to 1893 and again from 1895 to 1898. One of the four one-room schoolhouses built in 1794, the East School was located at 45 Mountain Road until February 2000, when it was razed. From left to right are the following: (front row) Alice Winn, Patsy Brady, Mary Young, John Graham, Lizzie Graham, Henry Graham, and Cassie Young; (middle row) Frank Winn and Willie Winn; (back row) Mary Brady, Elva Marion, Cora McIntire, and Ida Stone. (Courtesy of the Burlington Archives, No. 359.)

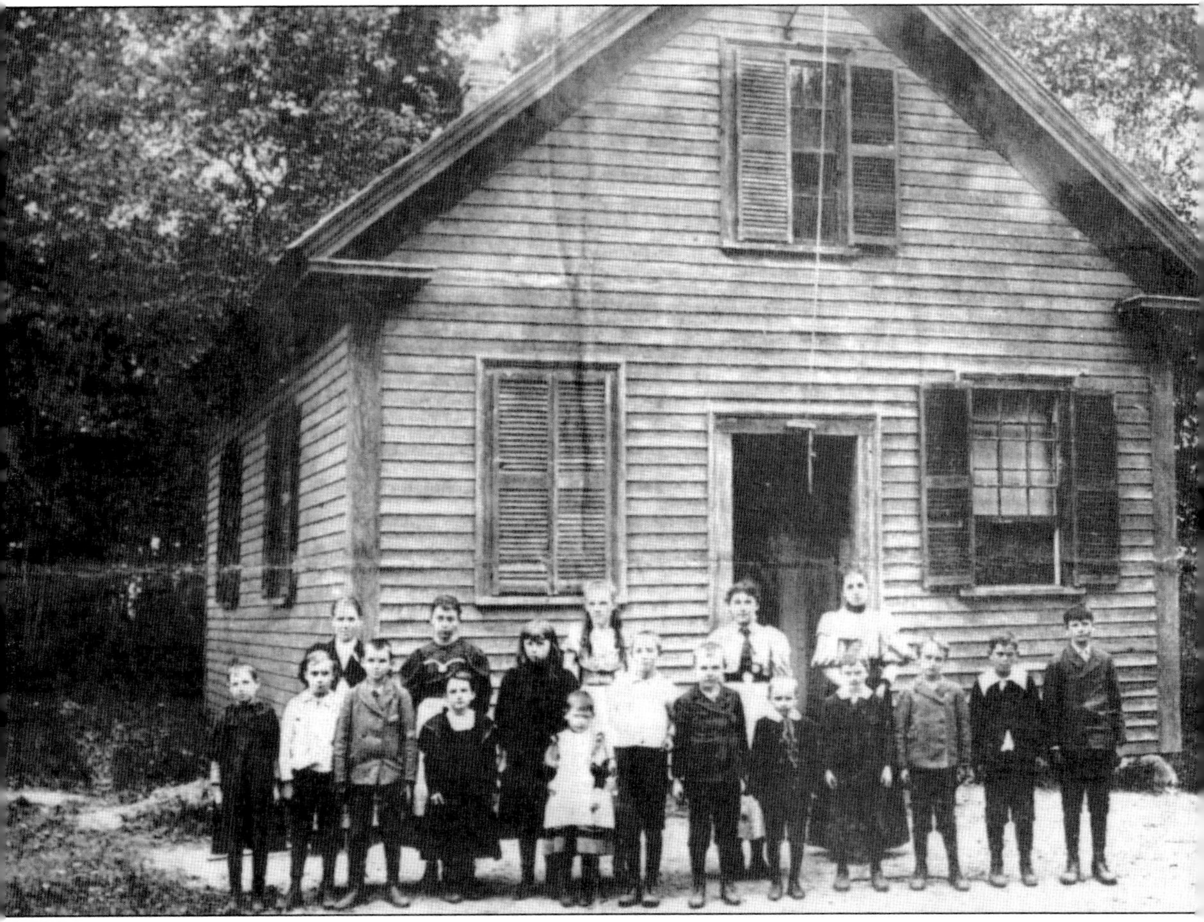

The South School was located at the junction of Lexington Street and Blanchard Road and was also known as the Capt. James Reed District School. After the opening of the Union School in 1898, the one-room schoolhouses became obsolete and the buildings were used as private homes and public property. South School was sold and moved farther down Blanchard Road to become a private residence. By the 1950s, the building was falling apart and was later demolished. (Courtesy of the Burlington Archives, No. 198.)

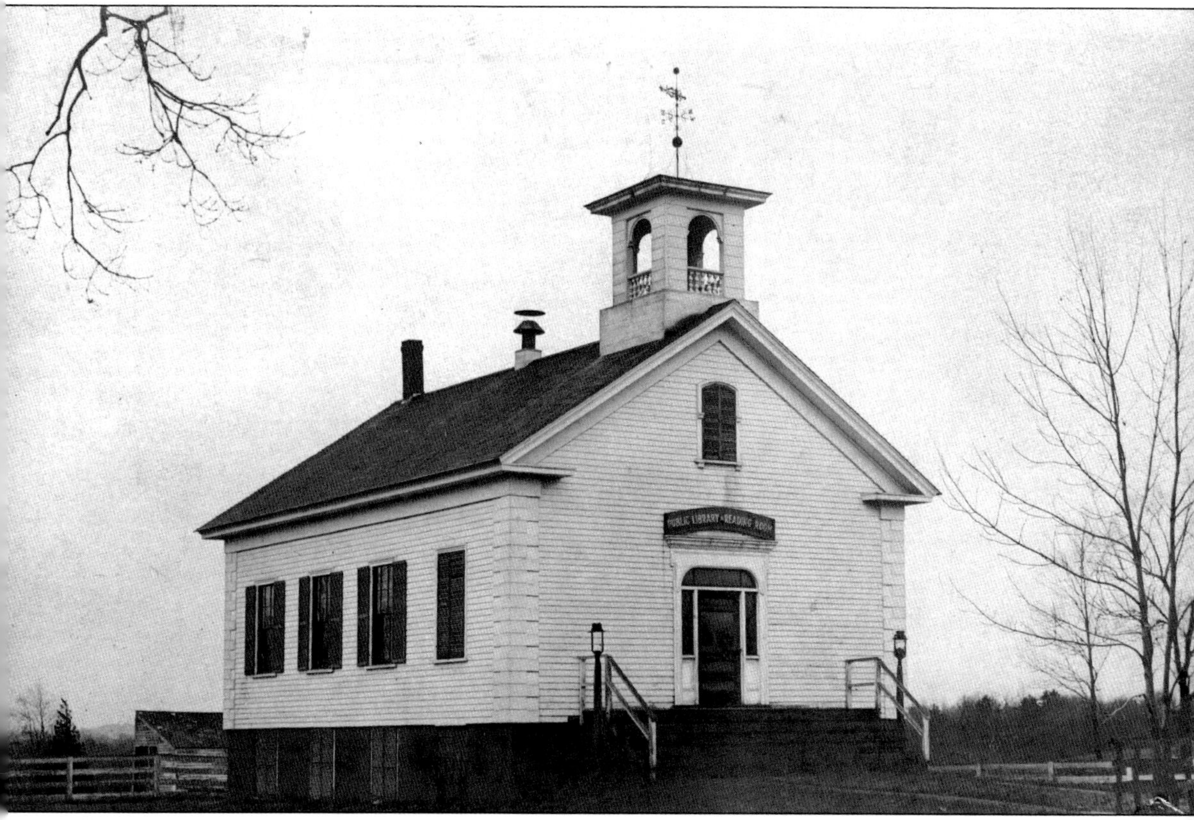

The historic Center School of 1855 is a front-gabled, wood-framed schoolhouse designed in the transitional Greek Revival and Italianate style. It was built to provide a modern, well-equipped school for Burlington students living in the center of town, since the one-room schoolhouses in various parts of town were filled to capacity. In 1897, the building became Burlington's first library. Today, it is the Burlington Public Museum (operated by the Burlington Historical Commission) and serves as the center of the town's historical preservation movement. (Courtesy of the Burlington Archives, No. 194.)

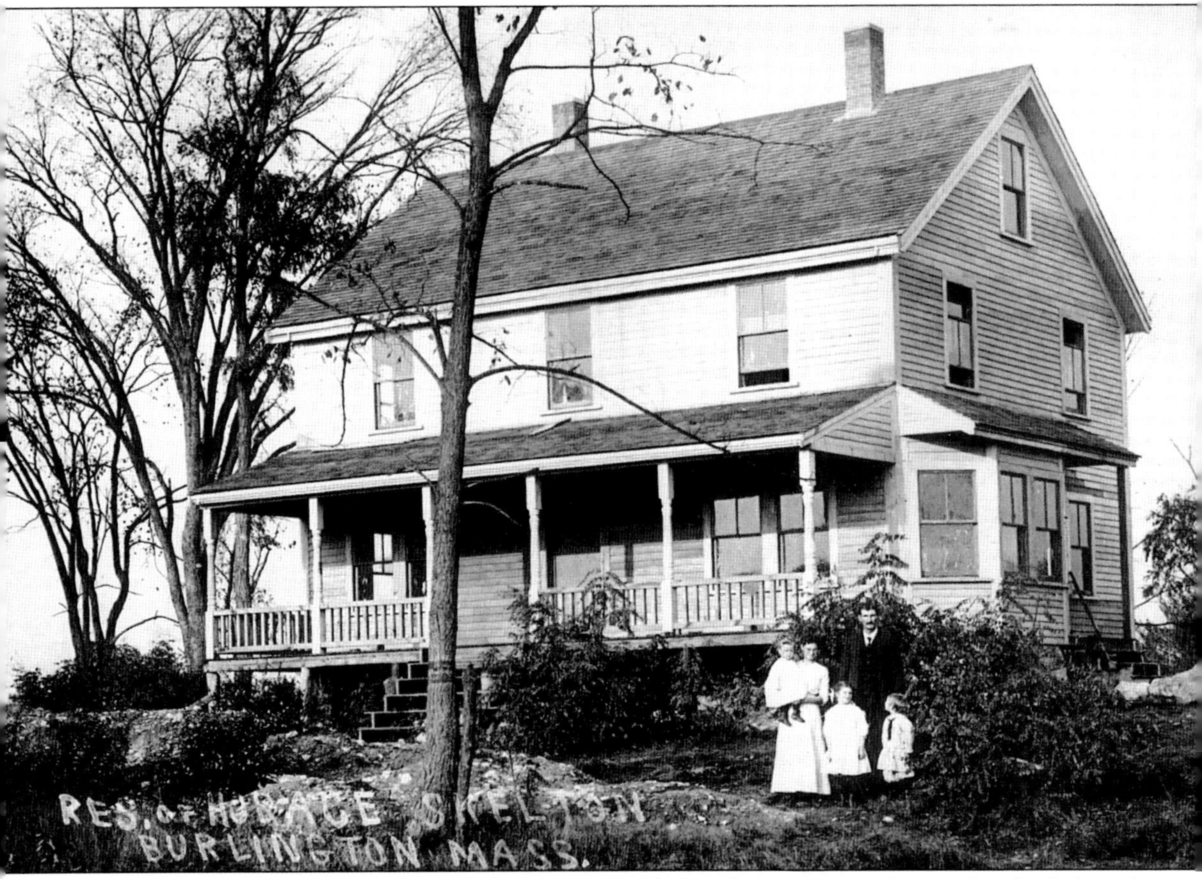

Located on Francis Wyman Road, the Horace B. Skelton house is a good example of a Colonial Revival farmhouse of the early 20th century. Skelton was one of four brothers who were very influential in Burlington society and politics throughout the 20th century. He is featured with his young family in this image. The baby girl in the arms of her mother is Iona Skelton Ganley, one of the current owners. (Courtesy of the Burlington Community Scholarship Committee.)

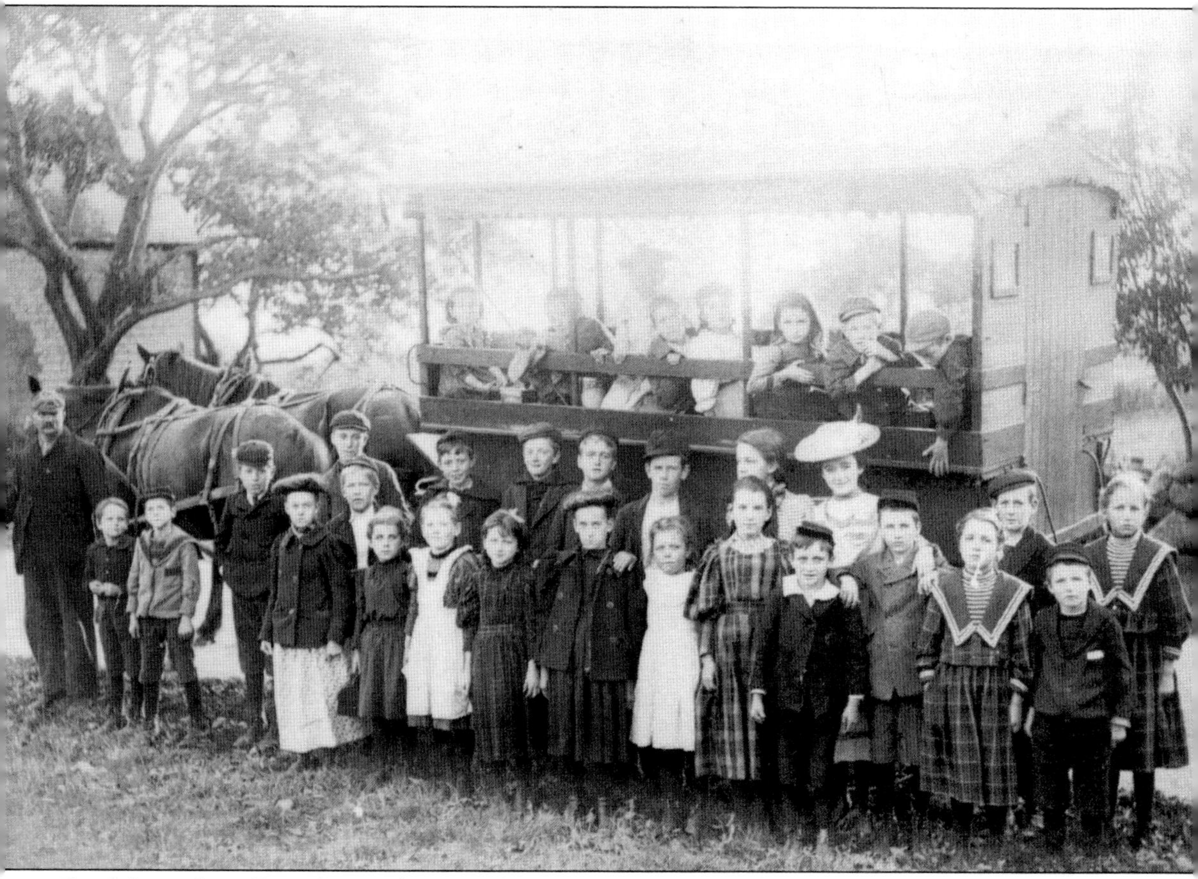

Frank Lounsbury Barnaby was born in Nova Scotia *c.* 1865 and married Mary C. Jennings in Burlington on November 29, 1888. By 1890, the Barnabys were residing in Burlington and had five children. In March 1899, Burlington Town Meeting approved $400 to run a school bus service, and Barnaby became one of the first Burlington school bus drivers. During the early 20th century, Joseph Howe used a four-wheeled, glassed-in carriage that was known as the Barge. The vehicle in this 1902 image seems to be an earlier version of the Barge. (Courtesy of the Burlington Archives, No. 418.)

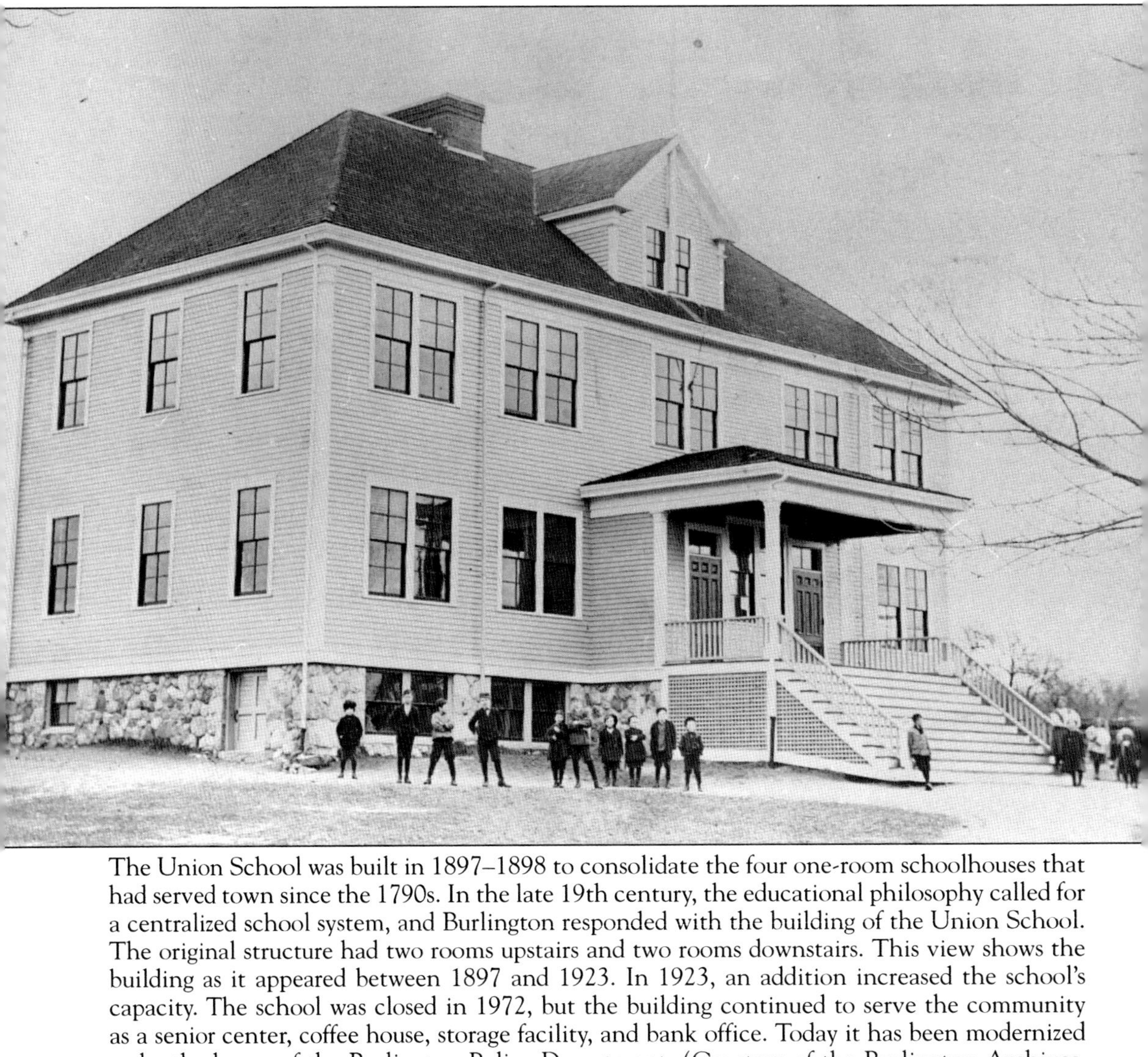

The Union School was built in 1897–1898 to consolidate the four one-room schoolhouses that had served town since the 1790s. In the late 19th century, the educational philosophy called for a centralized school system, and Burlington responded with the building of the Union School. The original structure had two rooms upstairs and two rooms downstairs. This view shows the building as it appeared between 1897 and 1923. In 1923, an addition increased the school's capacity. The school was closed in 1972, but the building continued to serve the community as a senior center, coffee house, storage facility, and bank office. Today it has been modernized to be the home of the Burlington Police Department. (Courtesy of the Burlington Archives, No. 437.)

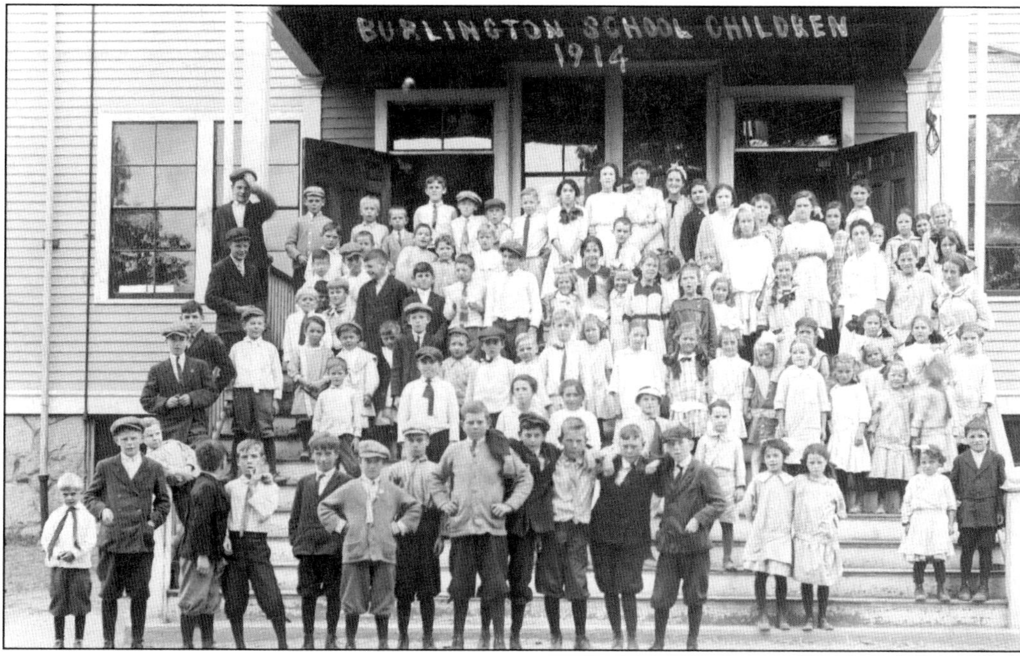

The entire school population of Burlington appears in this photograph taken on the steps of the Union School. According to town archive sources, the students pictured represent the total number of students in the Burlington school system in 1914. (Courtesy of the Burlington Archives, No. 8.)

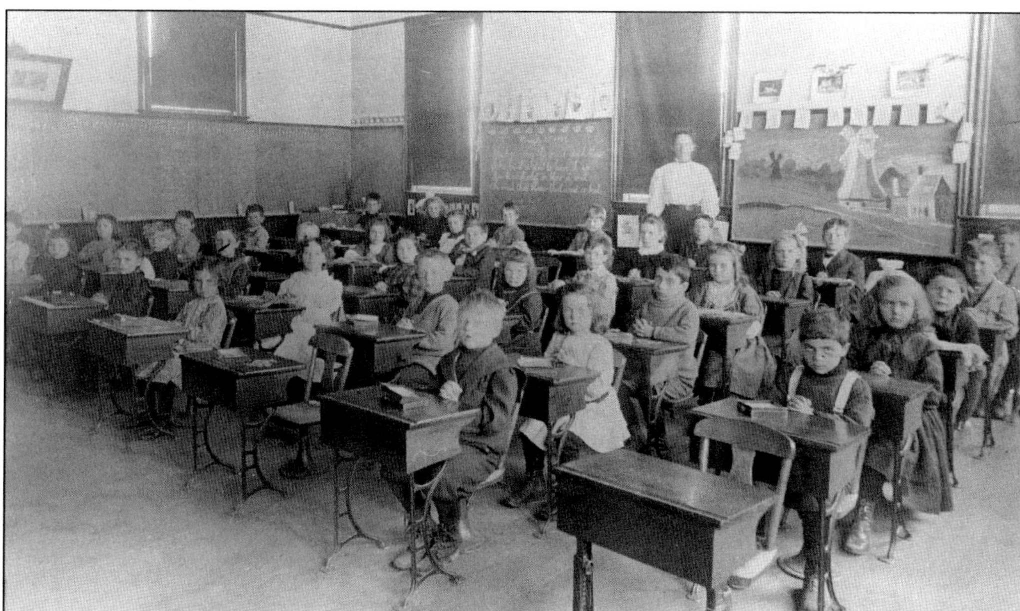

A very large class of students is shown in a Miss Thompson's classroom—possibly Susie G. Thompson (1908–1909)—in the Union School in the early 20th century. According to town historian Ed Fogelberg, the blackboard on the rear wall reads: "Which ever way the wind doth blow / Some heart is glad to find it so / Then blow it east or blow it west / The wind that blows—that wind is best." (Courtesy of the Burlington Archives, No. 9.)

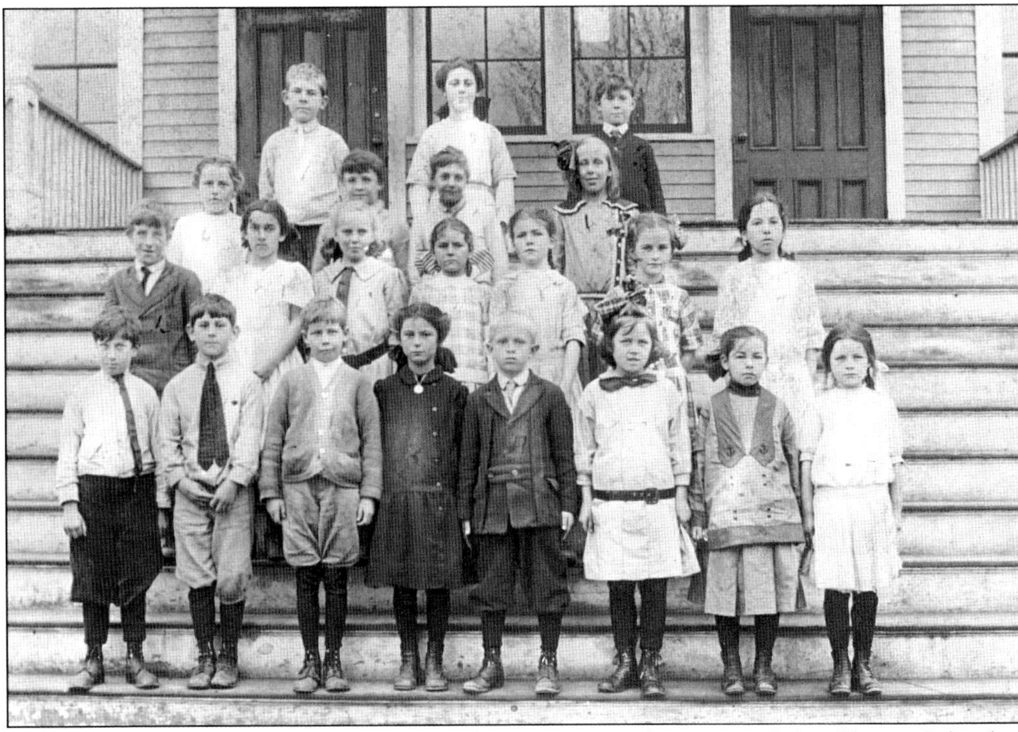

In this 1914 photograph, Burlington students pose on the steps of the Union School at 45 Center Street. The Union School was built in 1897 and was a major innovation in the consolidated school movement of the late 19th century. (Courtesy of the Burlington Archives, No. 14.)

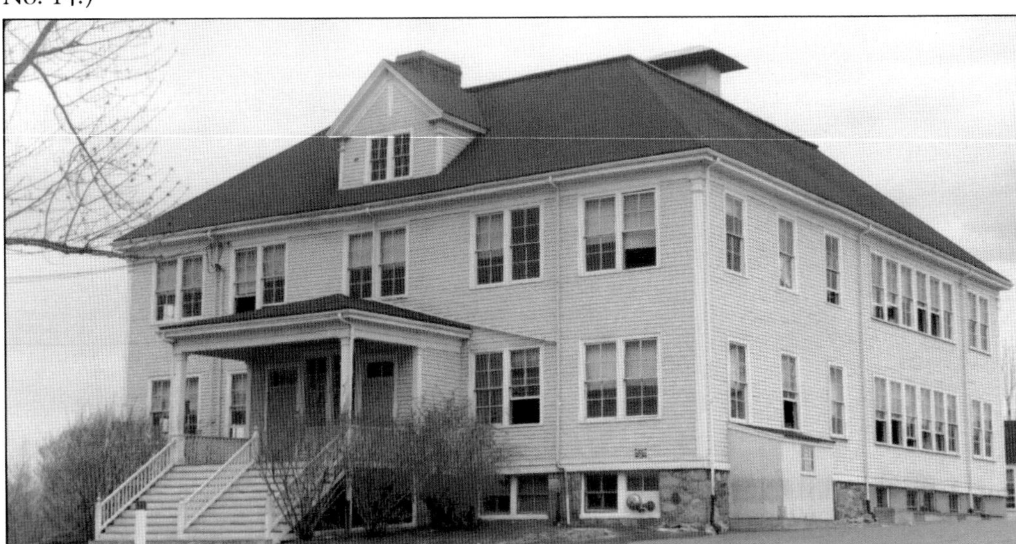

This view of the Union School shows the original four-room, up-and-down layout as well as the 1923 addition that doubled its size. The Union School is significant as an over-100-year-old municipal building that occupies a strategic position on the town common and in Burlington's proud record of preservation of historic schoolhouses. (Courtesy of the Burlington Archives, No. 178.)

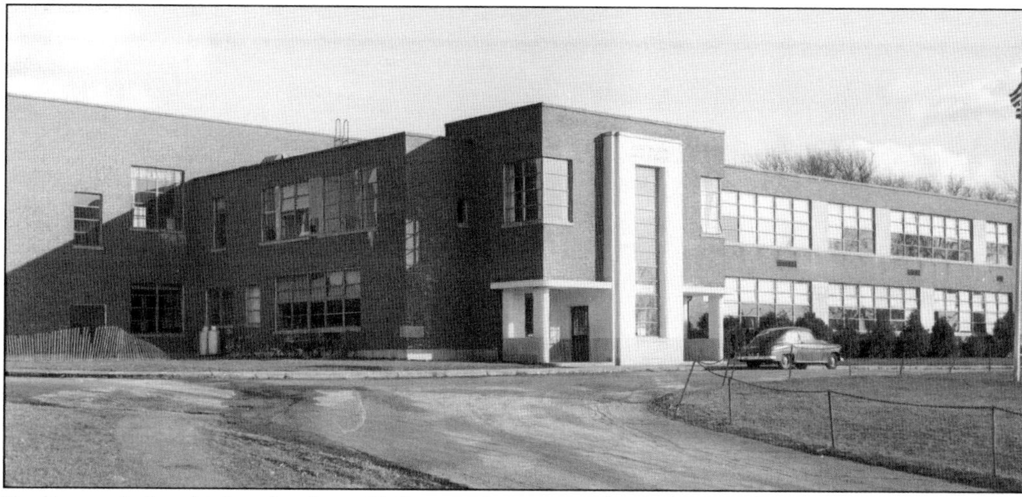

Burlington's first high school, at 61 Center Street, was built during the Great Depression with funding from the Works Progress Administration, one of Franklin D. Roosevelt's New Deal programs. According to sources from the Burlington Archives, there was a population boom during the 1930s when people left the cities of the area to seek more favorable economic conditions in the country. Lexington and Woburn had been taking Burlington students in their high schools but stopped doing so in the 1930s. The building was designed by architect J. Williams Beal and Sons and was erected in 1939. (Courtesy of the Burlington Archives, No. 294.)

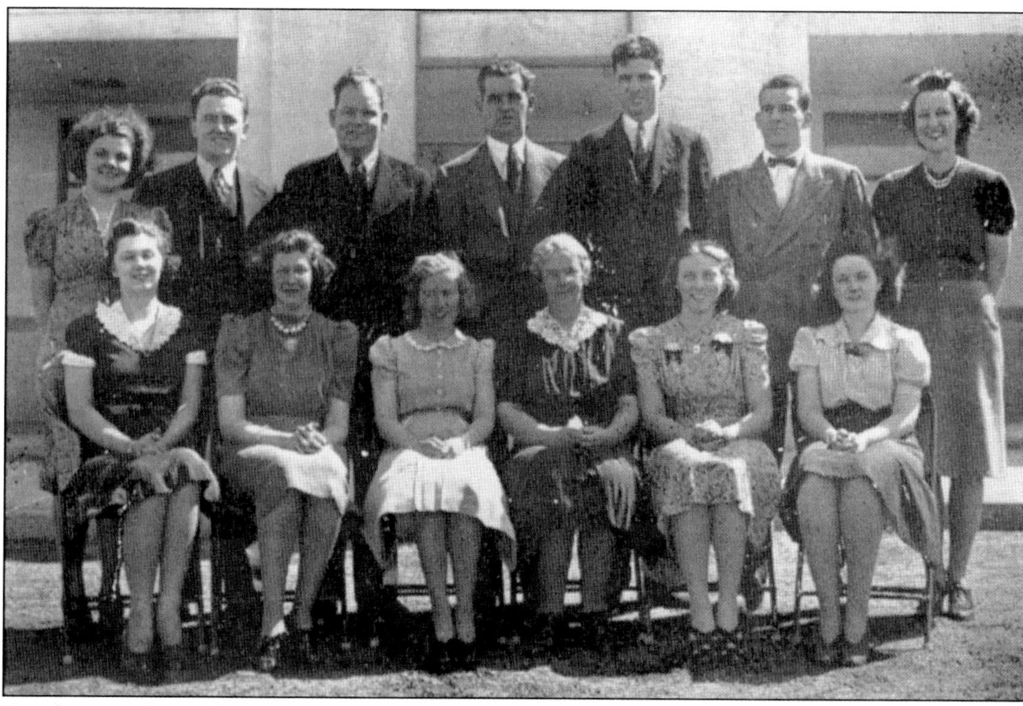

Faculty members of Burlington's junior-senior high school are shown in the 1940s. They are, from left to right, as follows: (front row) D. Donovan, H. Pearson, G. Burke, W. Andrews, E. Lambert, and E. Trickey; (back row) M. DeMone, G. Higgins, D. Dunnan, H. Norton, T. Higgins, R. Lawry, and C. Lee. (Courtesy of the Burlington Archives, No. 210.)

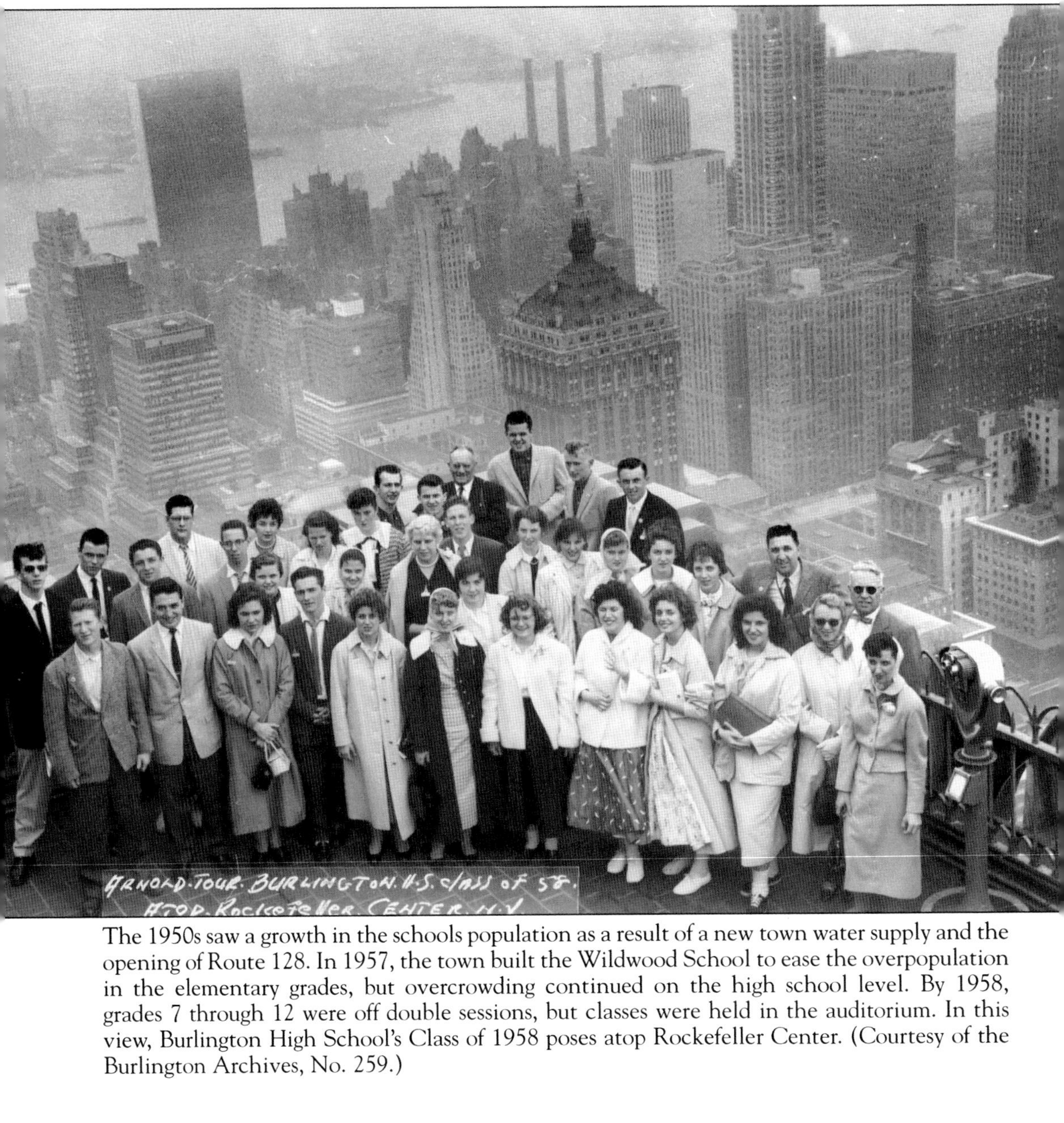

The 1950s saw a growth in the schools population as a result of a new town water supply and the opening of Route 128. In 1957, the town built the Wildwood School to ease the overpopulation in the elementary grades, but overcrowding continued on the high school level. By 1958, grades 7 through 12 were off double sessions, but classes were held in the auditorium. In this view, Burlington High School's Class of 1958 poses atop Rockefeller Center. (Courtesy of the Burlington Archives, No. 259.)

Four

LANDSCAPES

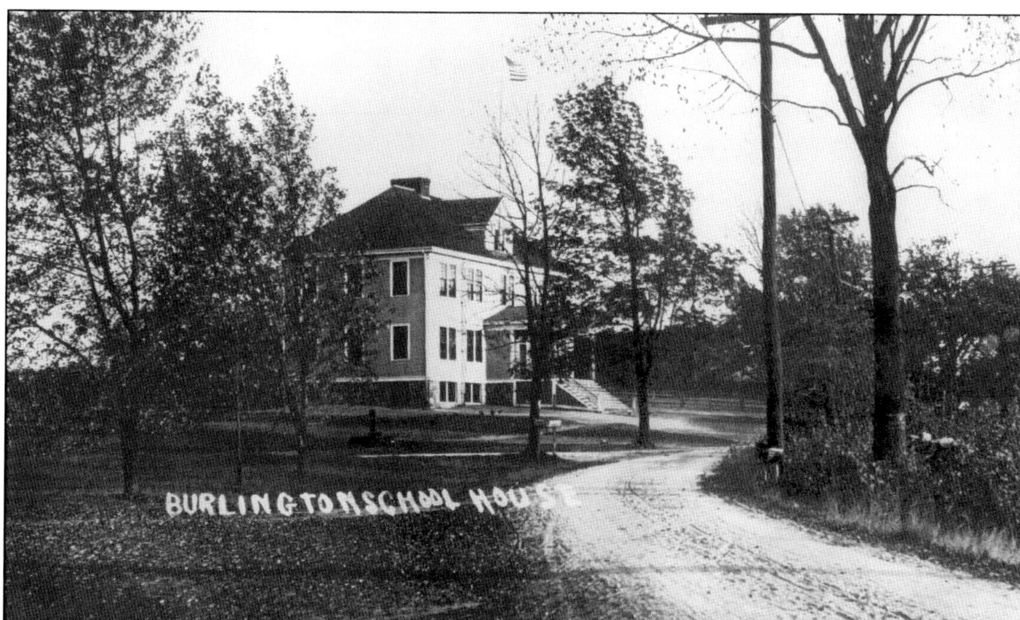

This photograph shows an unpaved Center Street with the Union School in the background. The image was captured sometime between 1910 and 1923. Burlington received electricity between 1910 and 1911. Electric poles are seen in this photograph, and the Union School is without its 1923 addition. (Courtesy of the Burlington Archives, No. 512.)

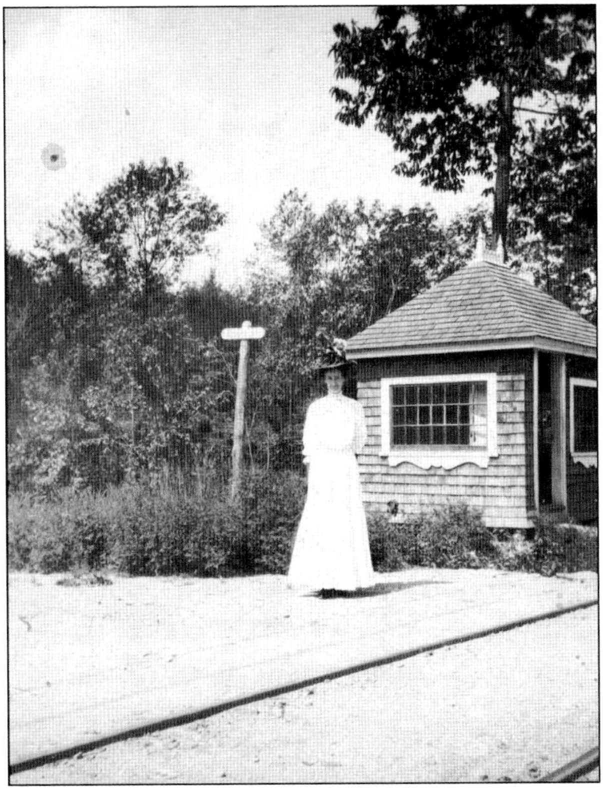

Although the railroad bypassed Burlington, streetcar lines did exist. This scene shows a woman waiting at the corner of Winn and Sears Streets c. 1910. In 1906, the Boston and Northern Street Railway Streetcar Company built tracks from Woburn to Burlington. The route went along Winn Street to Cambridge Street and into Billerica. The company built Sears Street from Center to Winn Street, and put a waiting room at the foot of Winn Street. (Courtesy of the Burlington Archives, No. 139.)

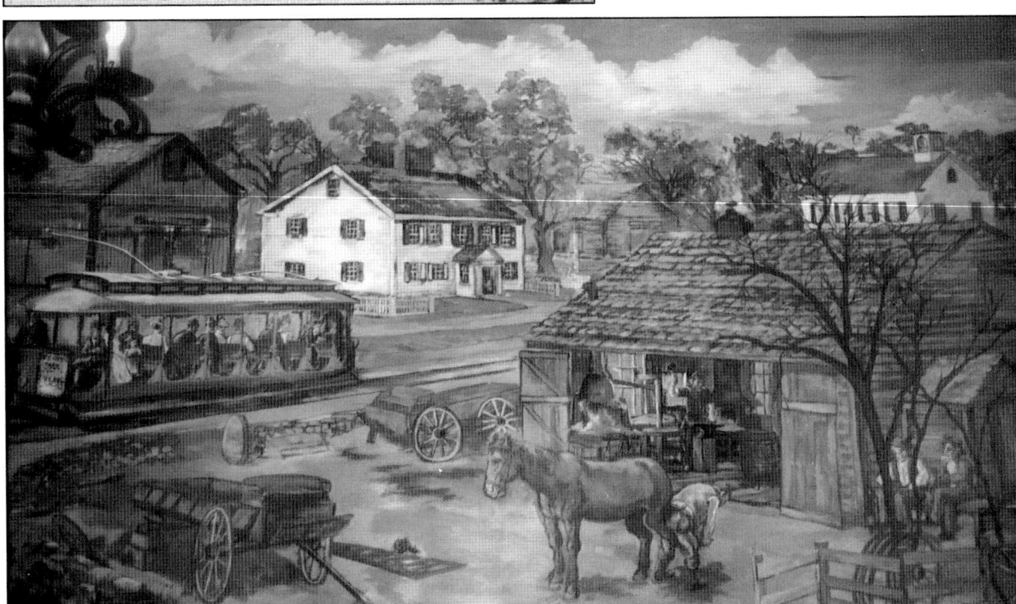

Burlington's town common at the turn of the century was a vibrant, colorful location. In this mural, which occupies a corner of the entryway to the Burlington Public Museum, a streetcar proceeds down Bedford Street. The white Colonial is the Gen. John Walker house, and the white building on the far right is the Center School of 1855. The blacksmith shop in the foreground is doing a brisk business. (Courtesy of R.J. Costa.)

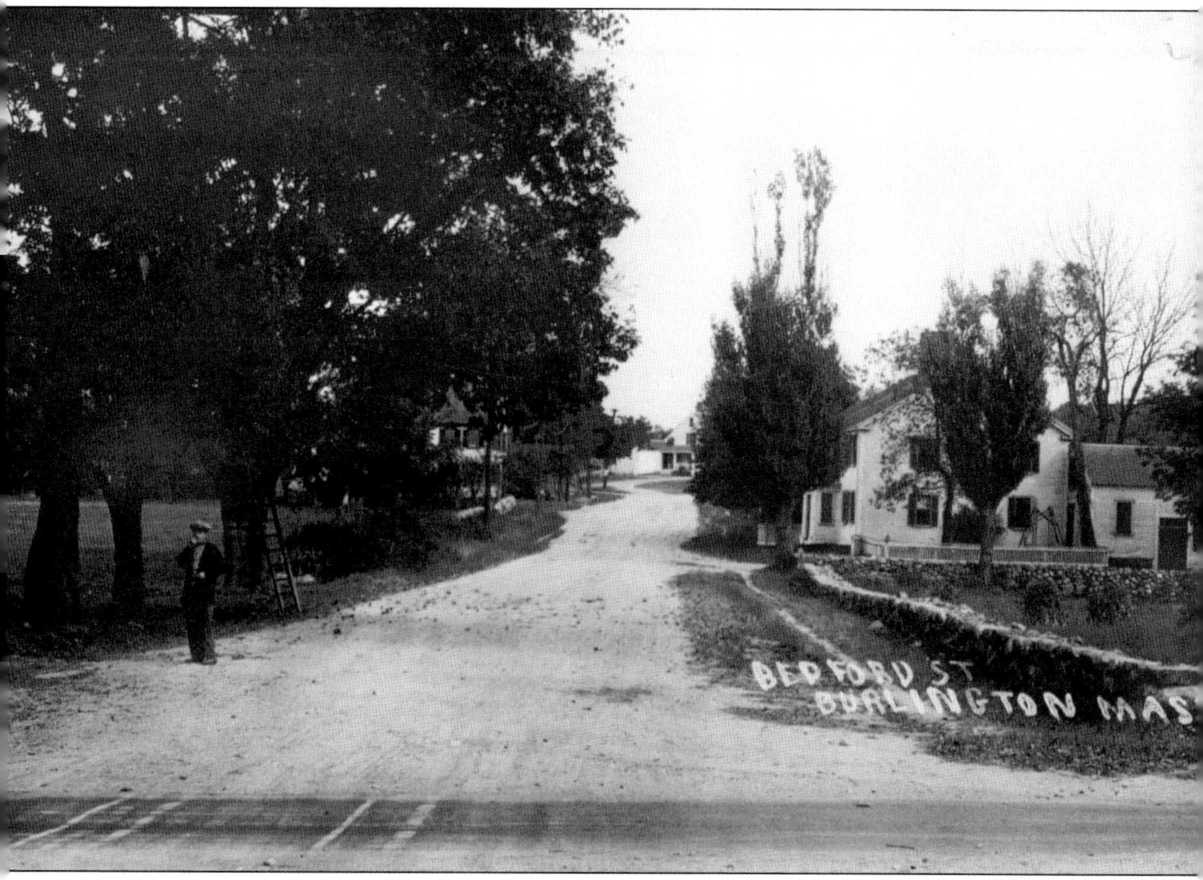

The intersection of Bedford Street and "the state road" is shown *c.* 1900. On the right is the Maj. Gen. John Walker house. Walker was the son of Revolutionary War commander Capt. Joshua Walker. Pres. John Adams gave John Walker his commission of general in 1798 during the undeclared war with France. John Walker married Lucy Johnson, who was a direct descendant of Capt. Edward Johnson, one of the principal founders of the town of Woburn. In the background center of the photograph is part of the Grand View Farm complex. In the left center can be seen the Humphrey Prescott house, which once stood on the town common across from the Walker house. This house was moved before 1950 to 36 Bedford Street. (Courtesy of the Burlington Archives.)

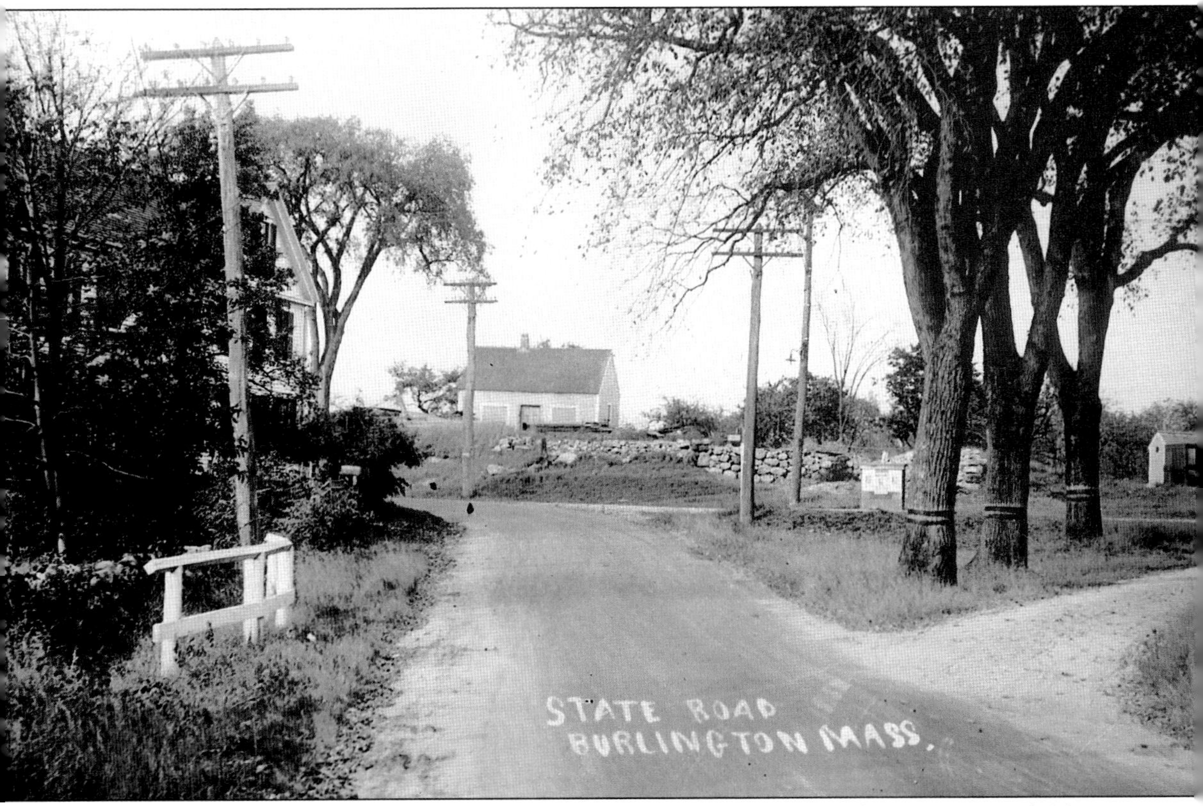

The three elm trees on the right stood at the intersection of Cambridge, Center, and Olympia Way, in the triangle where the town scales were kept. The scales were vital in an agricultural community for weighing farm products. The large elm tree on the left hides the Gleason-Bennett-Simonds house, which was once owned by town benefactor Marshall Simonds. In his 1905 will, Simonds bequeathed the town (where he was born) a sum of money and his farm, to be used as a public park. (Courtesy of the Burlington Archives, No. 431.)

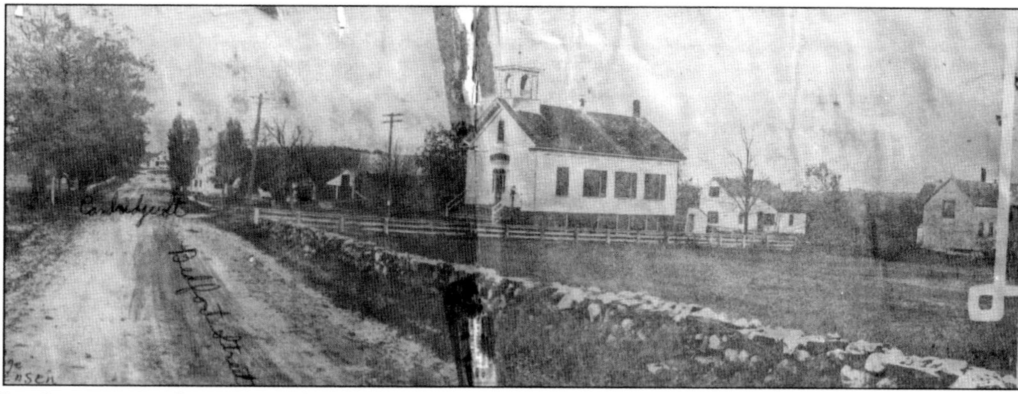

Looking east, this view of the intersection of Bedford and Cambridge Streets may have appeared as part of an article in an issue of the *Ladies Home Journal* in 1906. The photograph shows the Center School when it was used as a library. Burlington's first library was housed in this building through the efforts of Mr. E.S. Barker in 1897. The building to the far right is part of the William Edward Carter heel shop complex. Bedford Street appears unpaved. (Courtesy of the Burlington Archives, No. 517.)

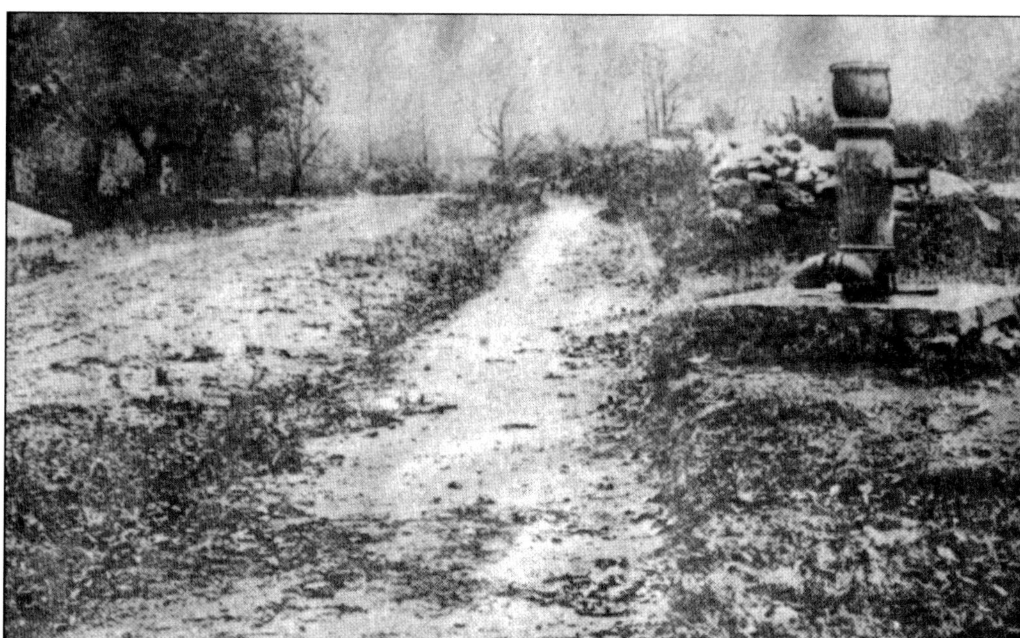

The "town pump" was located on the town common opposite the Silas Cutler general store. In this scene, the "highway" (Cambridge Street) leading to the schoolhouse passes in front of the pump. The Silas Cutler general store was a connected farmhouse complex that originally stood were today's town hall annex is situated. (Courtesy of the Burlington Archives, No. 505.)

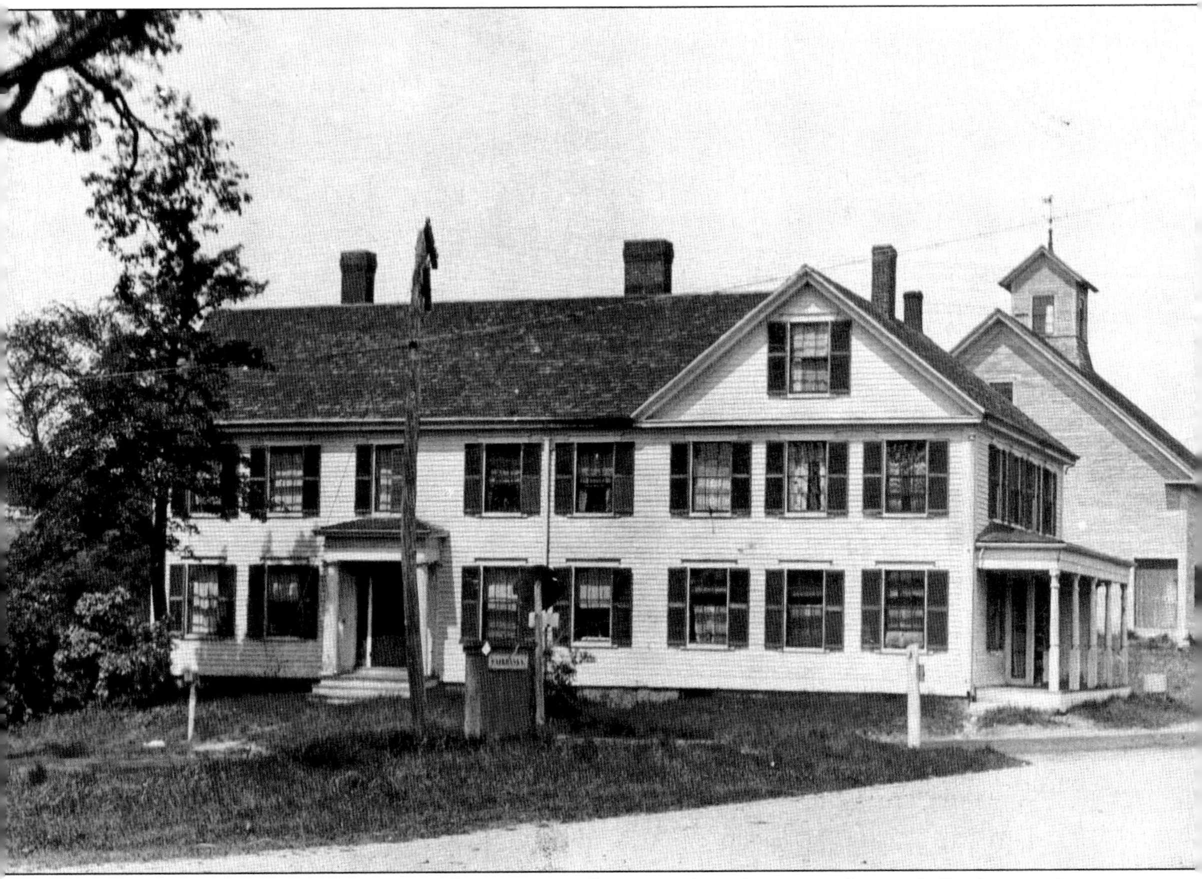

This imposing combination of various architectural styles once housed Burlington's town library and was the property of one of the most generous benefactors in town history, Marshall Simonds. Around 1920, the two halves of the structure were separated and moved to Mill Street and Sears Street, and both are still standing today. The house and barn had to be moved when the state decided to straighten Cambridge Street, which made a large S-shaped turn around the property. (Courtesy of the Burlington Archives, No. 331.)

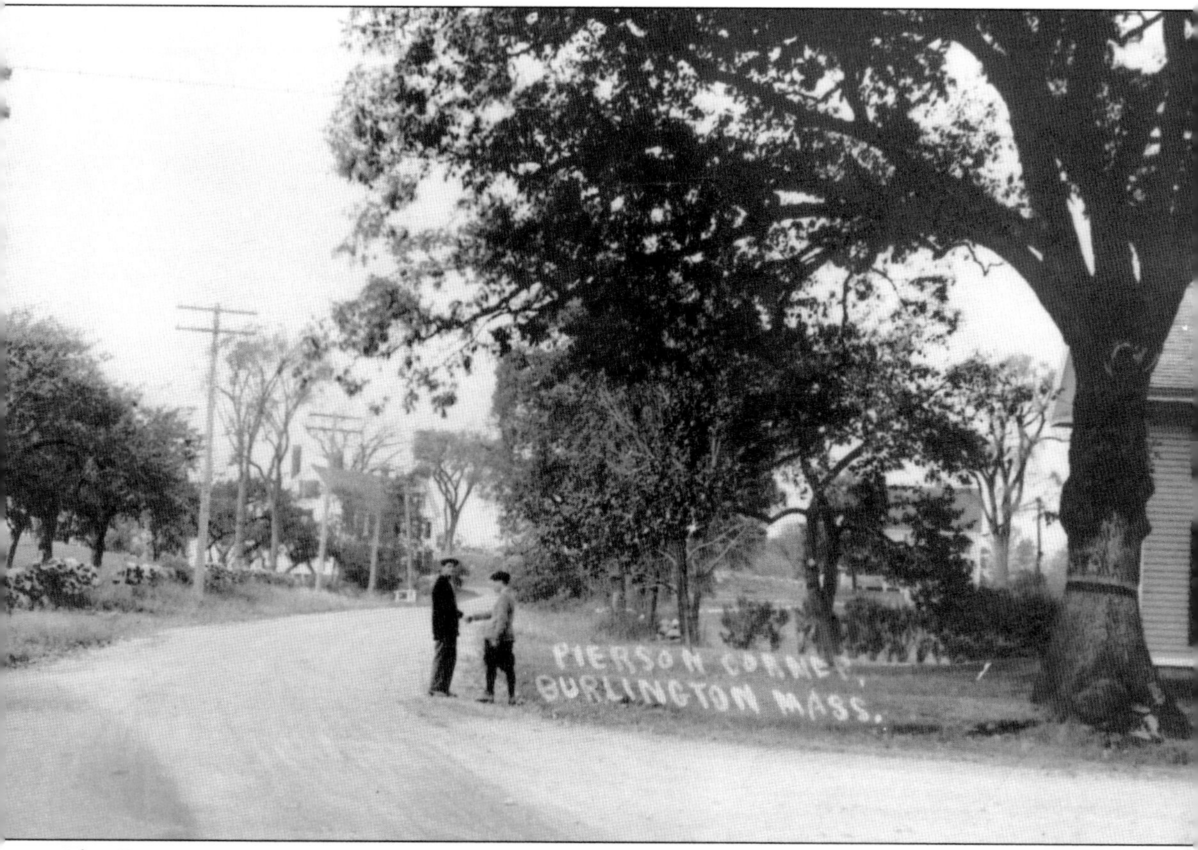

The Pearsons-Symmes house stood on the town common at the corner of Bedford and Cambridge Streets. The house was built by Horace Pearsons c. 1827–1864 and was later moved to 10 Sears Street. Here, William Henry Walker and Crawford Bennett (both from notable Burlington families of the 19th century) are standing on Cambridge Street (Route 3A). The Gleason-Bennett-Simonds house is visible on the far left. (Courtesy of the Burlington Archives, No. 337.)

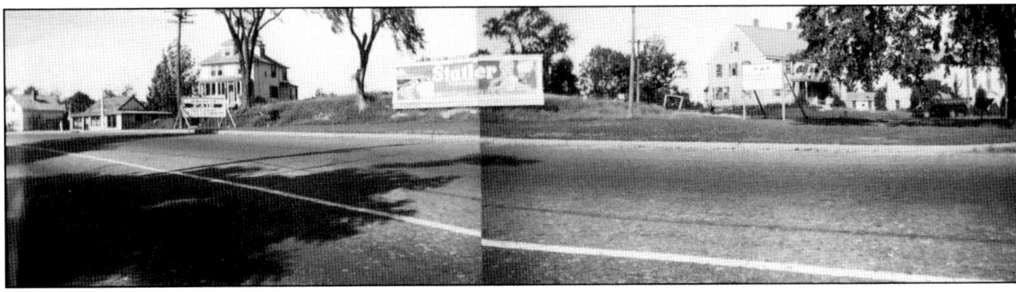

This c. 1930 photograph shows, from left to right, the house of Charles Foster, the Dearborn store, the Charles Dearborn house, the Statler Tissues billboard, the Wood Tavern, and the second town hall. By 1960, all had disappeared from the town common. The Wood Tavern stood on the site of the present-day fire station. The second town hall occupied the spot where the town hall annex is located. Charles Dearborn (1866–1938) operated Burlington's telephone exchange. (Courtesy of the Burlington Archives, No. 205.)

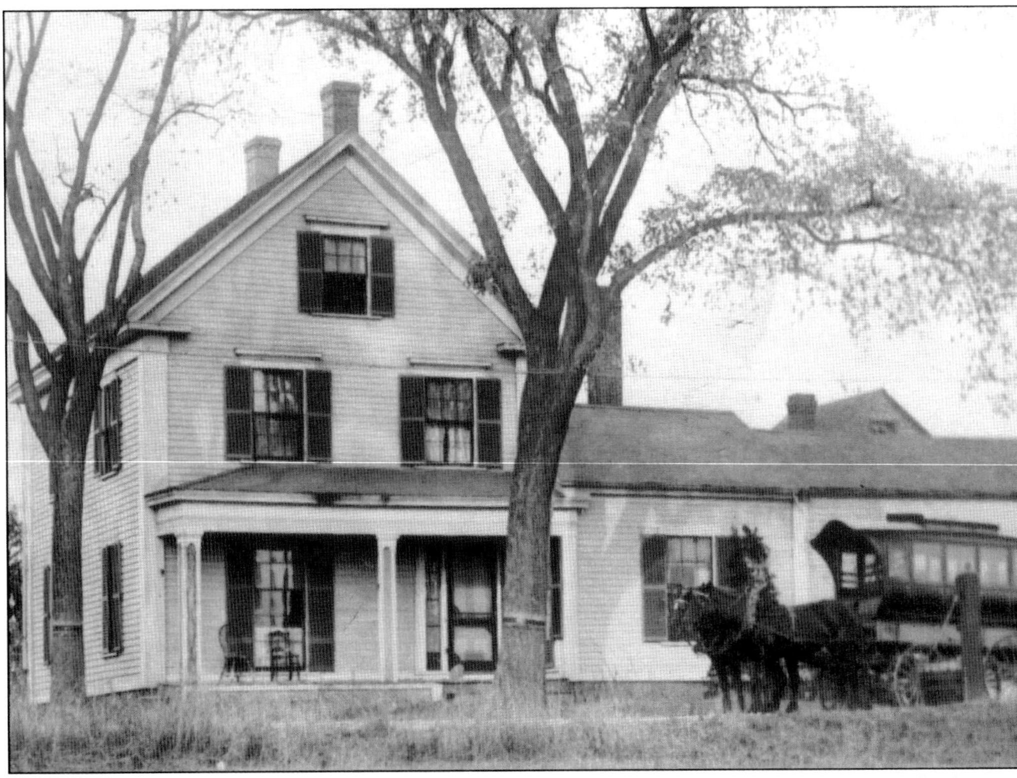

The Silas Cutler general store stood next to the Wood Tavern and was originally located where the town hall annex is today. In this early-1900s image, "the Barge" is parked in front of the store. The Barge was used as Burlington's first school bus and was also used by the local mail carrier. The general store was associated with a number of owners, including the Cutler, Gleason, Carter, Stevenson, and Dodge families. The complex had a house on the left, a low store in the center, and a large barn on the right. The store operated until the 1940s. By 1968, however, all the buildings had been demolished to make room for the new town hall. The site was historically significant, for it housed the early Burlington post office and the town's library until 1879. (Courtesy of the Burlington Archives, No. 465.)

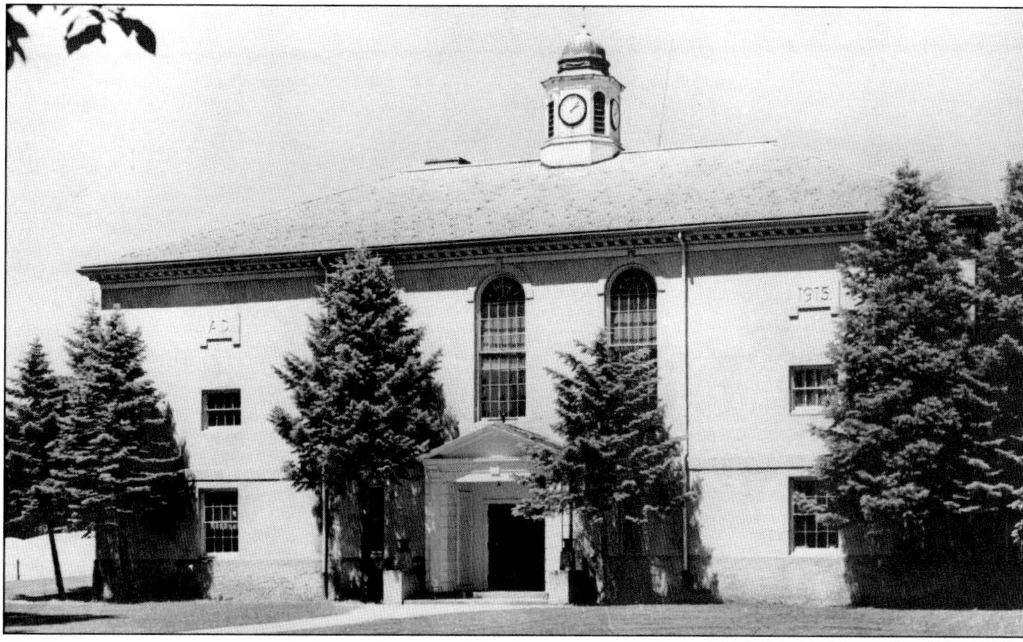

Burlington's second town hall was built in 1915 at the current location of the town hall annex. Architect Robert Coit designed the second town hall, which was a two-story stucco building with an auditorium that occupied the second floor. The auditorium had a stage on one end and a gallery on the other. The building also had an office for the selectmen and a vault for storage. Burlington's second town hall was demolished in 1969 to build a new police station. (Courtesy of the Burlington Archives, No. 17.)

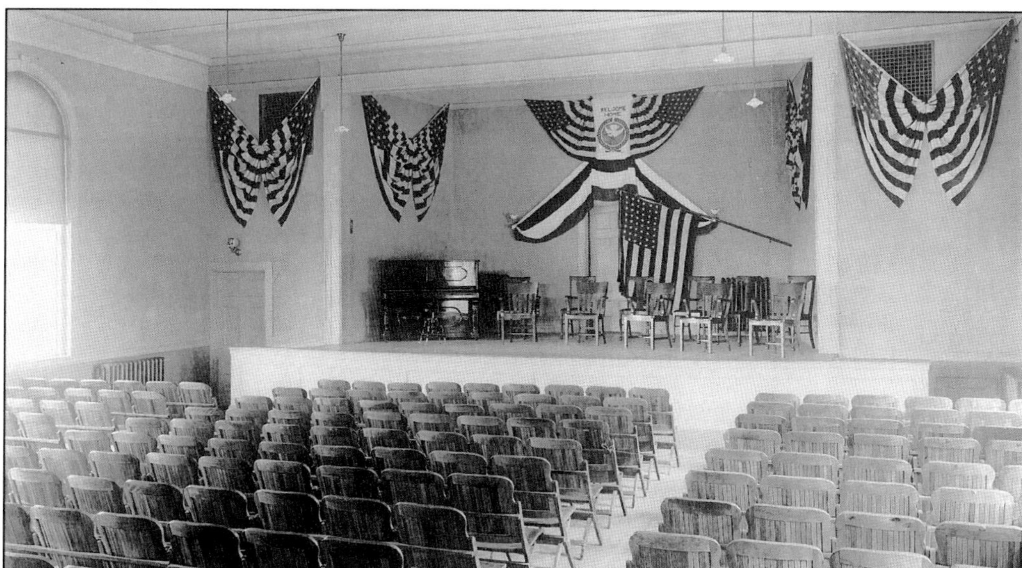

The auditorium of the second town hall was the scene of many important and spirited town meetings between 1915 and 1939. The town hall served as the political and social center of Burlington for decades. It was used to capacity until it was razed in 1969 to make way for a new police station. The site is now occupied by the town hall annex. (Courtesy of the Burlington Archives, No. 186.)

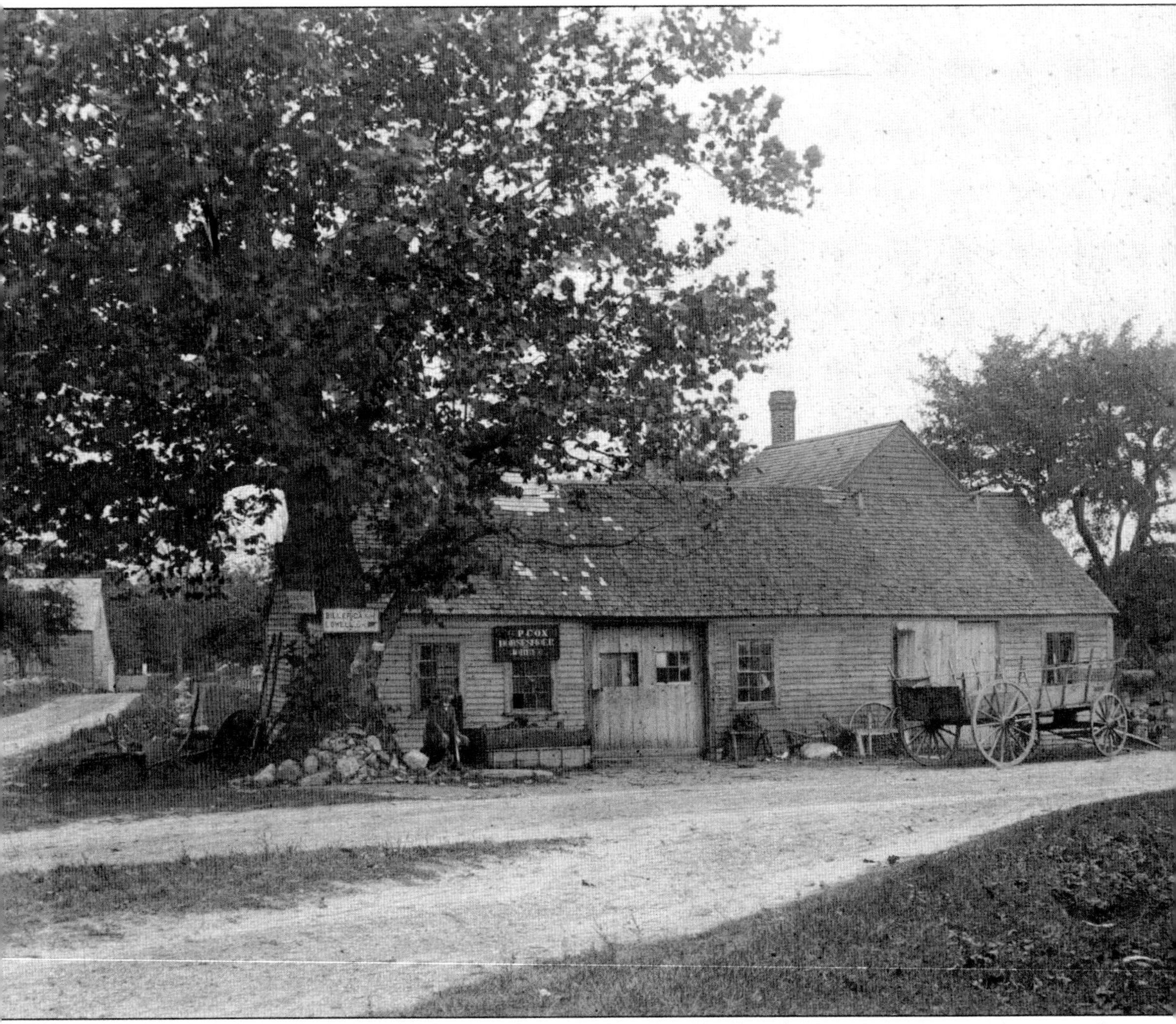

This blacksmith shop was located at the corner of Bedford and Center Streets in the triangle opposite today's police station. Local blacksmiths included Solomon Trull, Richard Alley, Henry P. Cox, and Fred Dockendorf. According to archival sources, Richard J. Alley ran the local blacksmith shop from 1842 until the 1890s. The weathervane on the Burlington Public Museum is considered to be Alley's work. (Courtesy of the Burlington Archives, No. 63)

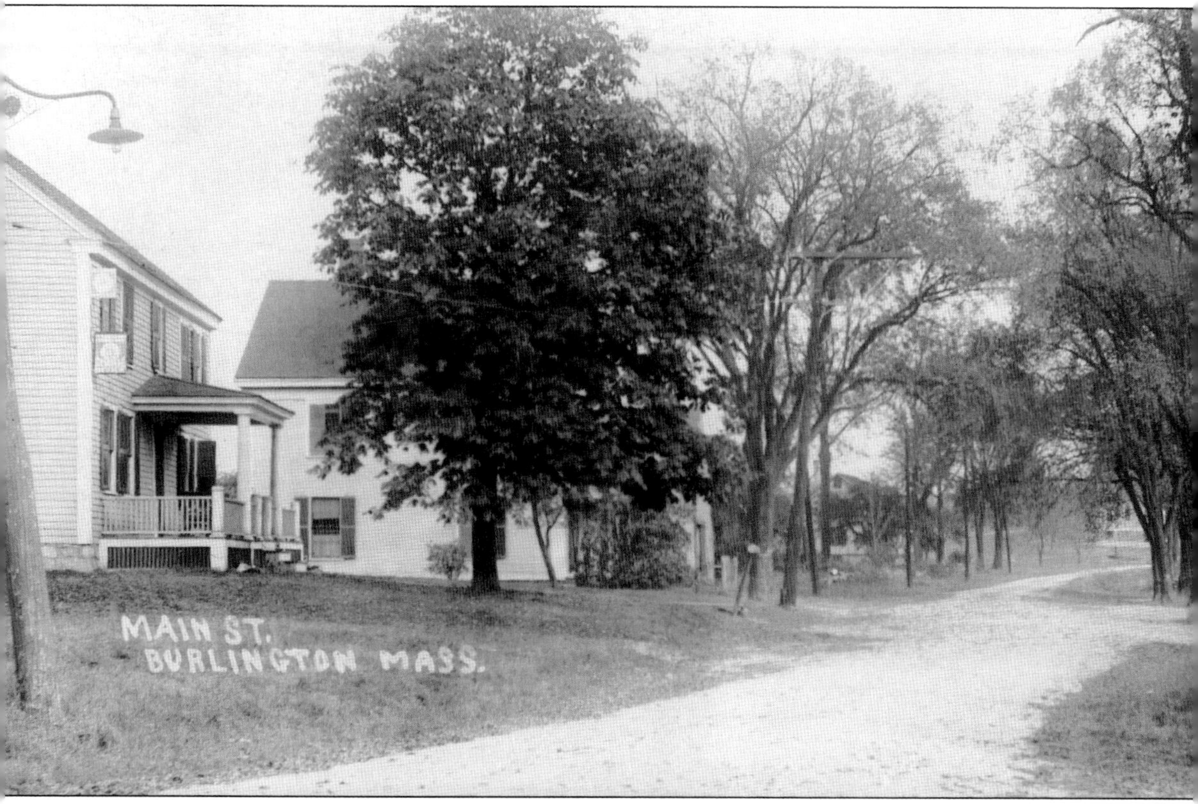

This is a view down Main Street from Cambridge Street c. 1900. Main Street is now called Center Street. It is the location of the town's major institutions, such as the town hall, police station, fire station, and financial institutions. The first house on the left is the Capt. John Wood house, which stood where the fire department is located today. The building was constructed before the Revolution and was a major community meeting place. The townwide celebration that took place upon Burlington's incorporation as a town in 1799 was held in the large ballroom on the second floor of this building. The town acquired the property and tore the building down in 1957. (Courtesy of the Burlington Archives, No. 78)

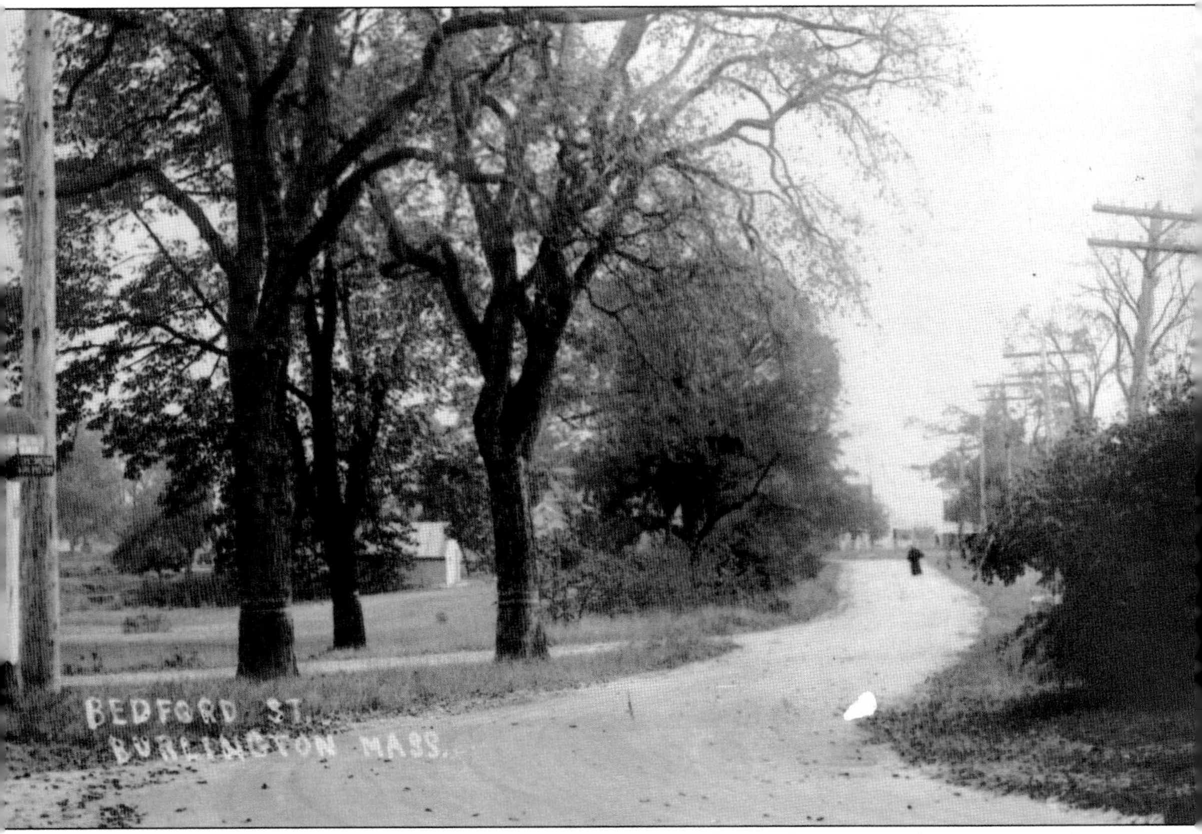

The location of this scene is somewhat of a mystery. The Burlington Archives suggest that it might be the intersection of Francis Wyman Road and Bedford Street early in the 20th century. The telephone poles indicate that it is sometime after 1910 or 1911, since electricity came to the town at that time. (Courtesy of the Burlington Archives, No. 284.)

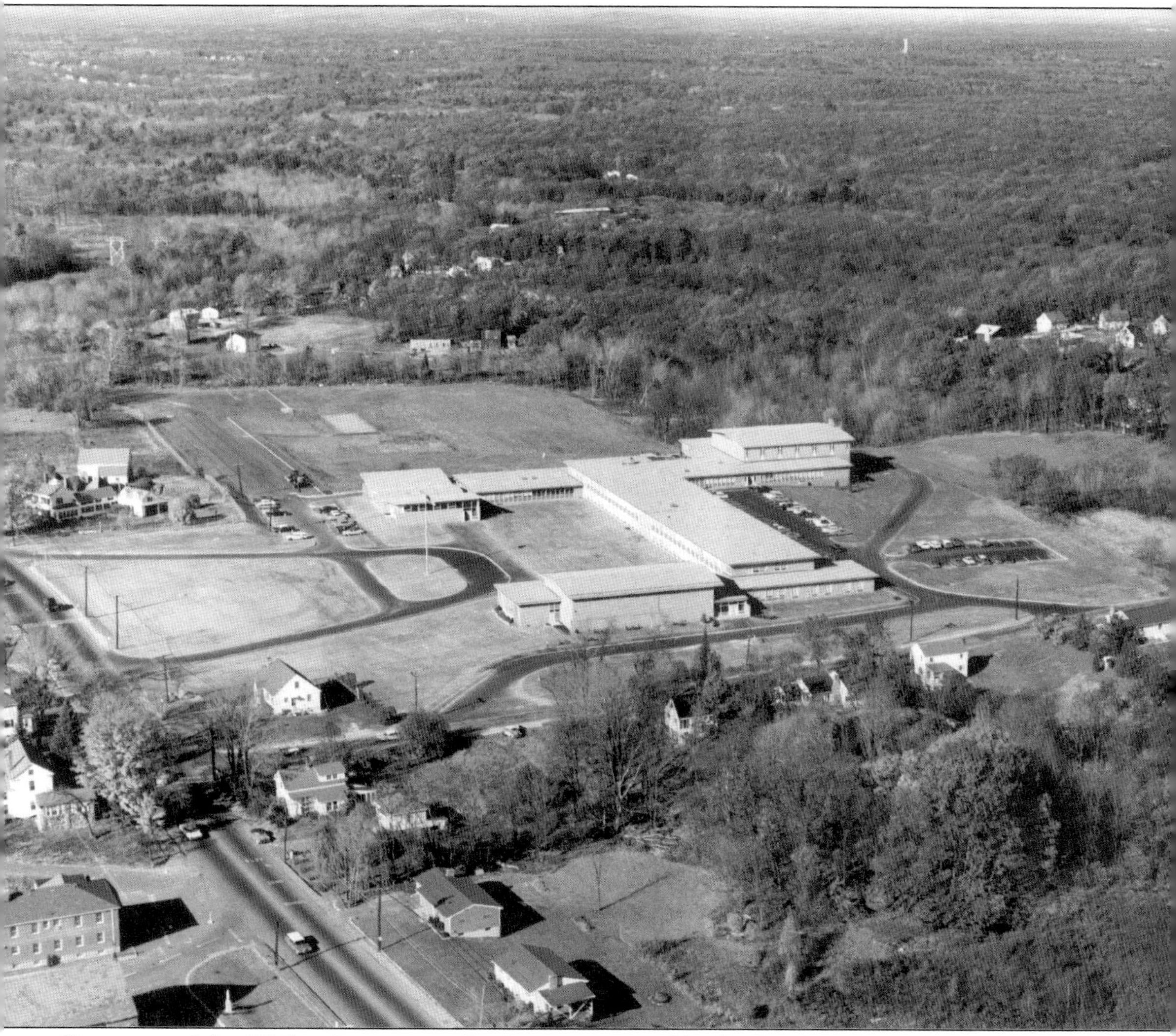

Once part of the Walker farm annex, Burlington's second high school was built in 1961 and is now the Marshall Simonds Middle School. In 1973, after a town competition and much debate, the building was renamed in honor of Marshall Simonds, one of chief benefactors of the town. In his 1905 will, Marshall Simonds left land to the town for use as a park and town common. He also directed a sum of money to be spent for the building of a high school and a location for a new town hall. (Courtesy of the Burlington Archives, No. 25.)

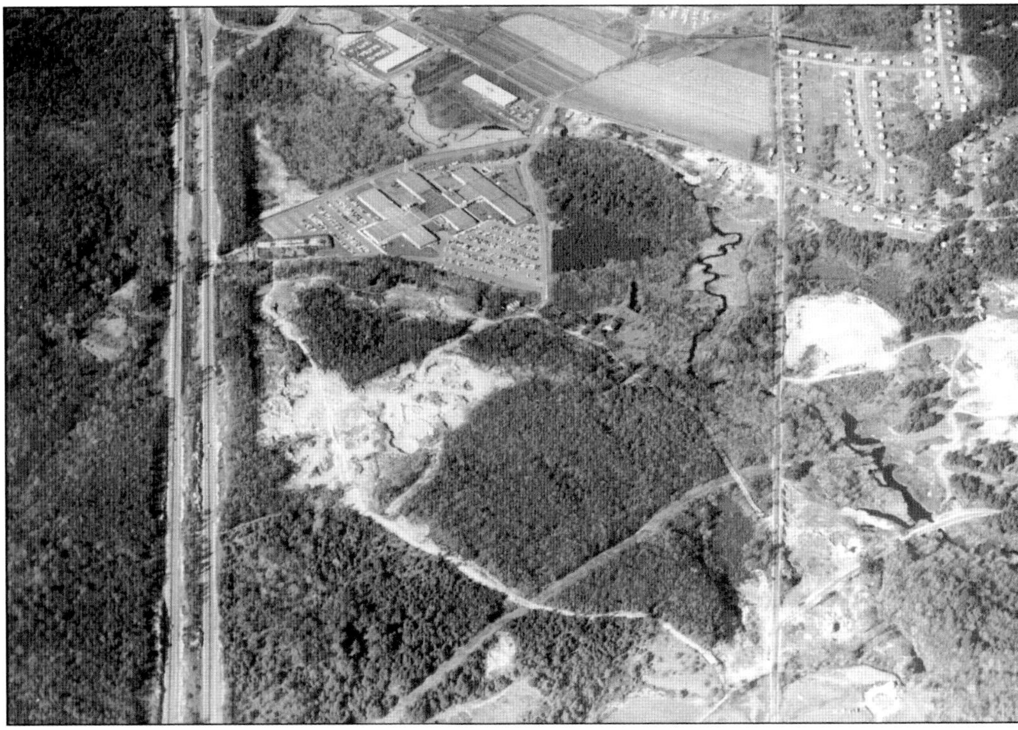

In this aerial view from the 1960s, the focus is on Middlesex Turnpike, Route 3, and Bedford Street. Now the area is the home of the Burlington Mall, industrial parks, and giant computer firms. (Courtesy of the Burlington Archives, No. 454.)

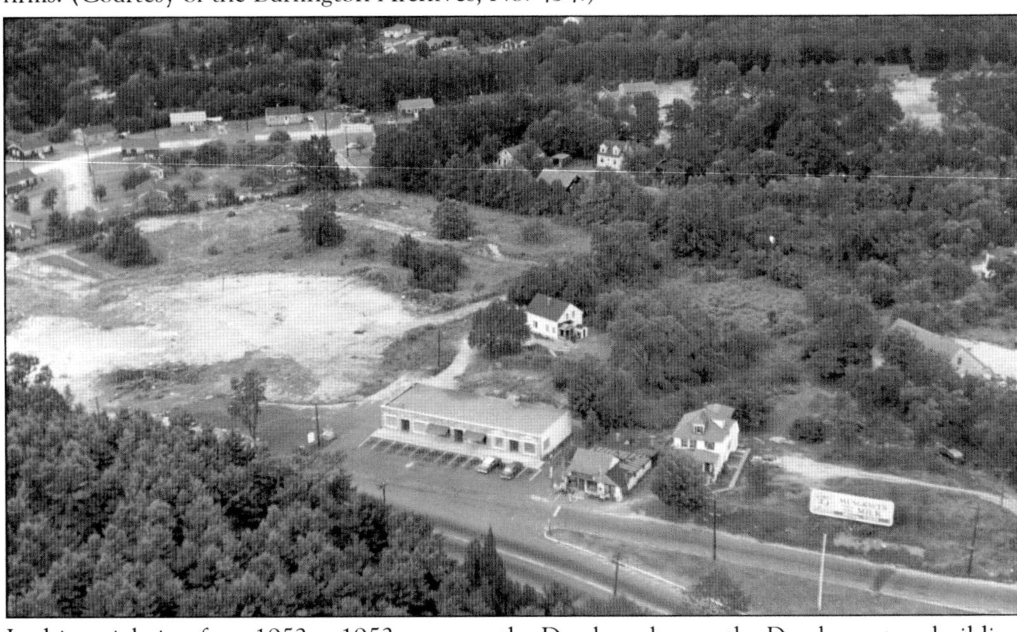

In this aerial view from 1952 or 1953, one sees the Dearborn house, the Dearborn store building, and the "new store" building (a retail strip today). In the center is the Doherty house. Forbes Avenue is at the top. The large open area on the left later became the home of Burlington's first supermarket, the IGA. (Courtesy of the Burlington Archives, No. 478.)

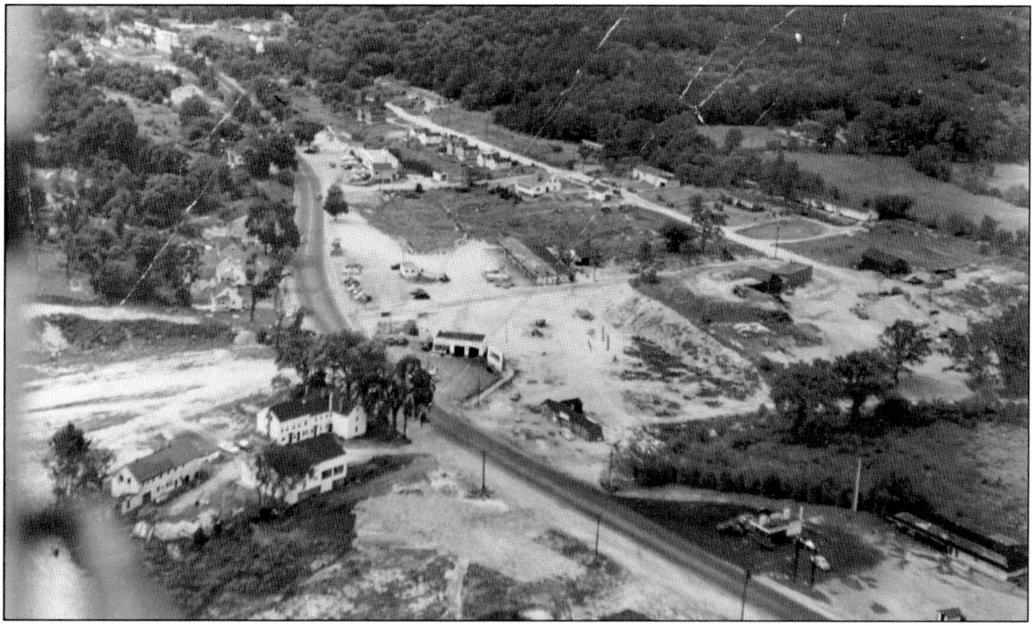

The large white building complex on the left is the Butters farmhouse, the approximate location of today's Brunswick Bowling Alley. In the 1940s and 1950s, the buildings were used as the Joman's Auction House. A popular drive-in restaurant called the Flying Saucer was located at the lower right of the image. Today, it is the location of the Dunkin' Donuts shop. (Courtesy of the Burlington Archives, No. 509.)

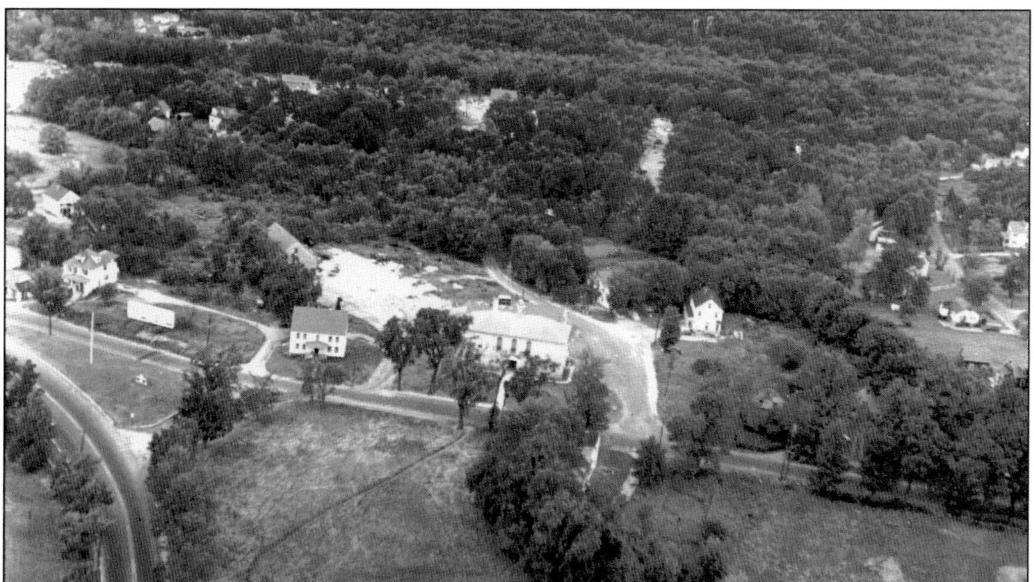

In the 1950s, Burlington's town common reflected the rural nature of the town at that time. In the center of the image is the second town hall. To the left is the Wood Tavern. Cambridge Street winds its way to the left, and Center Street runs through the middle, with Olympian Way connecting the two. The barn behind the Wood Tavern was the site of the annual Burlington Agricultural Fair, with exhibits there and on the town common. (Courtesy of the Burlington Archives, No. 422.)

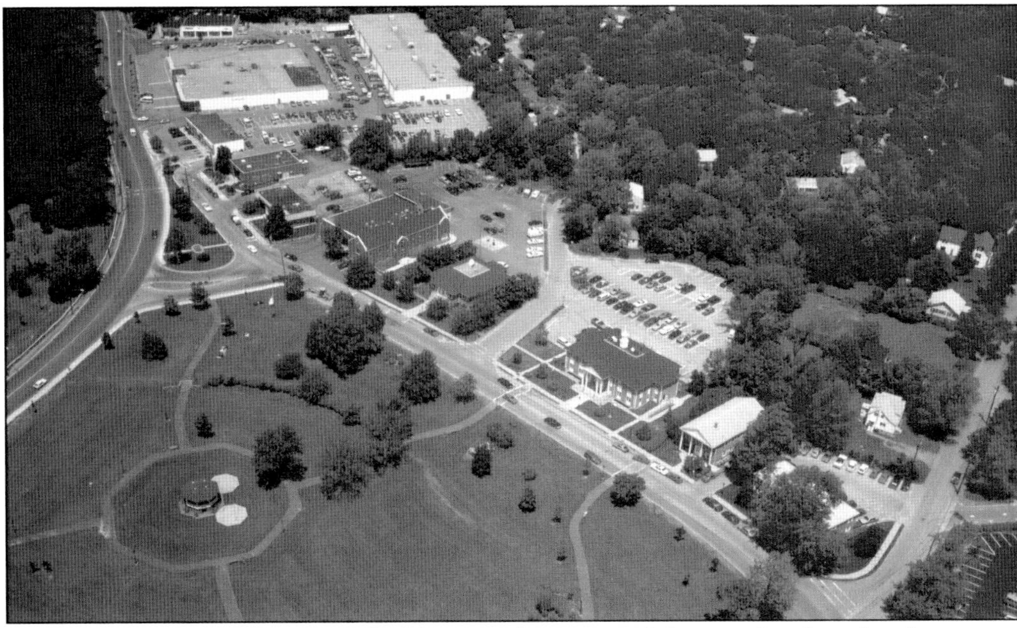

By the 1980s, the town common had become the center of the town's political and economic institutions. All private buildings and houses had been removed over the years, and a number of historic structures (such as the second town hall and the Wood Tavern) were razed to build modern structures. The common continues to serve the town as a place for community events and celebrations, as it has for over 200 years. (Courtesy of the Burlington Archives, No. 1.)

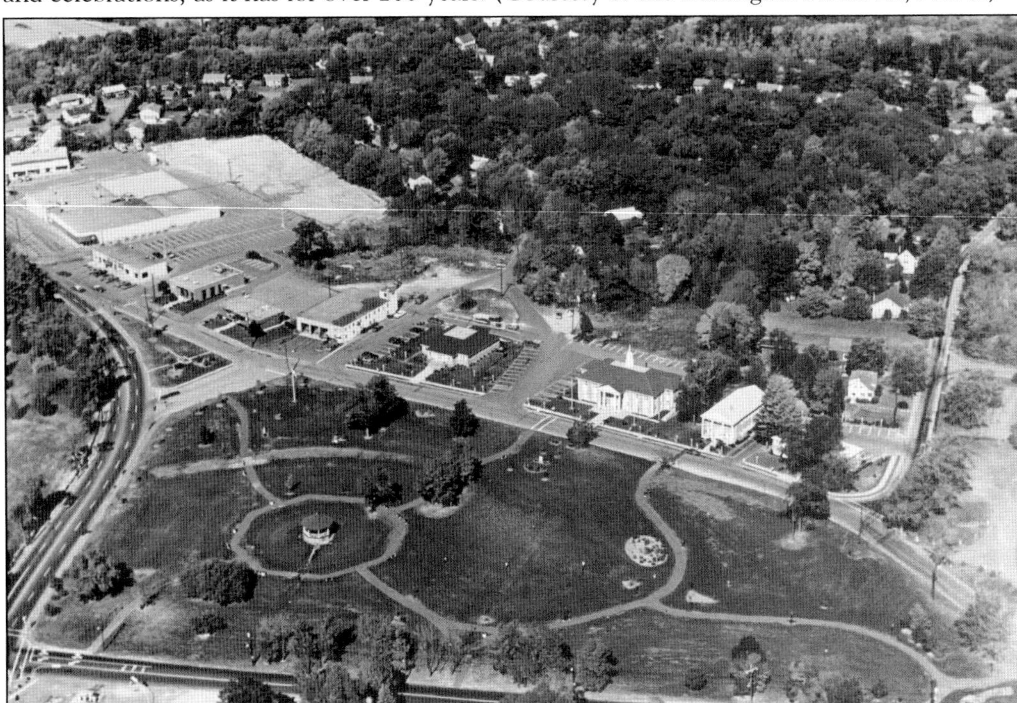

This photograph of the town common in 1973 shows Cambridge Street, Olympia Way, Center Street, Sears Street, and Bedford Street. (Courtesy of the Burlington Archives, No. 81.)

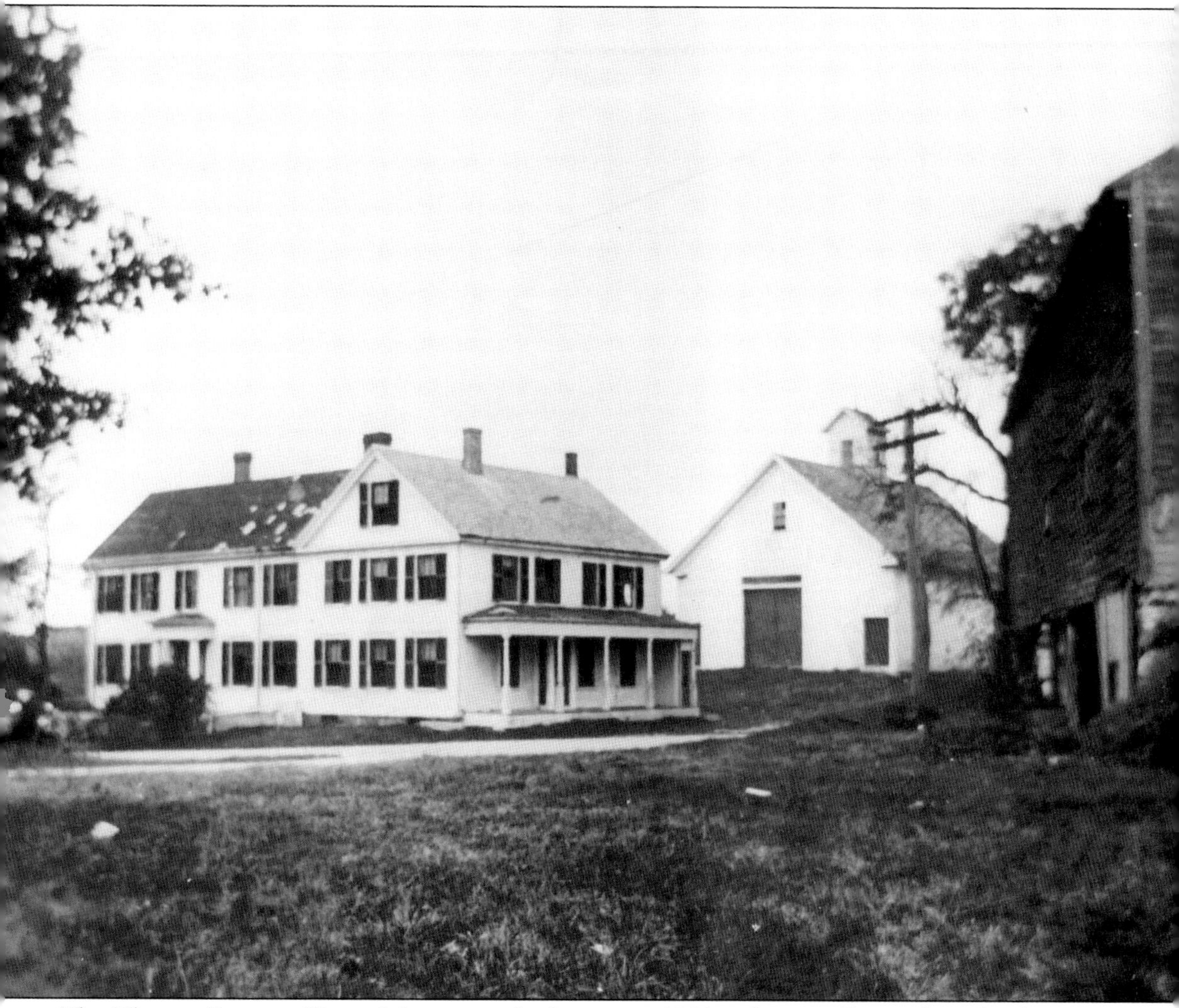

The Gleason-Bennett-Simonds house was built prior to 1851 and originally stood on the sharp curve on Cambridge Street across from Olympian Way. In 1920, the state straightened and widened Cambridge Street, and the house was split in two and moved. The town library was located in the house in a room that still survives at 2 Mill Street. Marshall Simonds purchased "the Block," as it was known, sometime before his death in 1905. One side of his original house is standing at 2 Mill Street, and the other half is located on Sears Street. (Courtesy of the Burlington Archives No. 52.)

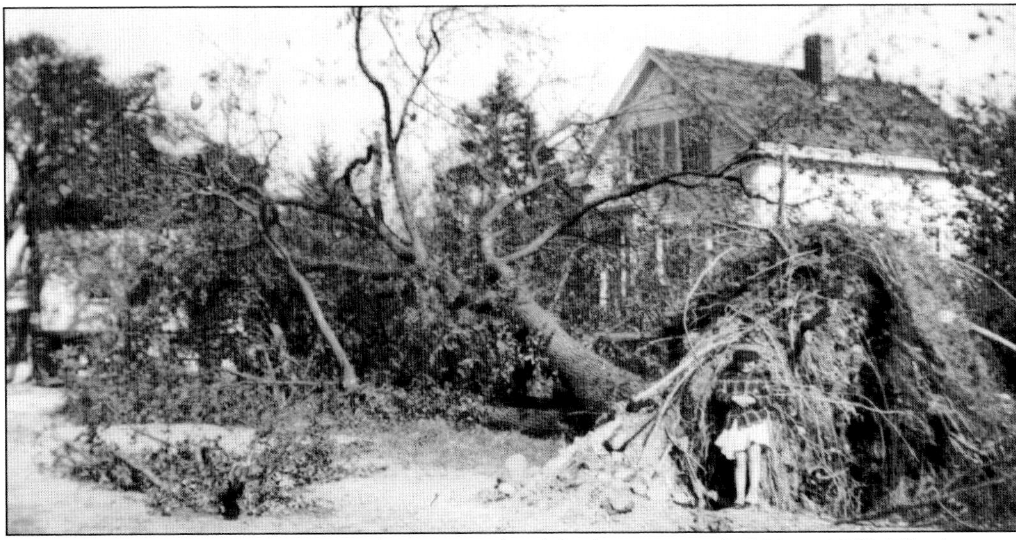

This large uprooted tree may have been a result of the hurricane of 1938 or 1953. The location is on Center Street at the home of Henrietta "Nettie" Richardson Foster. She and her husband, Charles Henry Foster, had a house and two acres in the center of town. Henrietta Foster was the town librarian from 1922 to 1939 and was known as "Aunt Nettie." (Courtesy of the Burlington Archives, No. 201.)

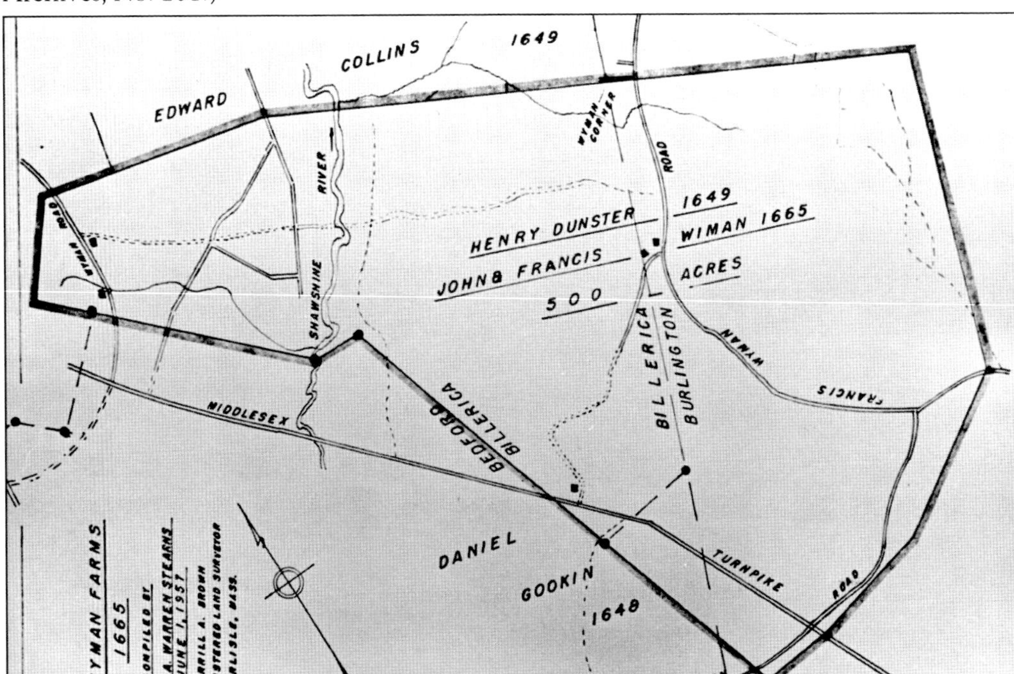

Francis and John Wyman immigrated to America from West Mill, England, in 1640. They were founders of the town of Woburn, owned large tracts of land in what is today Burlington, and founded one of the first industries in the area. The Wyman brothers operated tanneries in the Central Square region of Woburn. Over a period of 10 years, the Wyman brothers acquired 1,000 acres of land in what is present-day Burlington and Billerica. This map represents those land holdings. (Courtesy of the Burlington Archives, No. 463.)

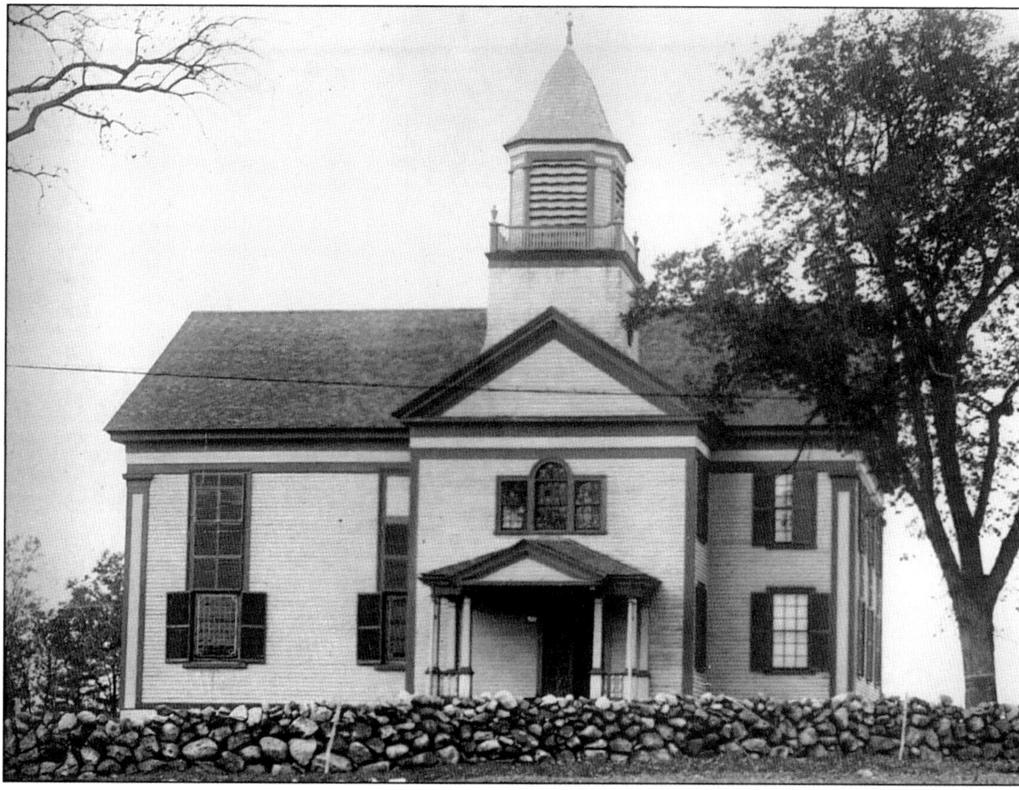

The Second Parish Meetinghouse (today's United Church of Christ Congregational) is significant as a Colonial meetinghouse with an active congregation that has served the town in many ways for more than 270 years. The building was raised on July 23, 1732, and had major renovations in 1846 and 1888. On March 9, 1990, the church was added to the National Register of Historic Places. (Courtesy of the Burlington Community Scholarship Committee.)

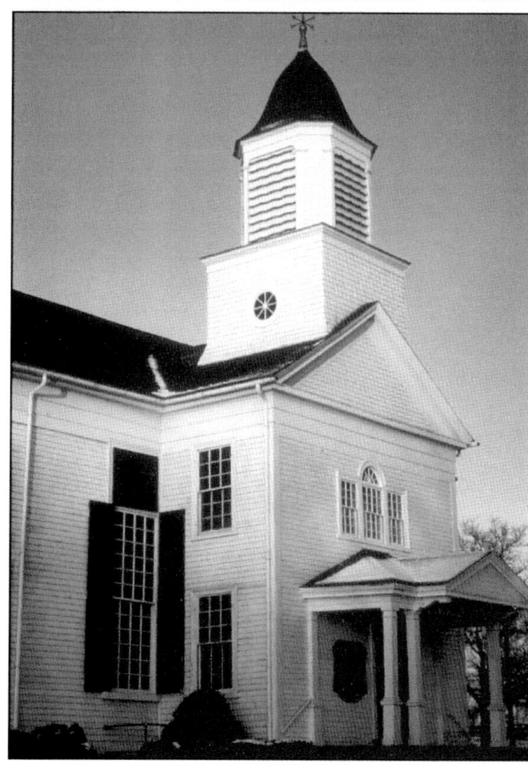

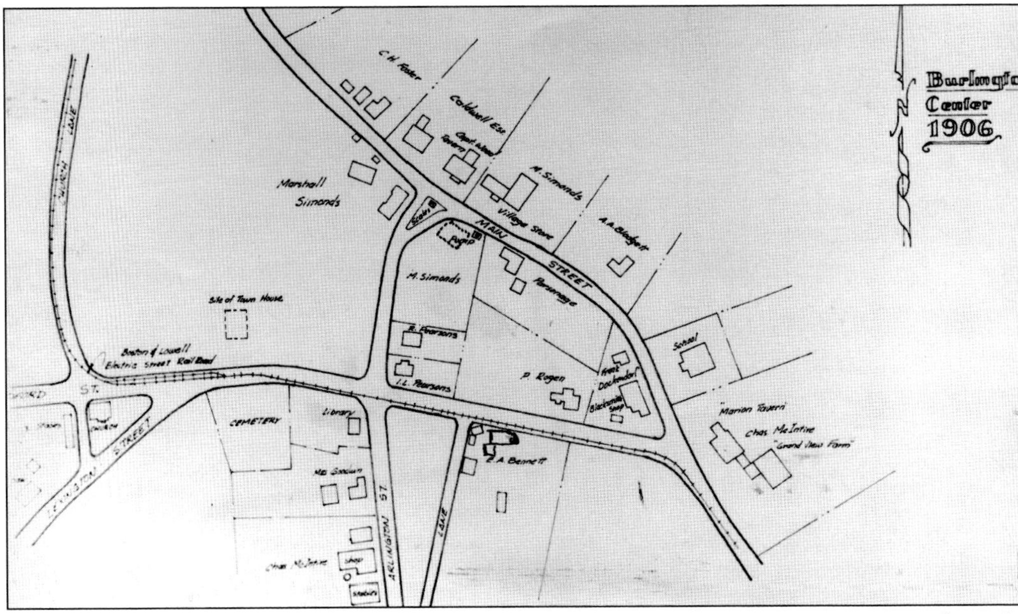

Drawn by town employee Al Nelson for Ed Fogelberg's *Burlington: Part of a Greater Chronicle*, this *c*. 1906 view of Burlington Center shows a number of interesting differences from the same area today. Notice the Boston and Lowell Electric Street Railroad tracks running from Church Lane to Bedford Street and down what was then called Main Street (now Center Street). As a result of the railroad, Sears Street was built by the company to connect Main Street to Winn Street. The center is carved up by private house and barn lots, and the blacksmith shop occupies a strategic location. (Courtesy of the Burlington Archives, No. 457.)

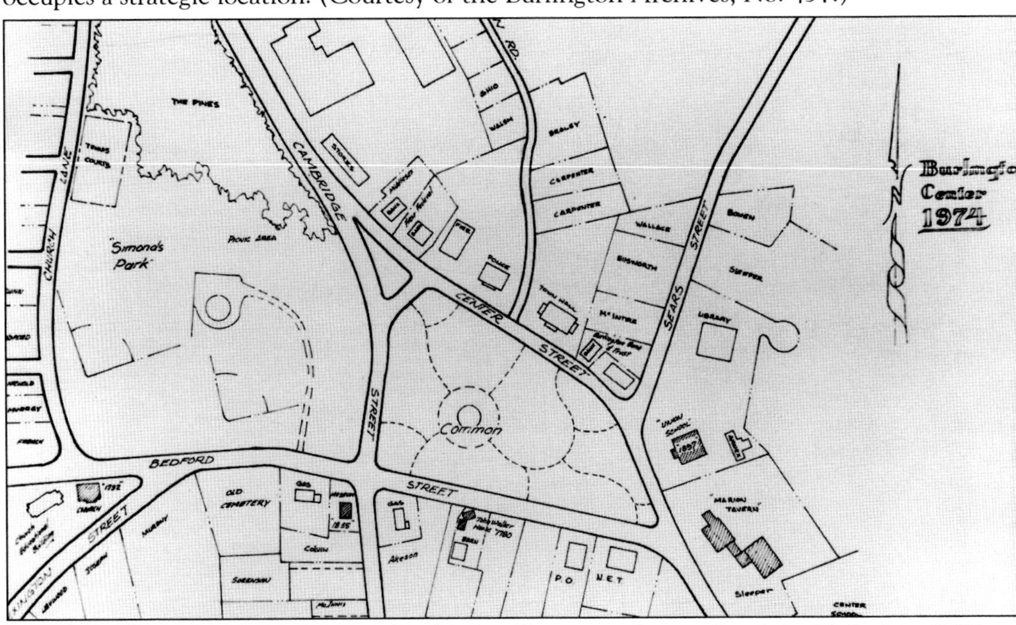

From the Al Nelson series of maps for the Fogelberg town history book (published in 1976 and expanded by the Burlington Bicentennial Commission for 1999), this view shows Burlington Center in 1974, with all private buildings removed from the common and the former Marshall Simonds farm turned into a large public park. (Courtesy of the Burlington Archives, No. 460.)

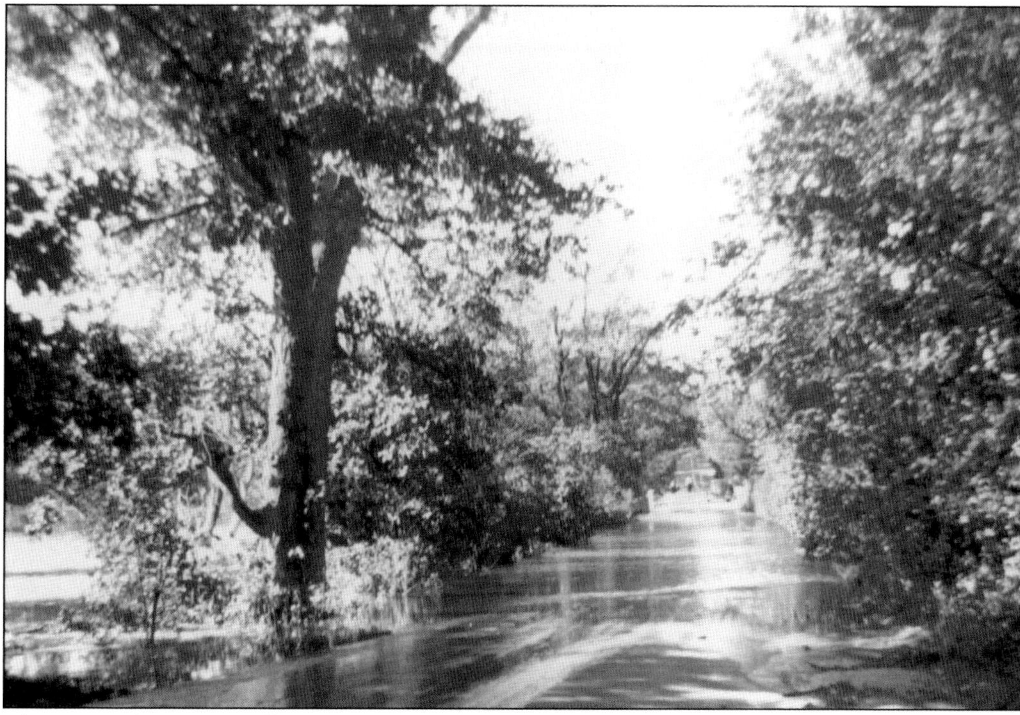

This view of Terrace Hall Avenue shows the results of the flooding of Vine Brook in the 1950s. According to sources from the Burlington Archives, the large tree on the left is where the first water treatment plant is located today. (Courtesy of the Burlington Archives, No. 368.)

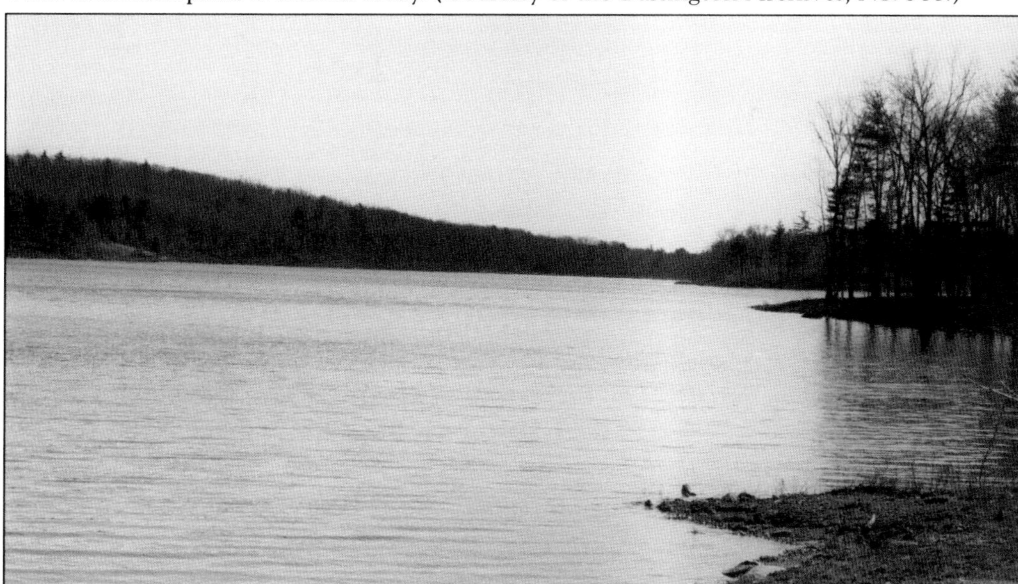

Once a small millpond with the working sawmill of Calvin Simonds and others, the reservoir was built by the firm of Whitman and Howard, beginning in 1971. The reservoir was to cover approximately 65 acres at a cost of $4.2 million. Today, the area offers residents a quiet, natural setting with conservation trails and other recreational opportunities. (Courtesy of the Burlington Archives, No. 283.)

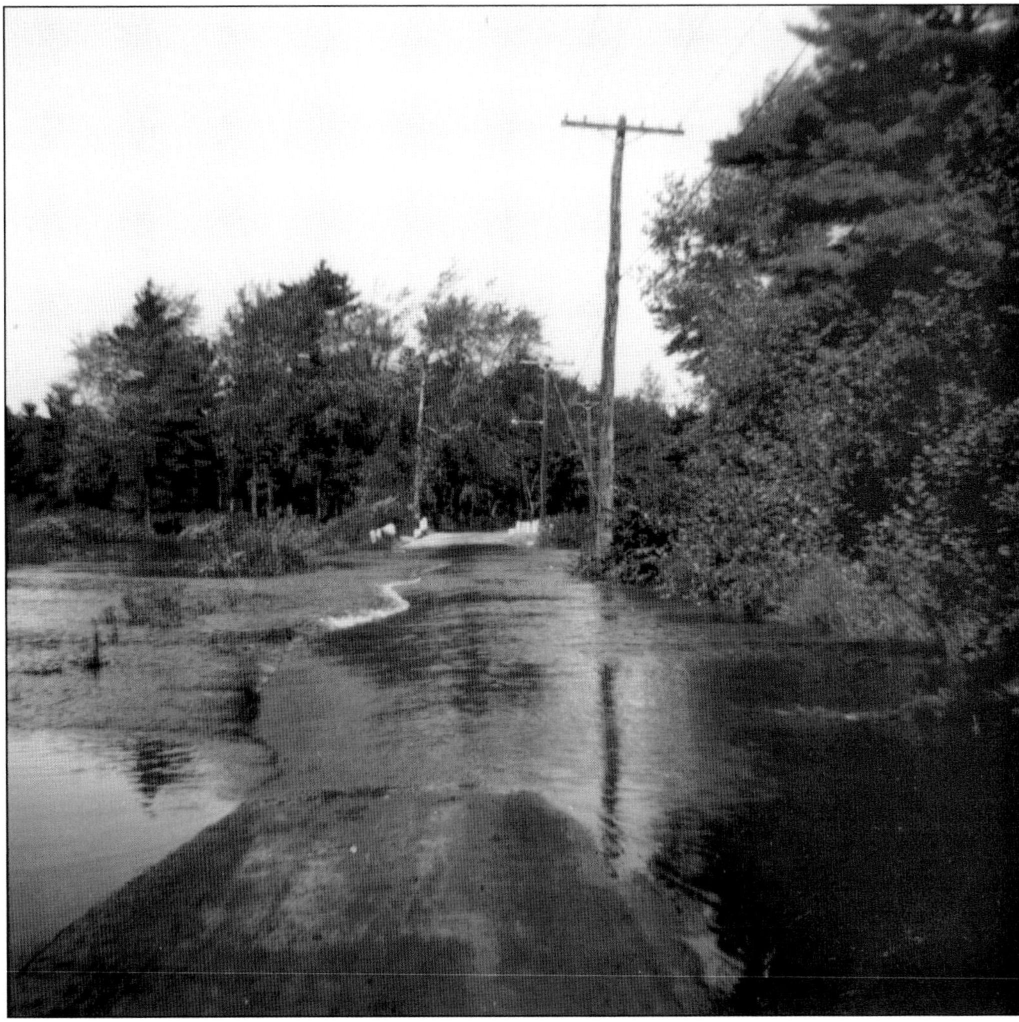

Severe flooding took place in the 1950s in this area of Terrace Hall Avenue. Over the years, Terrace Hall was known for being the location of the Simonds family homestead, where Marshall Simonds was born in 1825. Simonds left Burlington, became a successful businessman, and moved back to the area a wealthy man. (Courtesy of the Burlington Archives, No. 370.)

Five

Portrait Gallery

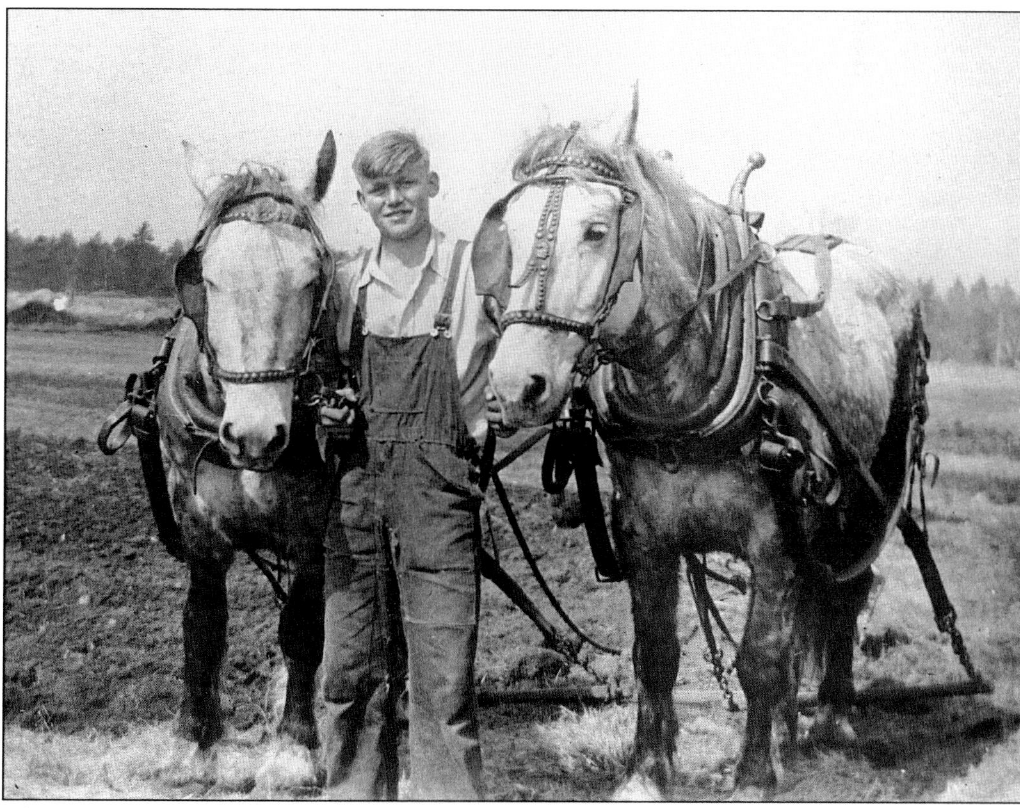

Clarence Bennett was born on May 2, 1919, in Burlington, the second son of Harold W. Bennett and Viola D. Mascho. He was the grandson of George Holden Bennett (1841–1919). This photograph was taken on the George Holden Bennett farm (on Francis Wyman Road), which included parts of Billerica and Burlington. The land was originally part of the 1,000 acres owned by brothers Francis and John Wyman in the 17th century. (Courtesy of the Burlington Archives, No. 93.)

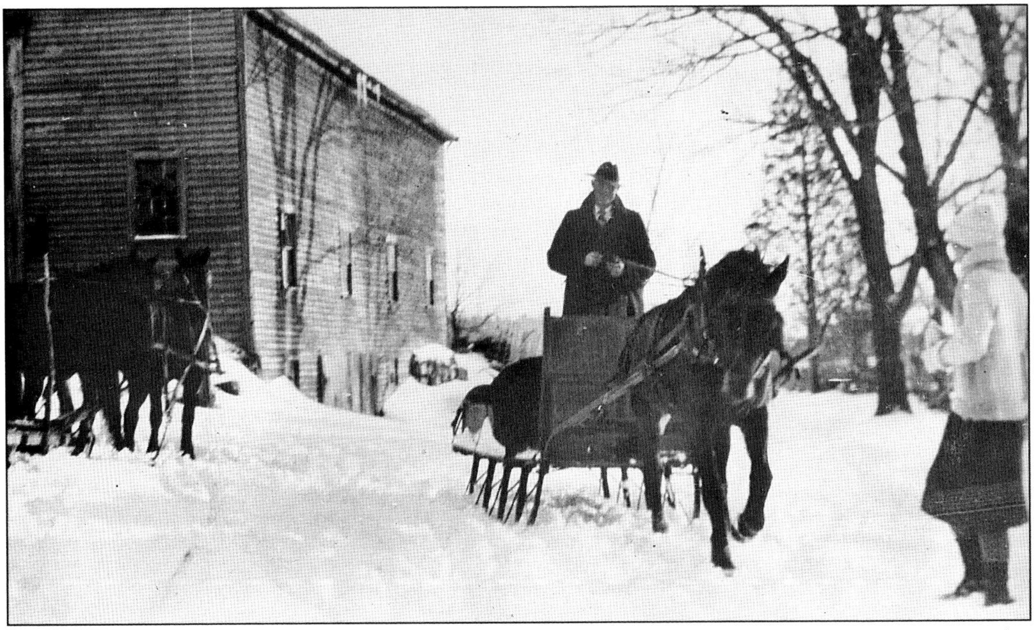

Joshua Holden Bennett (1899–1968) rides a sleigh outside the Walker barn in 1930. The Walker house and barn still stand at 9 Bedford Street, facing the town common. Bennett was the son of Edward Dana Bennett and Nellie Louise Sewall, whose marriage was the union of two significant early Burlington families. The property passed to Joshua Bennett in 1927. (Courtesy of the Burlington Archives, No. 429.)

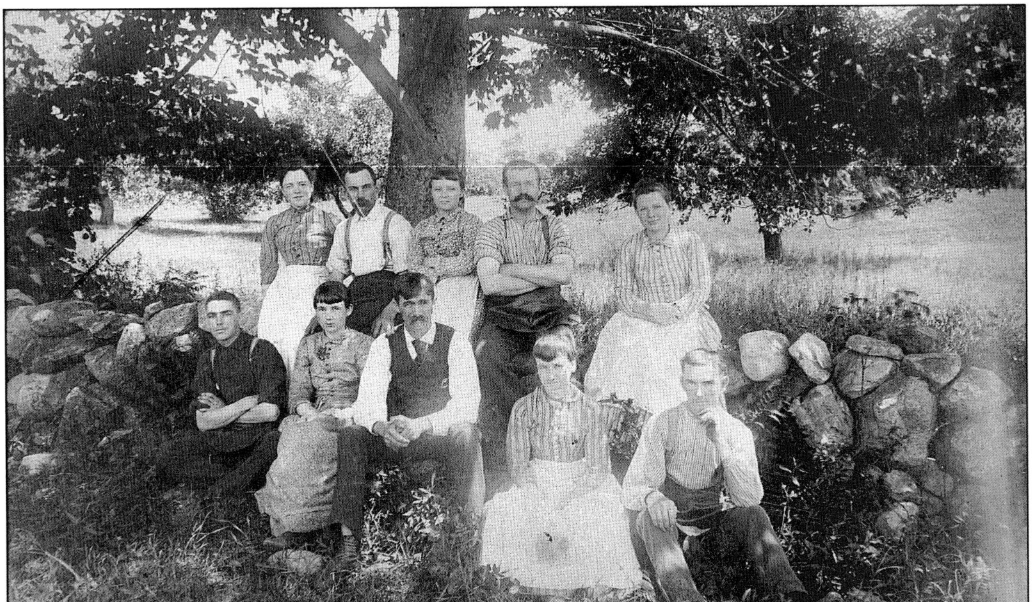

Reflecting the agricultural nature of the town in the late 1890s, farmers and friends pose for the camera. They are, from left to right, as follows: (front row) David Johnson, ? Hayes, George Getchell, ? Hayes, and Al Johnson; (back row) Abbie Abbott, Henry Harrington, Annie Murray, John Hutchinson, and unidentified. (Courtesy of the Burlington Archives, No. 262.)

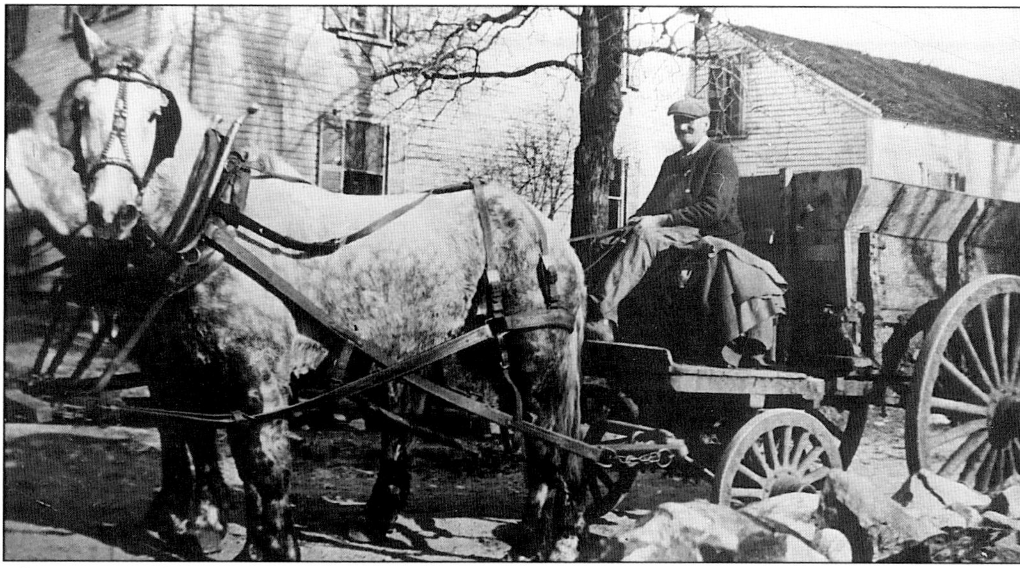

This picture of an unidentified man on a manure cart was taken *c.* 1930 outside of the Walker house, at 9 Bedford Street. At that time, the historic house (built by Joshua and John Walker during the Revolution) was owned by Joshua Holden Bennett. (Courtesy of the Burlington Archives, No. 77.)

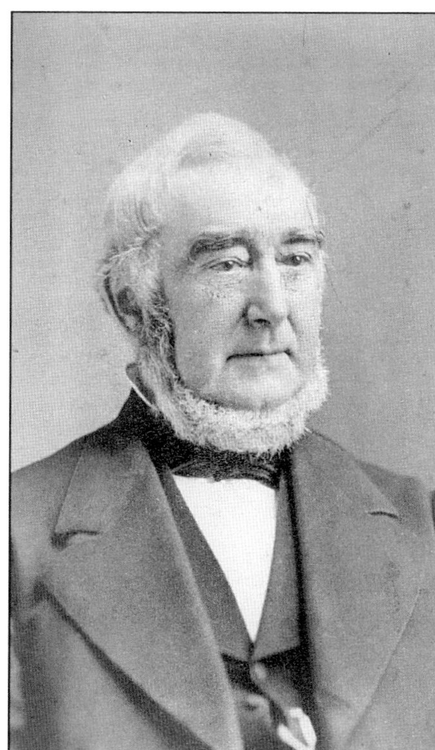

Sources from the Burlington Archives identify this portrait as either that of William Winn (son of Col. William Winn) or William H. Winn (grandson of Colonel Winn). Members of the Winn family were influential in town affairs for three centuries. (Courtesy of the Burlington Archives, No. 94.)

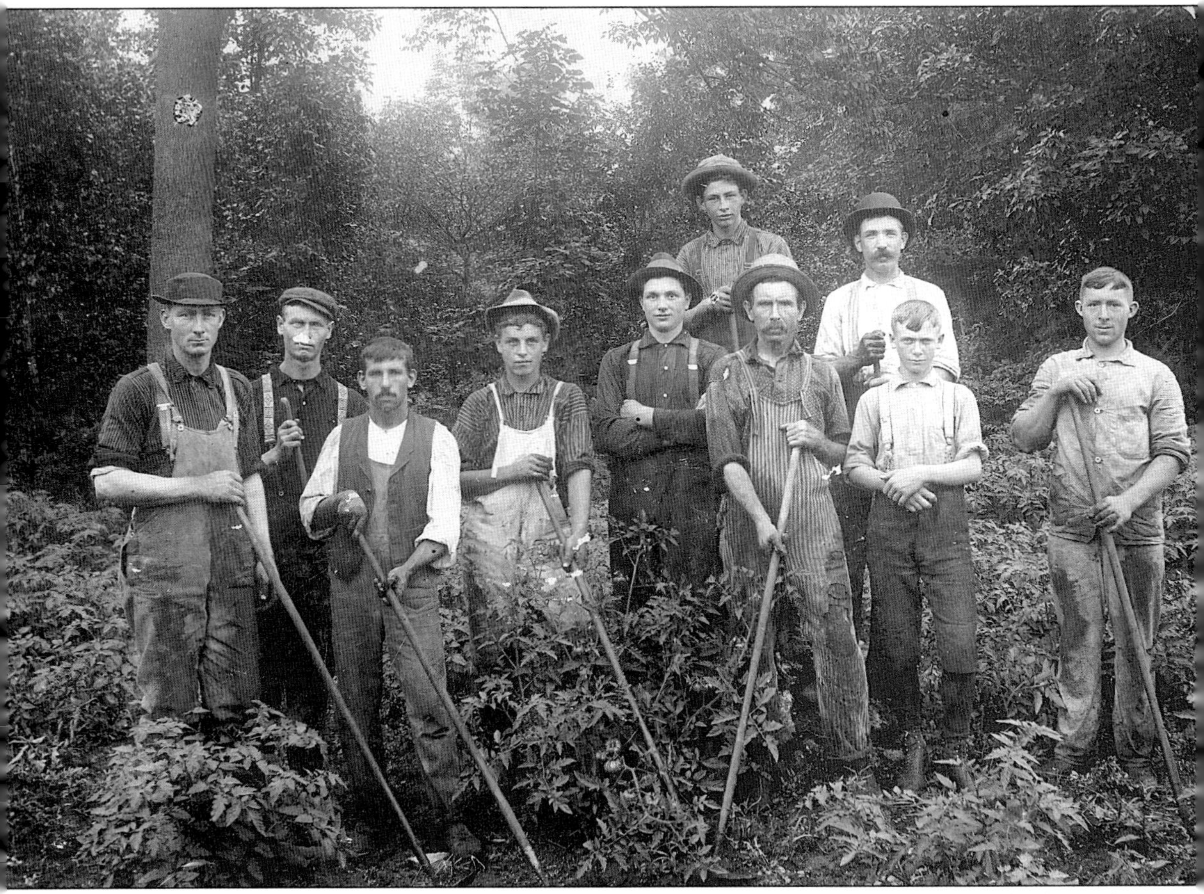

The Skelton family has a long and distinguished history in this area that dates back to the earliest settlements of Massachusetts. Skeltons were in this region during the American Revolution, the founding of Burlington, and its agricultural growth during the 19th century. The Skeltons lived in the Francis Wyman section of Burlington for more than 200 years. In this photograph, Orray Shedd Skelton (1876–1963) is on the far left with a group of field hands hoeing what seem to be tomato plants. His father, Bradford Skelton, traveled to the goldfields of California in 1851–1852. He returned after 1857, married, had four sons, and lived in the house that stands on Francis Wyman Road. (Courtesy of the Burlington Archives, No. 80.)

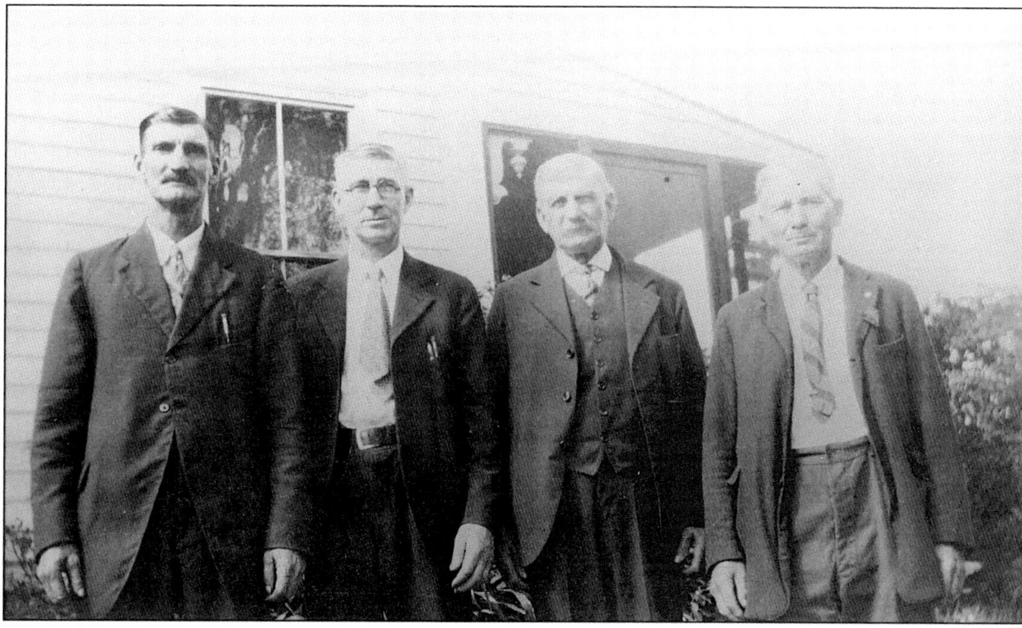

This photograph shows the four Skelton brothers—Horace Bradford, Orray Shedd, Walter Winn, and Lester Brown—sometime in the 1930s. The sons of Bradford Skelton and Almira Shedd Skelton, were all active in town government and community affairs. Horace served as selectman, moderator, and a member of the board of health. Orray was a town moderator and treasurer. Walter was named fire chief in 1935 and housed the first fire station on his property until 1937. (Courtesy of the Burlington Archives, No. 100.)

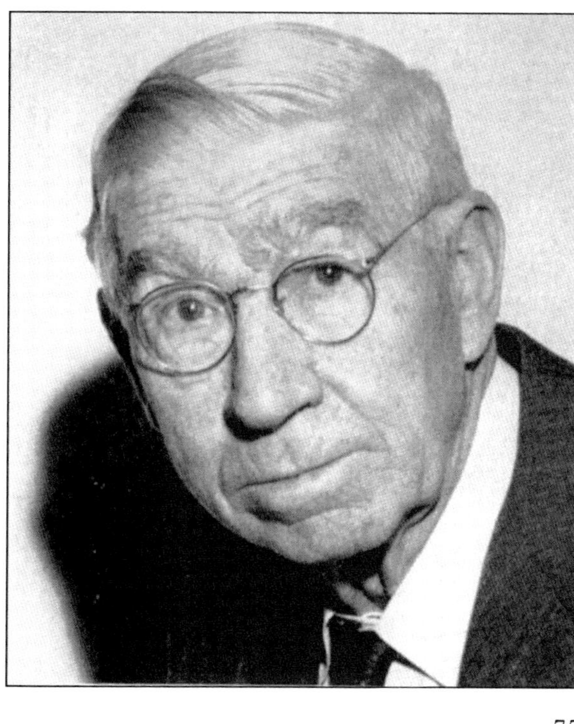

Orray Shedd Skelton was born on March 10, 1876, in Burlington. He married Carrie Augusta Nichols (1876–1914) on June 24, 1901, in Burlington. The couple had two children—Bradford Sumner Skelton and Marshall Winn Skelton. Orray served the town as constable, moderator, treasurer for 32 years, and library trustee. He was also a very active member of the United Church of Christ Congregational. The education building of that church was named in his honor. (Courtesy of the Burlington Archives, No. 84.)

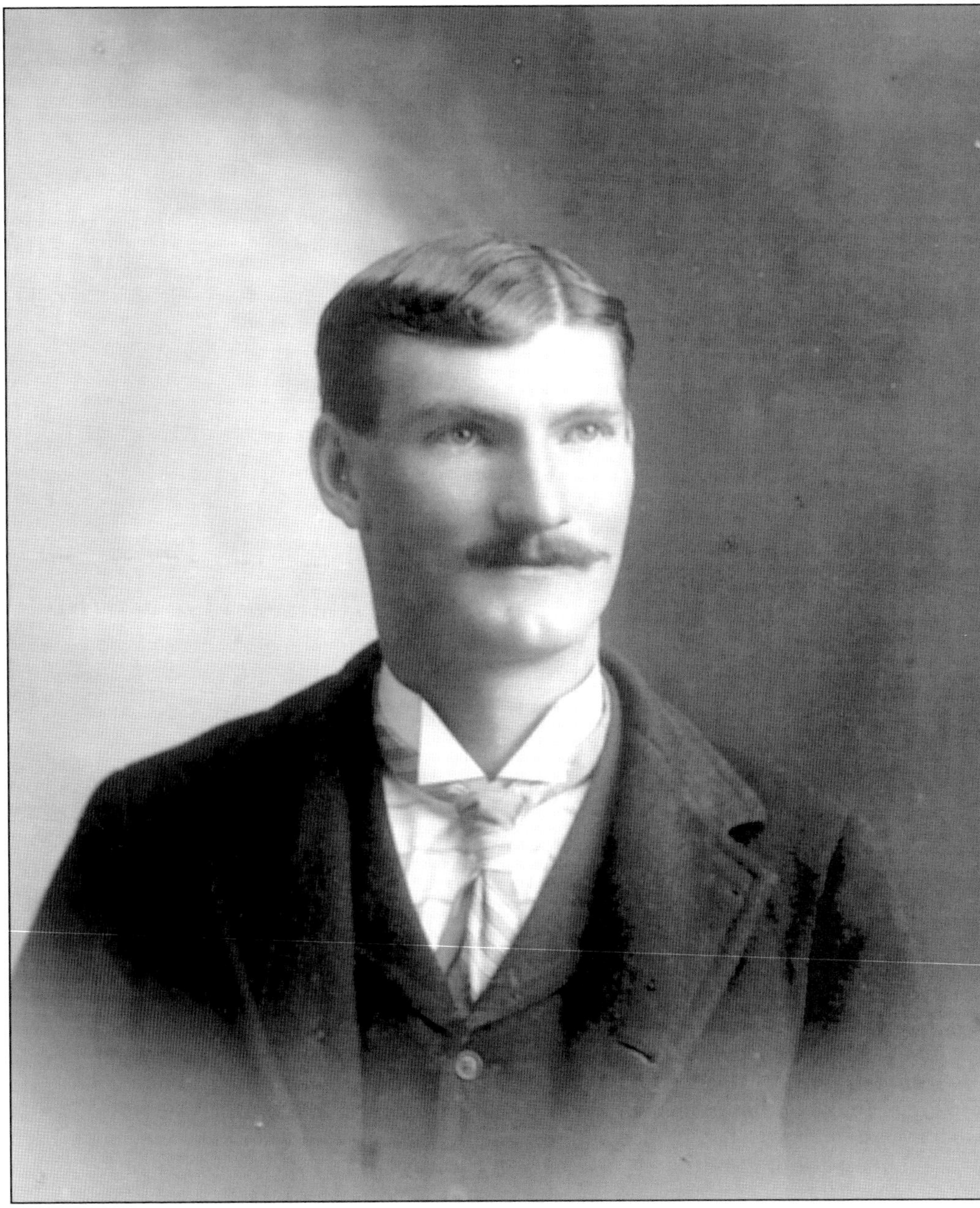

Horace Bradford Skelton was born in Burlington on May 23, 1879. He married Cora Frances Cleveland on May 17, 1906, and eventually had eight children, including Iona, the youngest. Horace operated a chicken farm and owned an incubator house, a brooder house, and a very large henhouse. The farm was located in the Francis Wyman Road area of Burlington on family land, the deed of which is said to date to Colonial times. The farmhouse still stands at Francis Wyman Road and is the home of Iona Skelton Ganley and her husband, Doey. (Courtesy of the Burlington Archives, No. 358.)

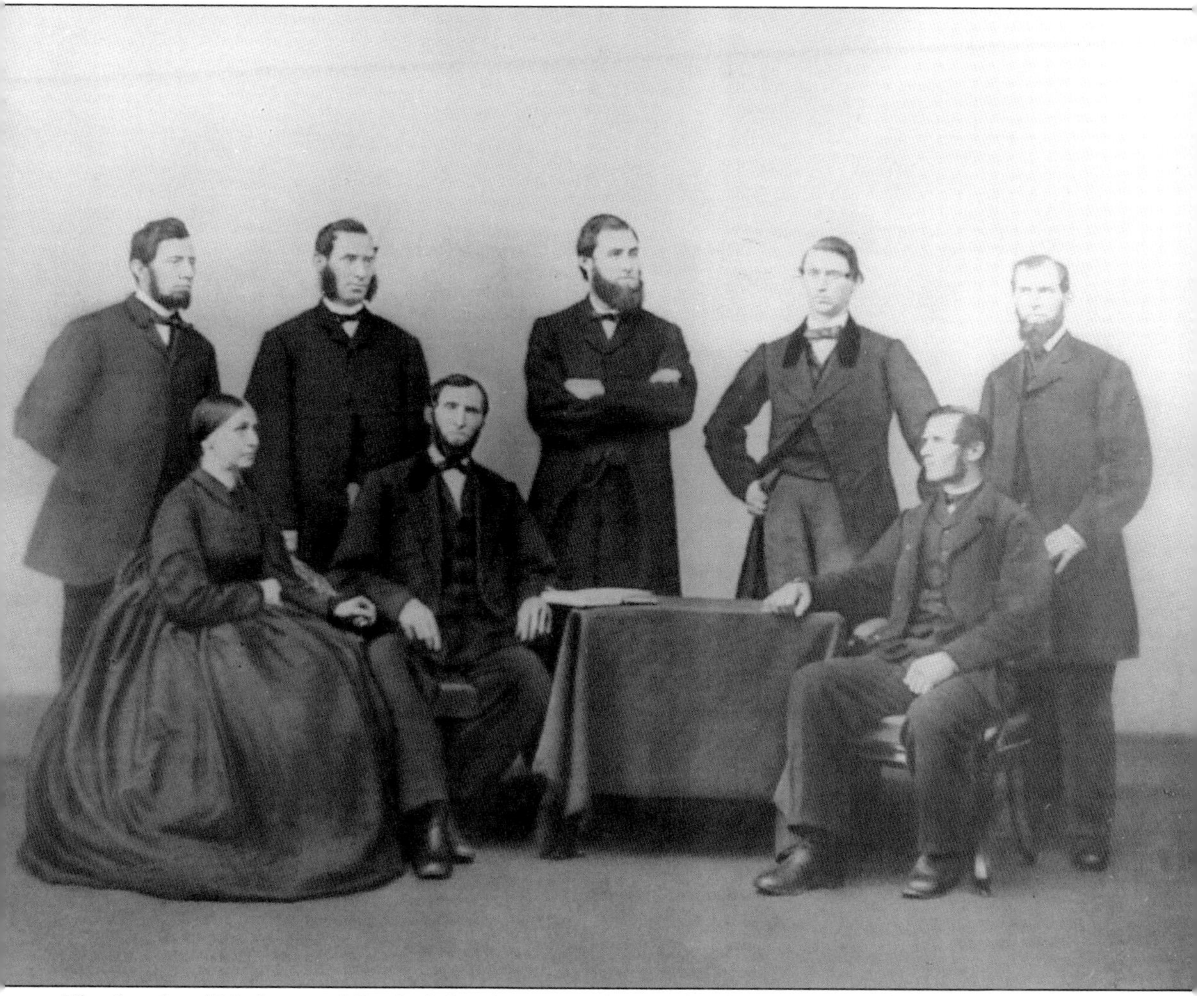

The family of Nathan and Rachel Crosby Simonds pose for the camera in this scene from the mid-19th century. Six of the eight Simonds children are included in this photograph (missing are the two namesakes, Nathan Simonds Jr. and Rachel). They are, from left to right, as follows: (front row) Rachel, Franklin, and Nathan Simonds; (back row) Otis, Marshall, David, Loammi, and George Henry Simonds. Marshall Simonds is the best-known Simonds in Burlington as a result of his generous gift to the town upon his death in 1905. (Courtesy of the Burlington Archives, No. 91.)

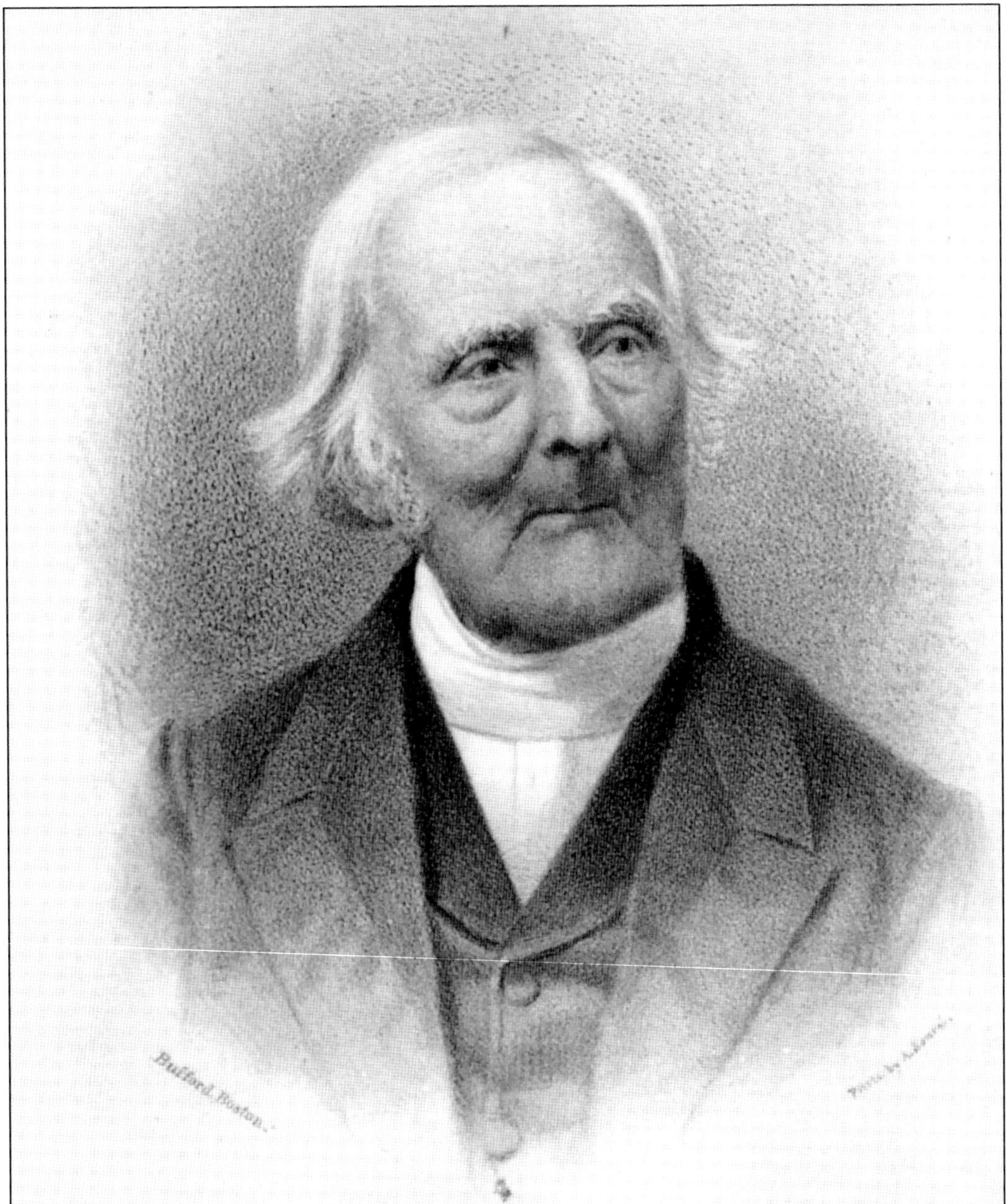

Samuel Sewall was born in Marblehead, Massachusetts, on June 1, 1785, the son of Chief Justice Samuel Sewall and Abigail (Devereux) Sewall. Samuel Sewall was a direct descendant of Judge Samuel Sewall, chief justice of the Province of Massachusetts from 1718 to 1728 and a major figure in the witch trials of 1692. Sewall attended Harvard College from 1800 to 1804. It was after his graduation that Sewall studied theology and later became a minister. Samuel Sewall came to the Burlington Congregational Church, today's United Church of Christ Congregational and was ordained on April 13, 1814. Sewall was also a historian, and his book A *History of Woburn* (the first published history of the area that is today Burlington) was published in the year of his death. Sewall died on February 18, 1868, and is buried in the Chestnut Hill Cemetery. (Courtesy of the Burlington Archives, No. 83.)

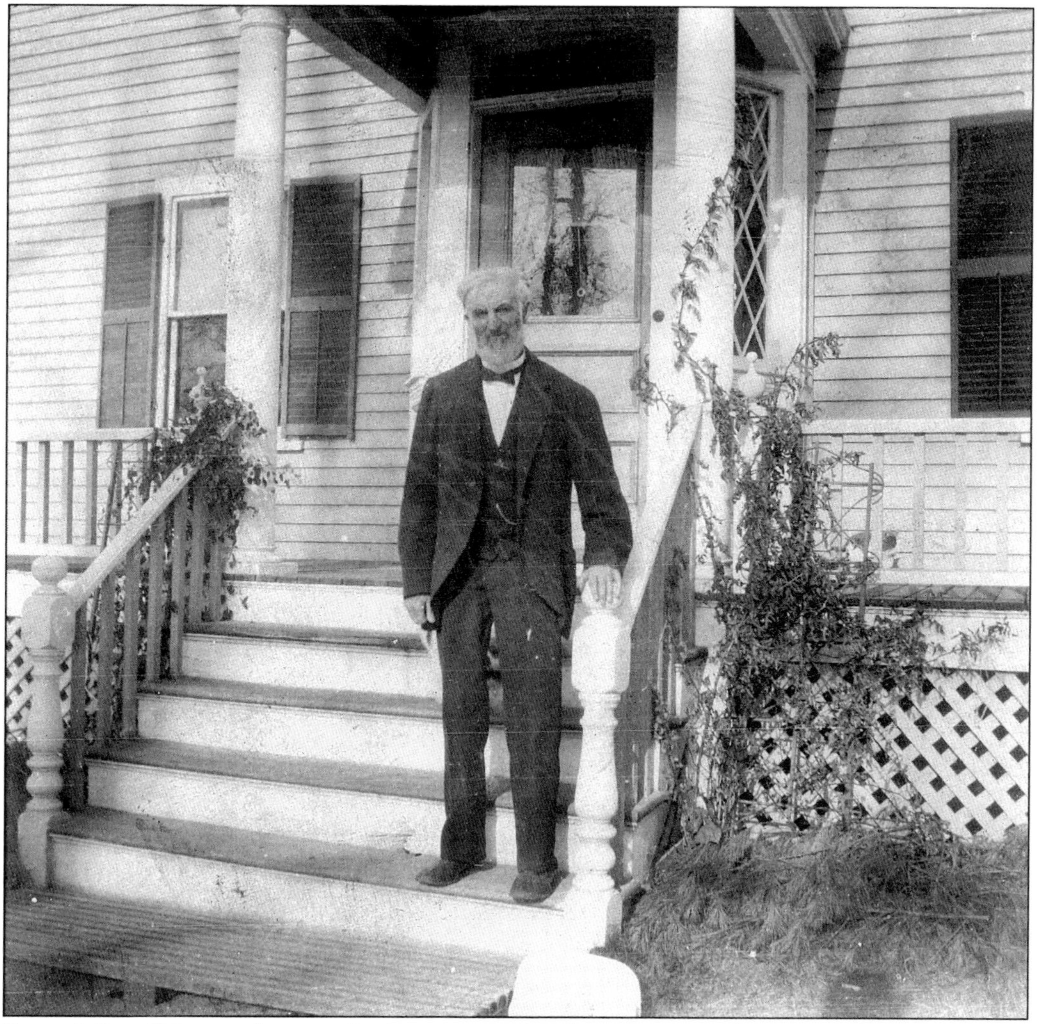

Samuel Sewall Jr. was born in Burlington on October 29, 1819, the son of the Rev. Samuel Sewall and Martha Marrett Sewall. Sewall Jr. married Elizabeth Brown on March 21, 1844, in Burlington and later had two children—Samuel and Martha Elizabeth. In this photograph, Sewall is standing on the steps of the second Sewall House, built in 1897 on the ruins of the first, which was destroyed in a fire on April 23, 1897. Samuel Sewall served in many of the town's elective positions, including selectman, assessor, school committee, and tax collector. He died in Burlington on November 16, 1903. (Courtesy of the Burlington Archives, No. 220.)

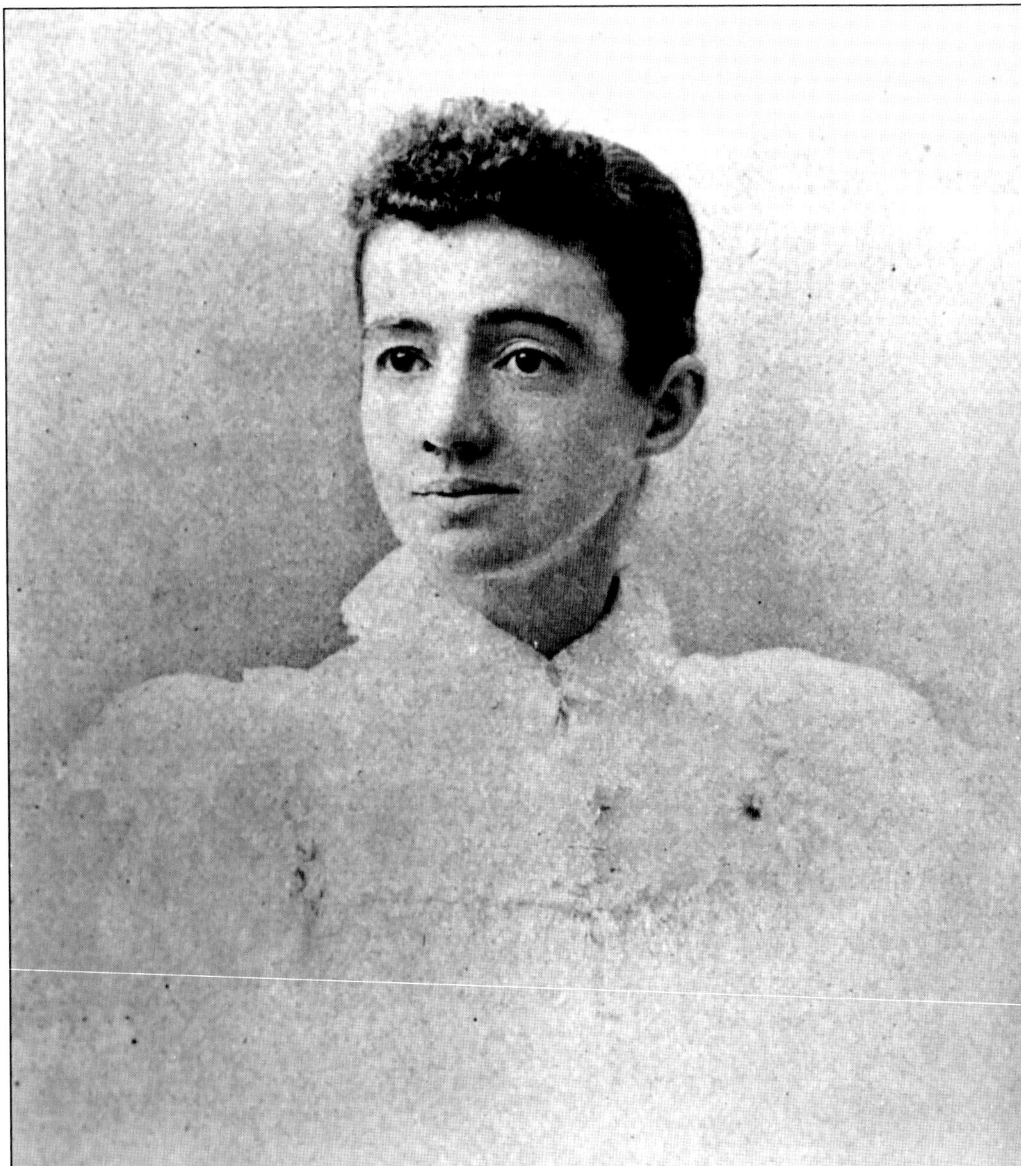

Martha Elizabeth Sewall Curtis was born in Burlington on May 18, 1858, the youngest child of Samuel Sewall Jr. and Elizabeth Brown Sewall. Martha was the granddaughter of Rev. Samuel Sewall and shared the family's love of history. She was an activist, historian, writer, and lecturer. In 1876, at age 18, she was chosen to be on the Burlington School Committee, the first woman to hold that position. She wrote and lectured in support of the women's rights movement. She wrote many articles on local history topics and published *Ye Olde Meeting House* in 1909. She died in Burlington on April 27, 1915. Her life was one of tragedy, losing two children and her husband to early deaths. (Courtesy of the Burlington Archives, No. 453.)

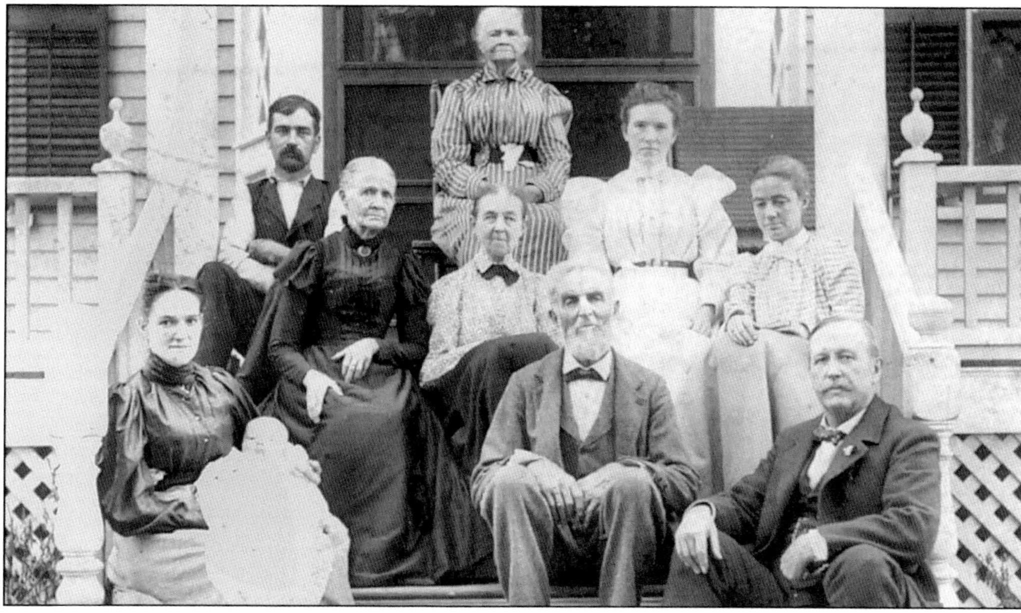

The family of Samuel Sewall Jr. poses on the steps of the second Sewall House *c.* 1899. The house, located at 40 Lexington Street, was built on the foundations of the historic mansion that was destroyed by fire on April 23, 1897. The people gathered are, from left to right, as follows: (front row) Nellie L. Bennett (holding Joshua Holden Bennett), Samuel Sewall Jr. (town clerk), and ? Hersey; (middle row) Mrs. Samuel Sewall, Martha Sewall Martin, and Martha Elizabeth Sewall Curtis; (back row) unidentified, Grandma Sewall, and unidentified. (Courtesy of the Burlington Archives, No. 92.)

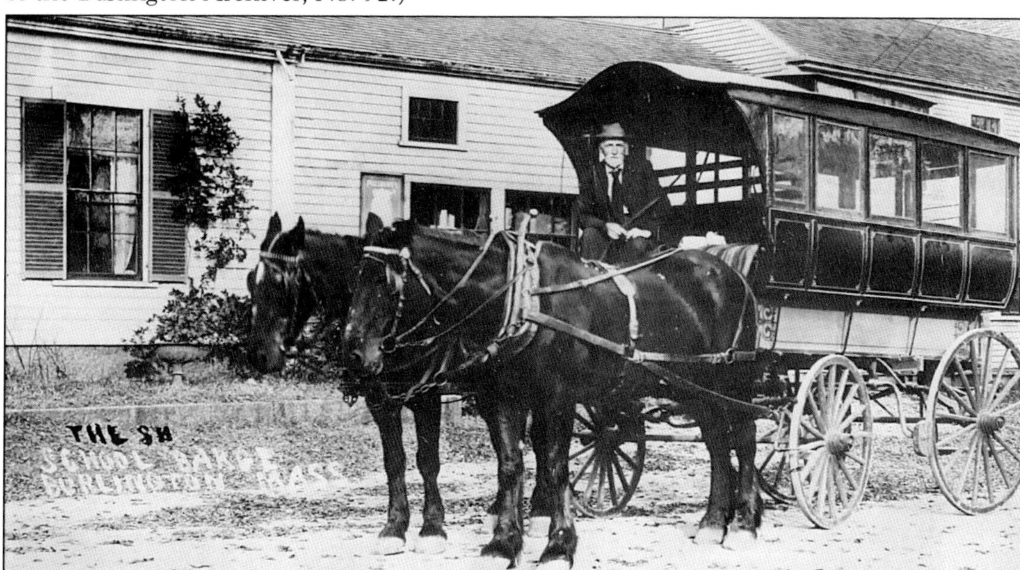

Located in the area where the town hall annex stands now, the general store has had a succession of owners and additions. By 1915, the entire complex was moved down Center Street to make way for Burlington's second town hall. The first Burlington school bus, known as "the Barge," is featured in this photograph with George F. Shaw at the wheel. (Courtesy of the Burlington Archives, No. 7.)

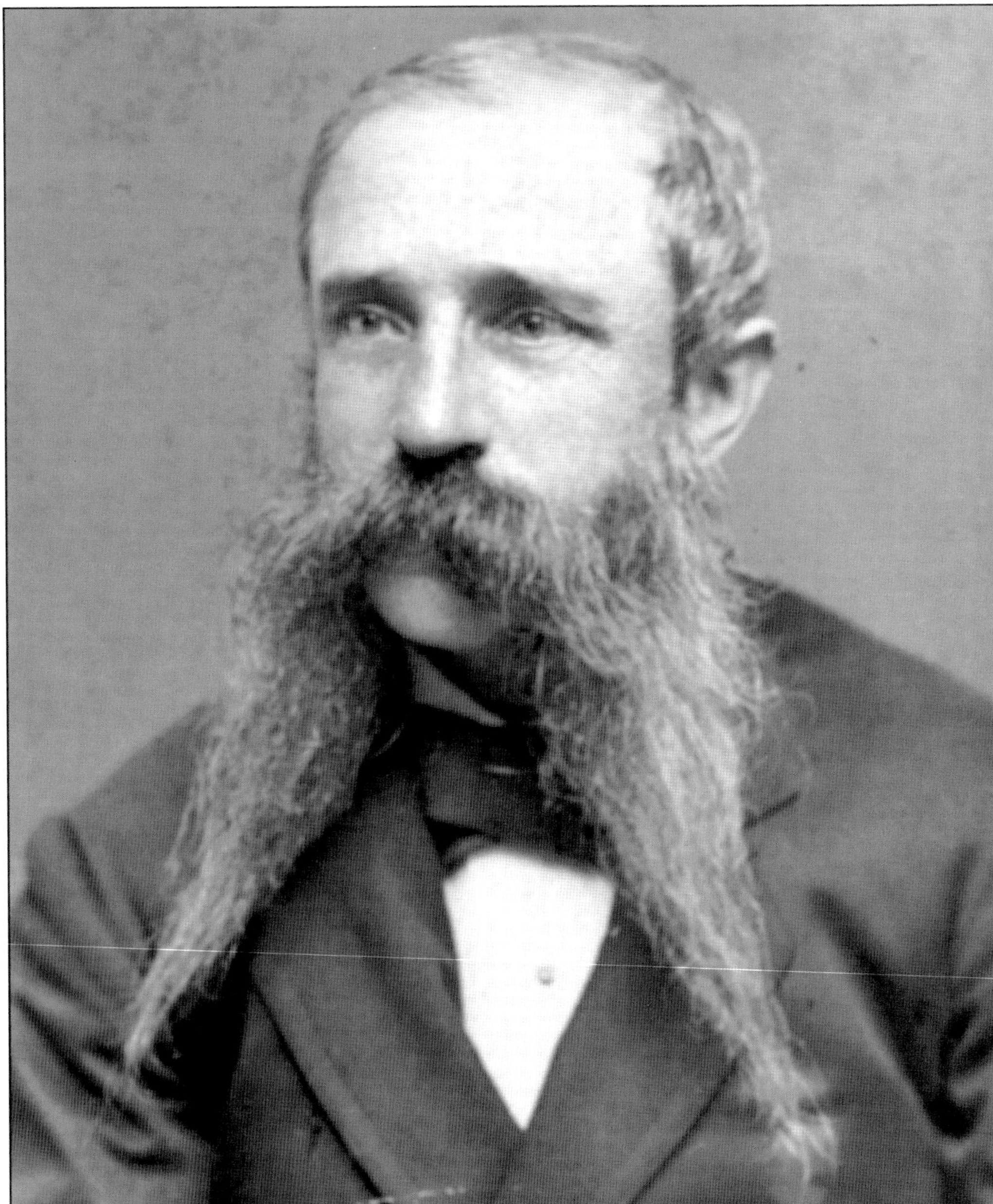

Ward Brooks Frothingham was born in Boston on November 26, 1828, the son of well-known clergyman Rev. Dr. Nathaniel Langdon Frothingham (1793–1870) and Ann Gorham Brooks. Ward Brooks Frothingham served as a lieutenant in the Civil War while his wife, Fanny Ward Frothingham, worked as a volunteer nurse. Reverend Frothingham, a good friend of Rev. Samuel Sewall, was captured with the rural charm of Burlington and had a mansion built in the Spruce Hill area of town in 1853. Ward Brooks Frothingham sold his father the land for the rural retreat from Boston. The Frothingham mansion, renovated and modernized, is Burlington's only surviving example of a mid-19th-century Palladian Italianate Villa–style house according to the 1999 *Historic Preservation Survey of Burlington*. (Courtesy of the Burlington Archives, No. 99.)

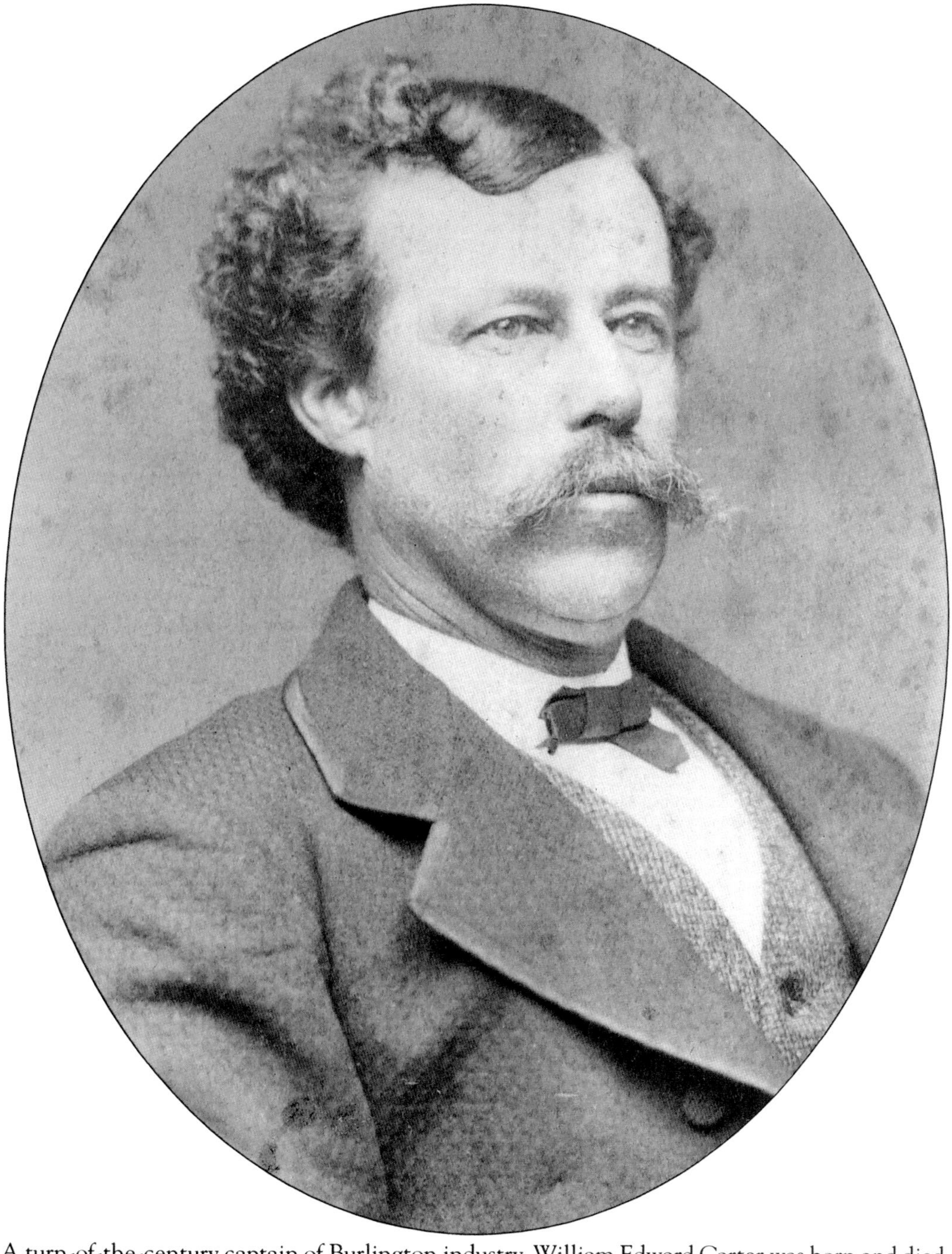

A turn-of-the-century captain of Burlington industry, William Edward Carter was born and died in Burlington. Carter—who was a direct descendant of Rev. Thomas Carter, one of the founders of Woburn—was born on November 6, 1843, and died on February 14, 1902, at his home on Arlington Street (now Cambridge Street). William Edward Carter was in the leather business and ran a shoe heel and stock factory on the corner of Cambridge and Bedford Streets sometime between 1880 and 1904. Carter's home was located at the corner of Center and Sears Streets, the site of the Colonial Building today. (Courtesy of the Burlington Archives, No. 98.)

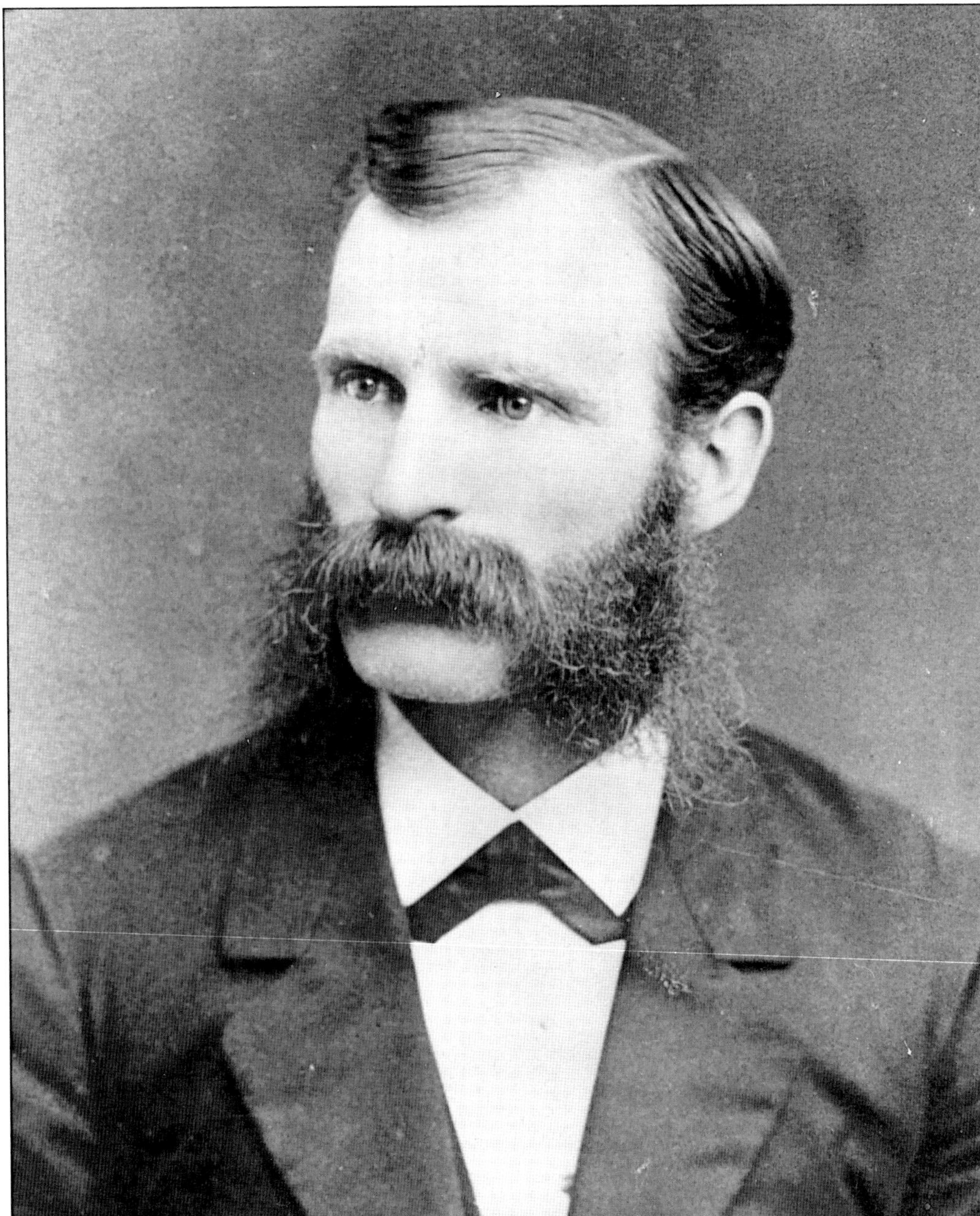

The Reed family has a long and distinguished history in the Burlington area as farmers, businessmen, and community servants. Thomas Isaiah Reed, born in Burlington in 1846, worked on his father's farm and learned the family business of smoking hams. Reed increased the business and developed a wide market that included Winchester, Medford, Boston, Chicago, and as far away as Constantinople. He was very involved in Burlington town affairs; he was elected to the school committee and served as a member of the first board of health. Foremost a farmer, Reed was the second president of the Burlington Agricultural Society and helped make the annual agricultural fair a success. He died in Burlington on July 20, 1933. (Courtesy of the Burlington Archives, No. 97.)

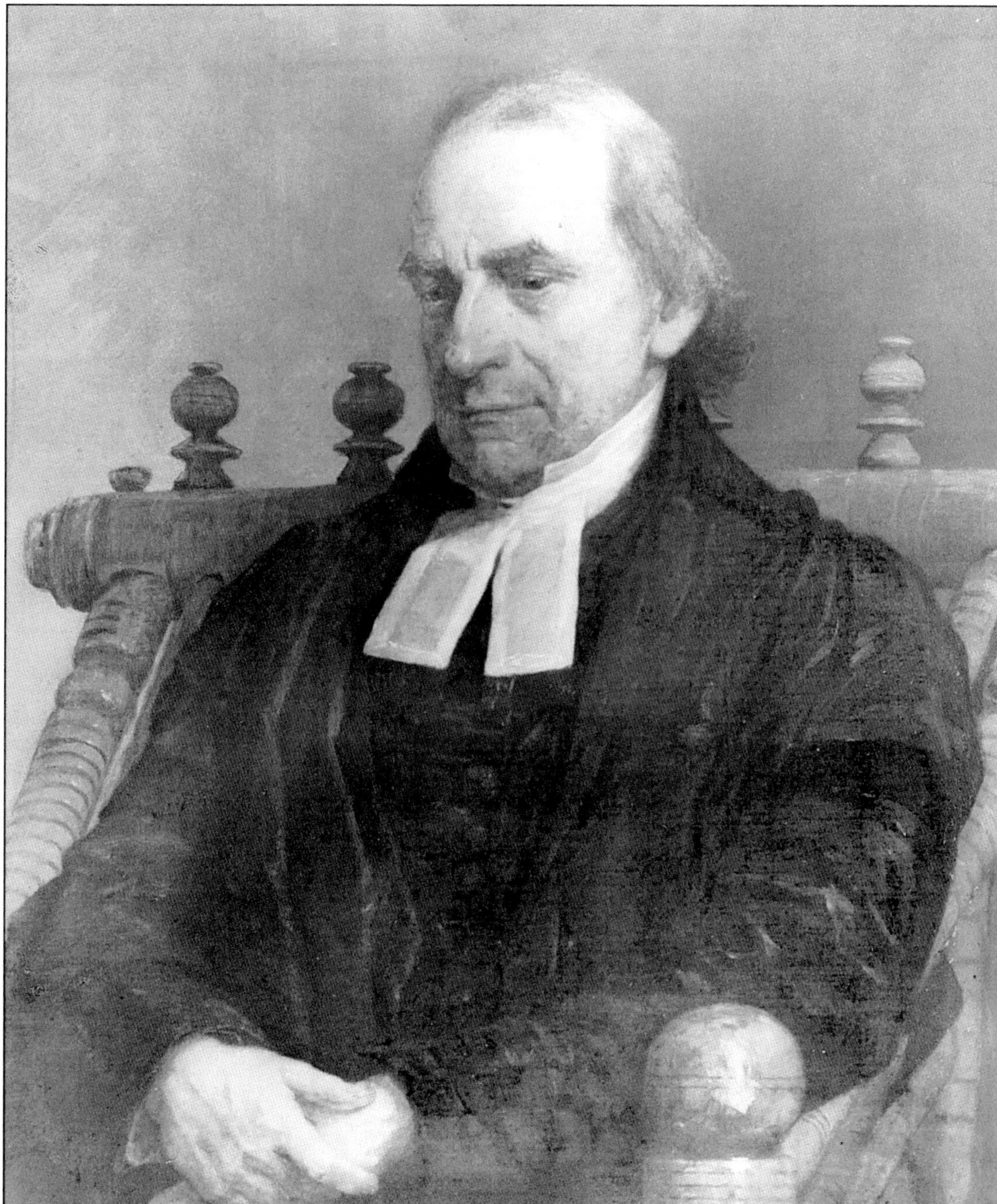

One of the most enlightened and intellectual men of the early 19th century, Rev. Dr. James Walker was born at 9 Bedford Street, Burlington, on August 16, 1794. Walker was a member of one of the most prestigious families in Burlington history. His father, John, was one of the leaders in the town's fight for independence from Woburn and was a general commissioned by Pres. John Adams in 1798. James attended Burlington schools and, in 1814, graduated from Harvard College. He returned to Burlington and taught at the West School. Walker was an ordained minister and a founder of the American Unitarian Association. To complete an illustrious career, Walker taught at Harvard College from 1839 to 1853 and was later selected to be president of Harvard College from 1853 to 1860. James Walker died in Cambridge on December 23, 1874. (Courtesy of the Burlington Archives, No. 90.)

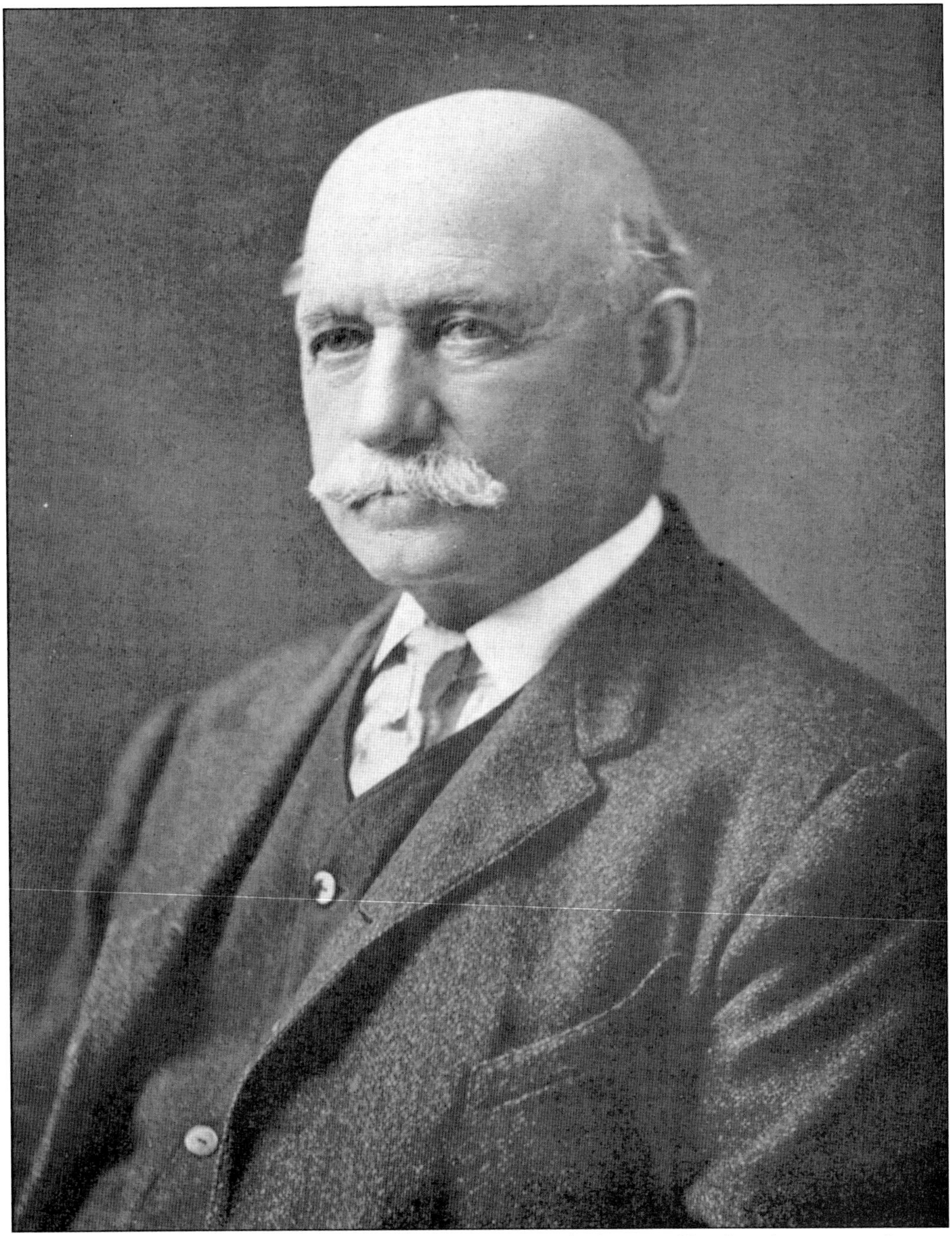

In 1870, Charles McIntire bought the Marion Tavern and 65 acres of land in the center of town. He added acreage and other property and operated a large dairy farm and milk-delivery service for a number of years. It was the McIntire family who renamed the historic property Grand View Farm for its panoramic view out to Mount Monadnock. (Courtesy of the Burlington Archives, No. 88.)

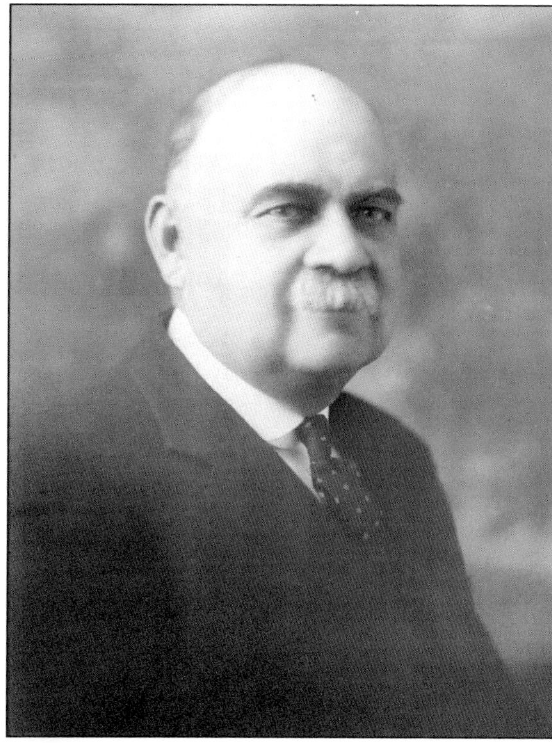

The eighth pastor called to the Congregational Church, today's United Church of Christ Congregational, was Rev. Charles H. Washburn, who was minister from c. 1888 to 1891 and from 1922 to 1931. In 1888, the historic Second Parish Meetinghouse was renovated, and Washburn hosted the rededication ceremony in December of that year. It was Reverend Washburn who introduced the idea of an organization to promote agricultural excellence, and the Burlington Agricultural Society was founded in October 1889. Louise W. Chaffin married Charles H. Washburn in 1886, and they had four sons and a daughter. (Courtesy of the Burlington Archives, Nos. 85 and 87).)

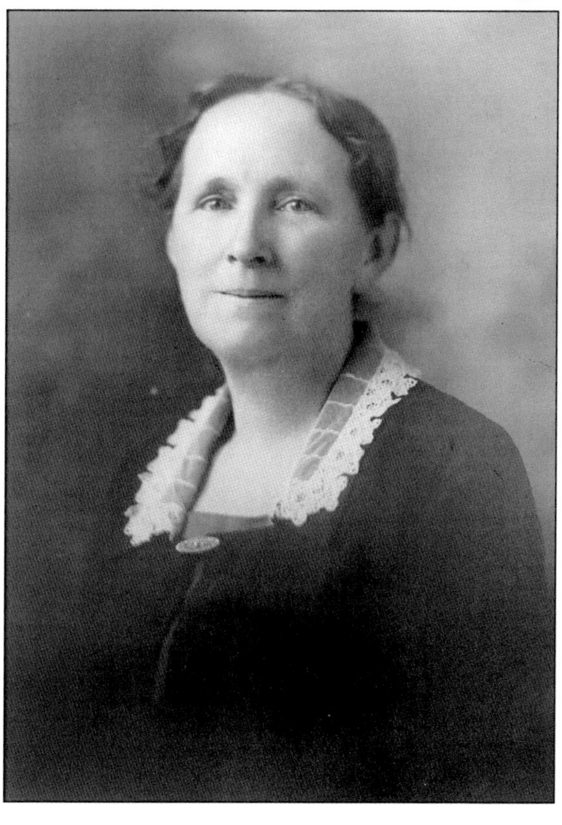

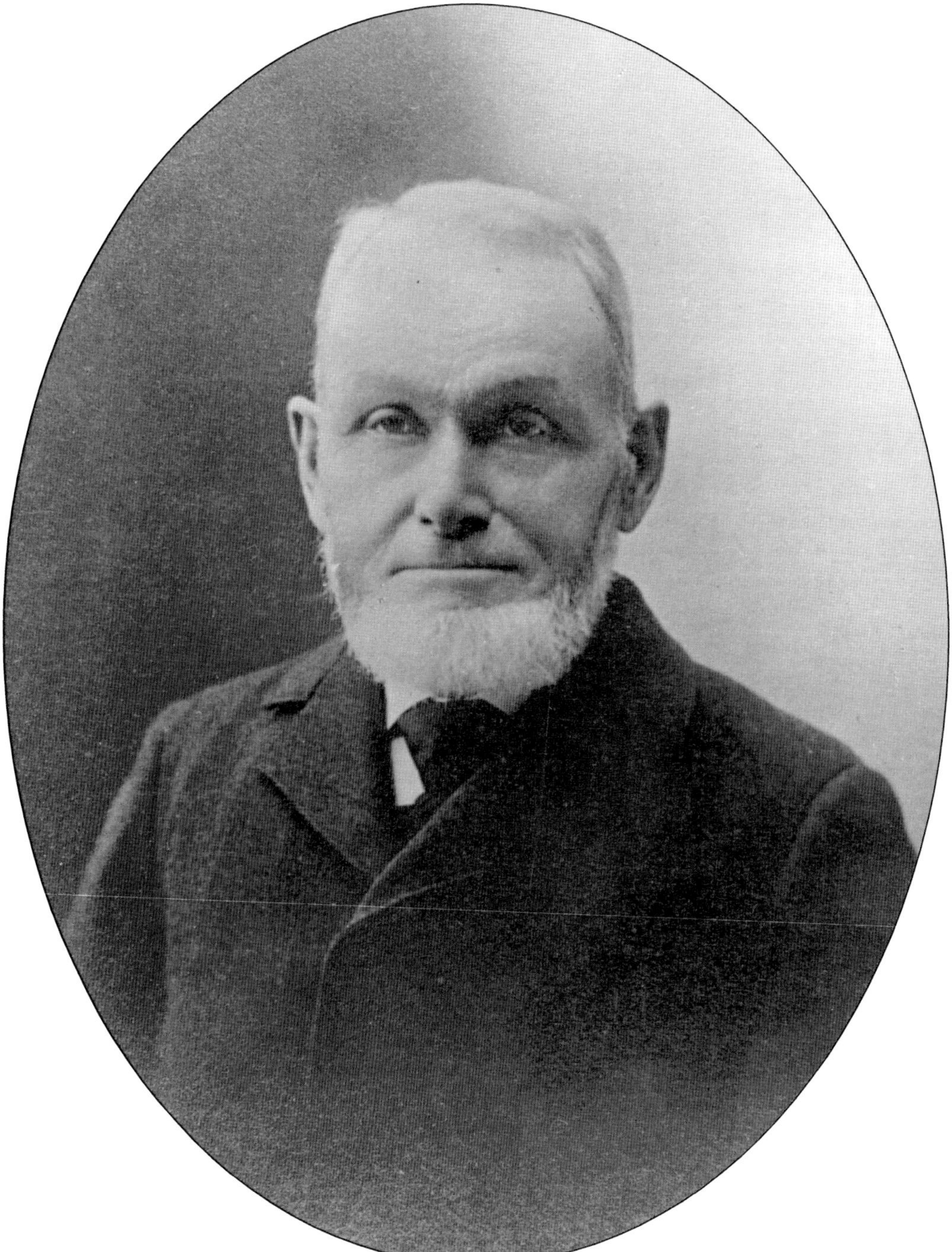

Augustus Prouty's house, built *c.* 1860, still stands on Prouty Road. He was born in 1828 in Hampden, Maine, the son of Aaron Prouty and Hannah Cary. He married Rachel B. Keith, had several children, and became a well-known citizen of Burlington. Prouty was a longtime member of the school committee and a strong advocate of the district school system, which was replaced when the Union School was opened in 1898. (Courtesy of the Burlington Archives, No. 357.)

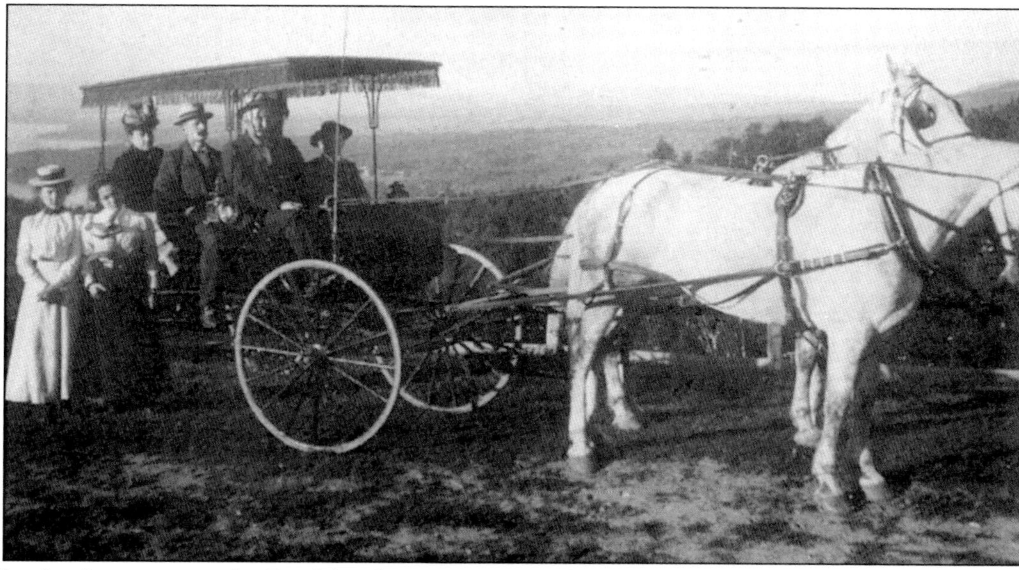

In this fine carriage, the Reed family poses on a Sunday afternoon in the late 19th century. This was the family of Frank Oliver Reed, who was born in Burlington on July 31, 1826. The family homestead is still standing at 23 Chestnut Avenue. The land and property may be traced to early settler John Reed (1660–1723), whose father, Ralph Reed (1630–1712), immigrated from England. (Courtesy of the Burlington Archives, No. 383.)

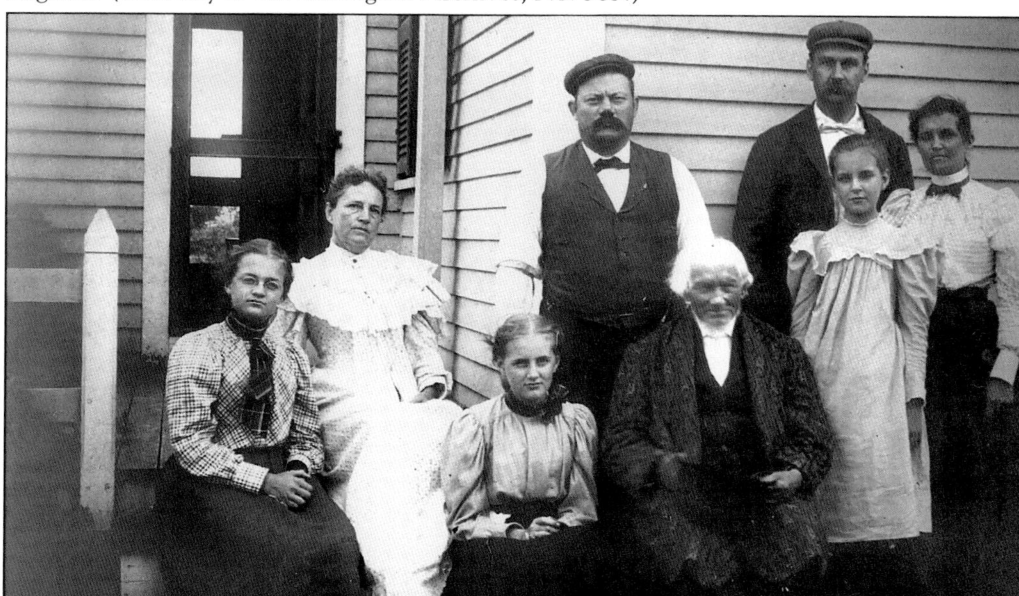

The individuals in this image are thought to be members of the Ken Brown family on the steps of their home at 110 Winn Street, *c.* 1898. The location, historically known as the Jonas Lawrence house, is Burlington's only example of a Greek Revival–style house. It is suggested that Jonas Lawrence may have built a framed structure on this site in 1799, the year of Burlington's incorporation as a separate town. The property was renovated *c.* 1840 in the Greek Revival style and again later by housewright and cabinetmaker William Lawrence. (Courtesy of the Burlington Archives, No. 46.)

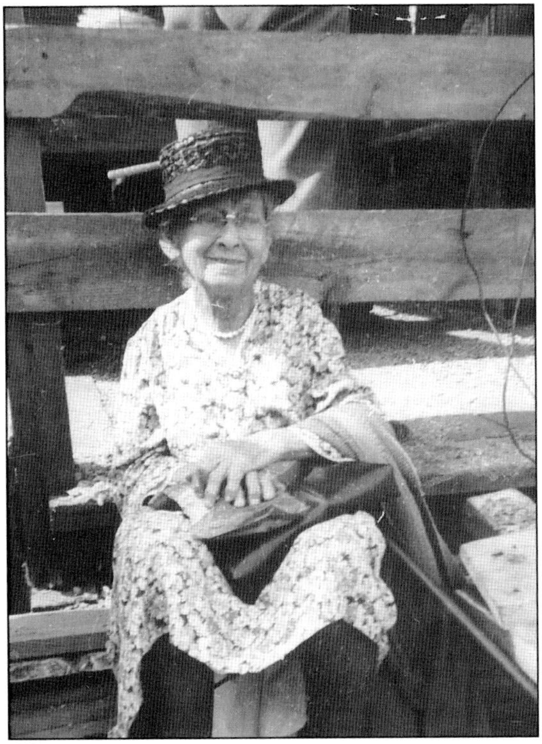

Henrietta Richardson Foster, town librarian in the 1920s and 1930s, is captured in this photograph at the Burlington Agricultural Fair sometime early in the 20th century. Henrietta Richardson was born in Billerica on October 8, 1859, and married Charles Henry Foster of Lexington. The family had a house and several acres of land in the center of town when Burlington's common was private land. Foster served as town librarian from 1922 to 1939 and was known as "Aunt Nettie." (Courtesy of the Burlington Archives, No. 105.)

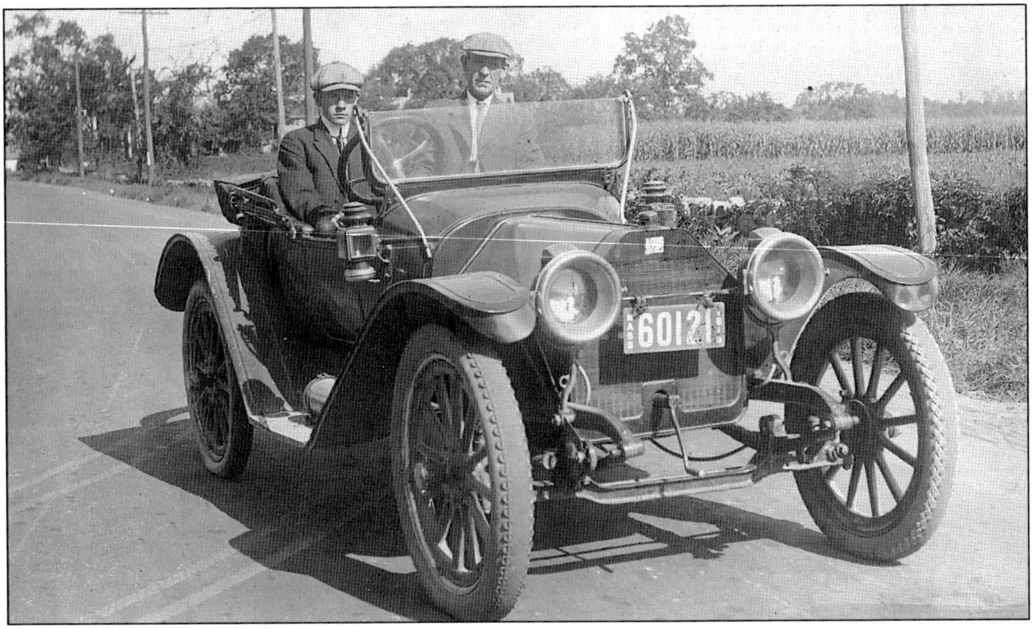

Charles Tobin Boston and his son John Lloyd Boston are out for a drive in the Pinehurst section of Billerica in this image from 1915. Charles was born in October 1868 in Halifax, Nova Scotia, and married Clara M. Shedd, a Burlington girl, on July 20, 1892. Charles was known locally as "Tobe" and was active in town government, winning elections as tax collector, constable, and highway superintendent from 1900 to 1933. John Lloyd Boston, their son, was born in Burlington on May 24, 1899. (Courtesy of the Burlington Archives, No. 519.)

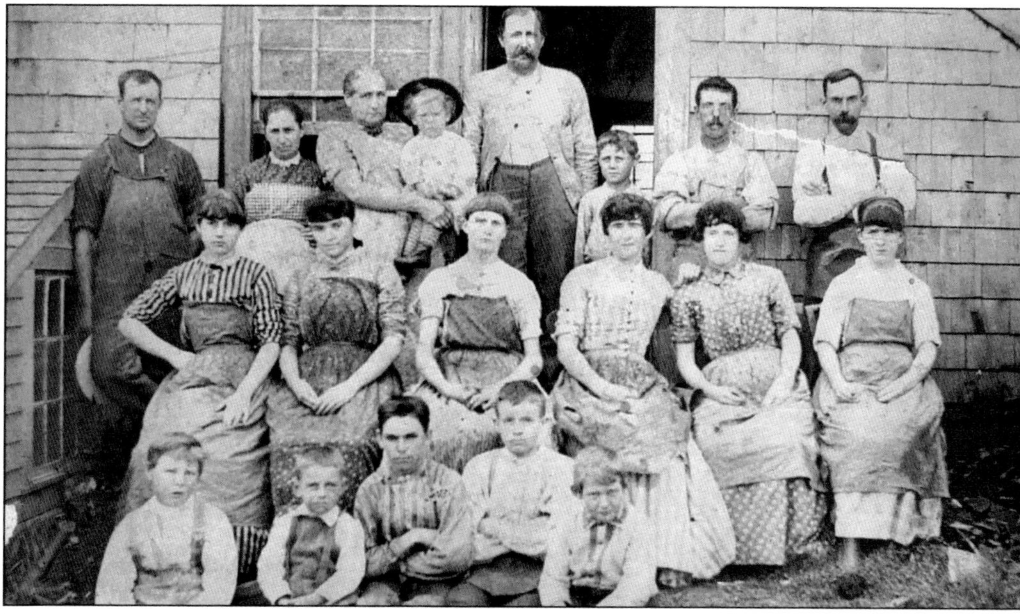

This group photograph was taken in front of "Uncle Dud's" shop, which may have been located in the center of town. The locals are identified, from left to right, as follows: (front row) Frank Pearsons, Harry Diloria, David Johnson, ? Chambers, and Roscoe E. Pearsons; (middle row) unidentified, unidentified, Tilley Chambers, unidentified, unidentified, and Mammie Carr; (back row) H. Pearsons, Pauline Deloria, Sarah Johnson (holding Horace Pearsons), George Lewis Tebetts, Carol Tebetts, Nathan Soper, and Henry Harrington. (Courtesy of the Burlington Archives, No. 252.)

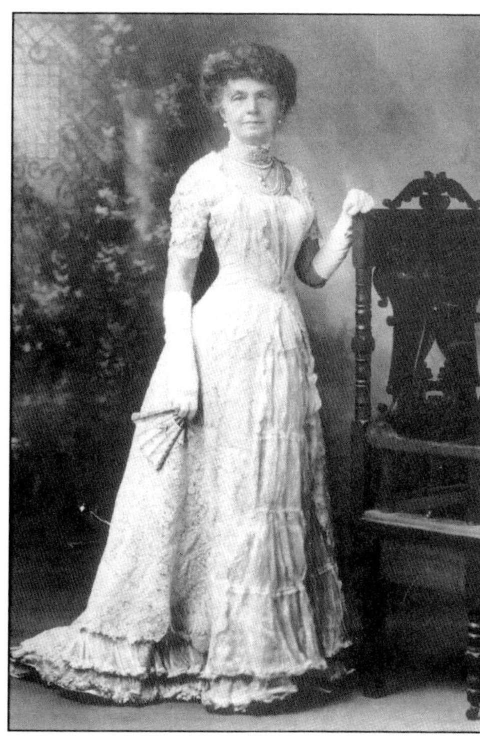

Mary Phelps Cowles Hall Cummings estate in 1900 totaled over 400 acres; nearly 300 were in Burlington and the rest in Woburn. In 1900, there were three large piggeries on the farm that was her property. Part of her land included Babylon Hill, where the Nike missile site was built in the 1950s and where the Northeastern University buildings are located today. Her second husband, John C. Cummings, was a banker and owner of one of the largest tanneries in Woburn. The Cummingses built a three-story Victorian mansion that was located at the intersection of Cambridge and South Bedford Streets. Mary Phelps Cowles Cummings died of bronchitis on December 23, 1927. As a result of a tax dispute with the town of Burlington, Cummings left her entire estate to the City of Boston for recreational uses. (Courtesy of the Burlington Archives, No. 257.)

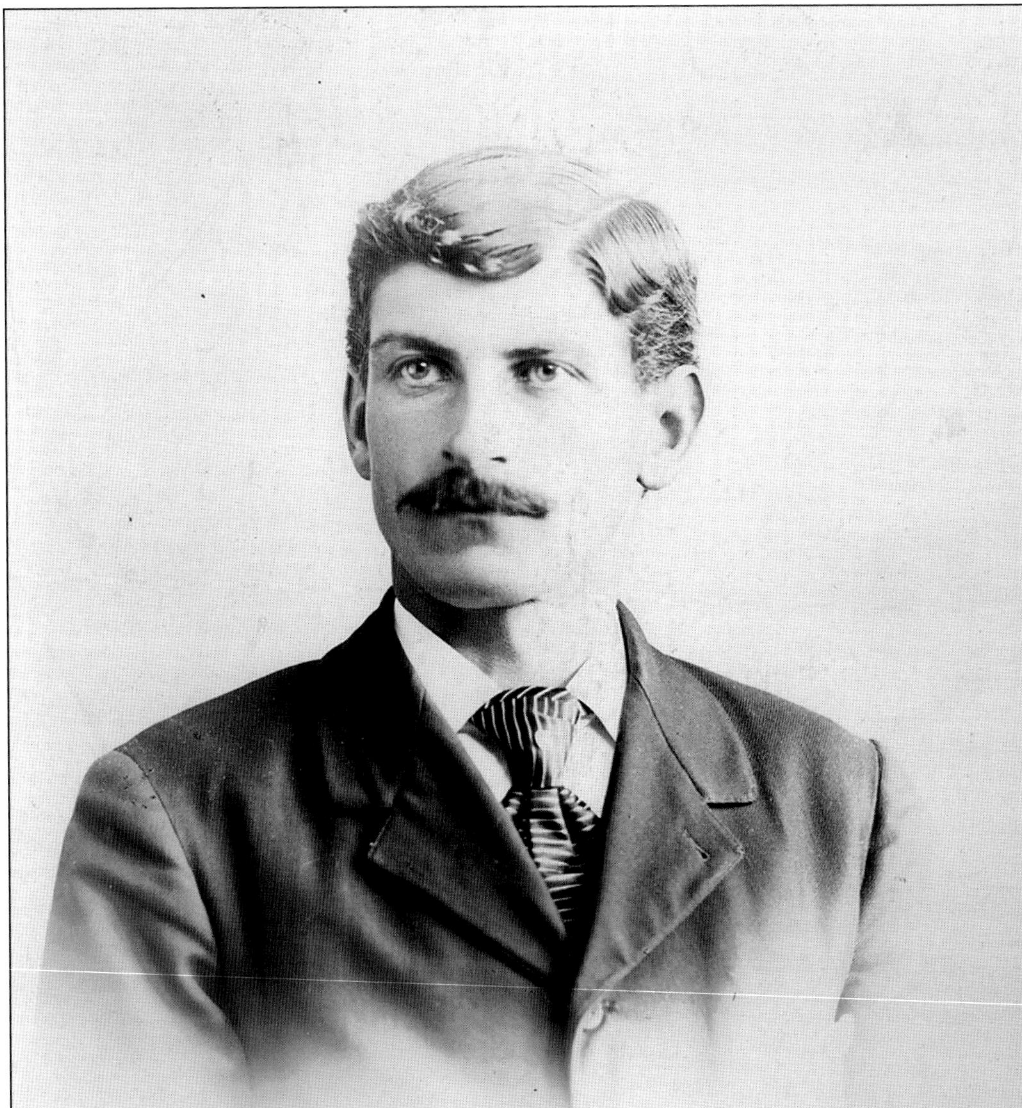

Walter Winn Skelton was the oldest son of Bradford Skelton and Almira Shedd and was born on October 1, 1864, in Burlington. Walter Skelton was the town's forest warden, serving from 1910 to 1945. He was named fire chief in 1935 and served until 1937. The first fire department was housed on his property at 92 Francis Wyman Road until 1937. Like his father and three brothers, Walter was actively involved in town government, serving as a selectman, a member of the school committee, and a member of the board of health. (Courtesy of the Burlington Archives, No. 343.)

Six

Farms, Farmhouses, and Barns

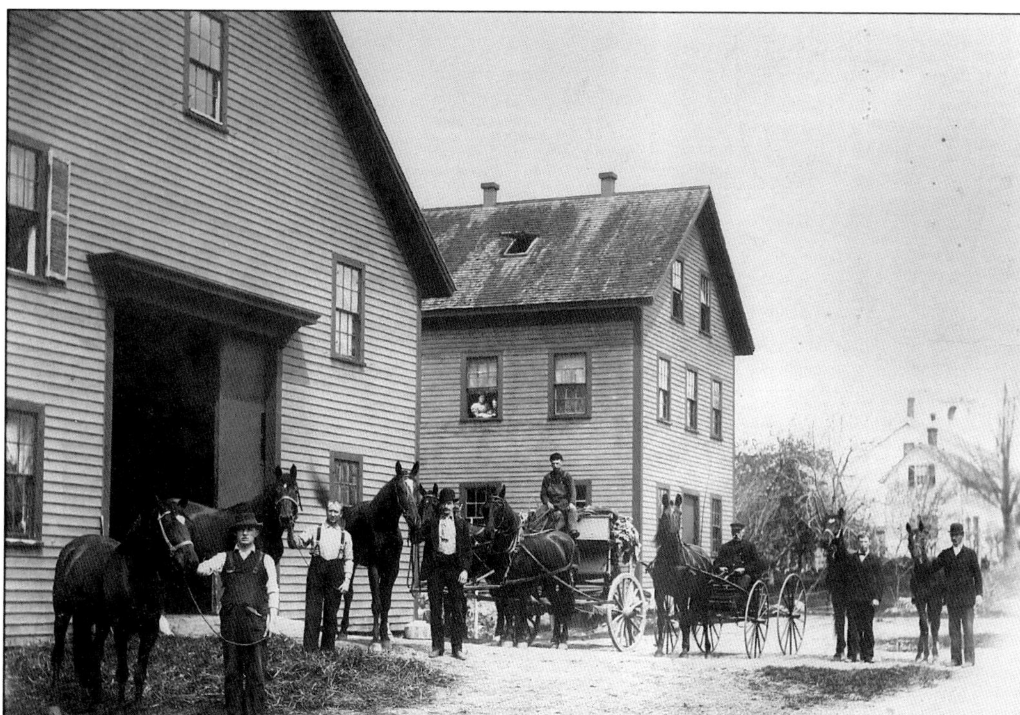

Standing on Cambridge Street, workers and their horses from the William Edward Carter Shoe Stock factory proudly pose for the camera near the horse barn. In this *c.* 1900 photograph, the Center School (now the Burlington Public Museum) is in the distance behind the Samuel Sumner Shedd house. Carter ran a heel shop or shoe stock factory near the corner of Cambridge Street and Bedford Street from 1880 to *c.* 1904. (Courtesy of the Burlington Archives, No. 48.)

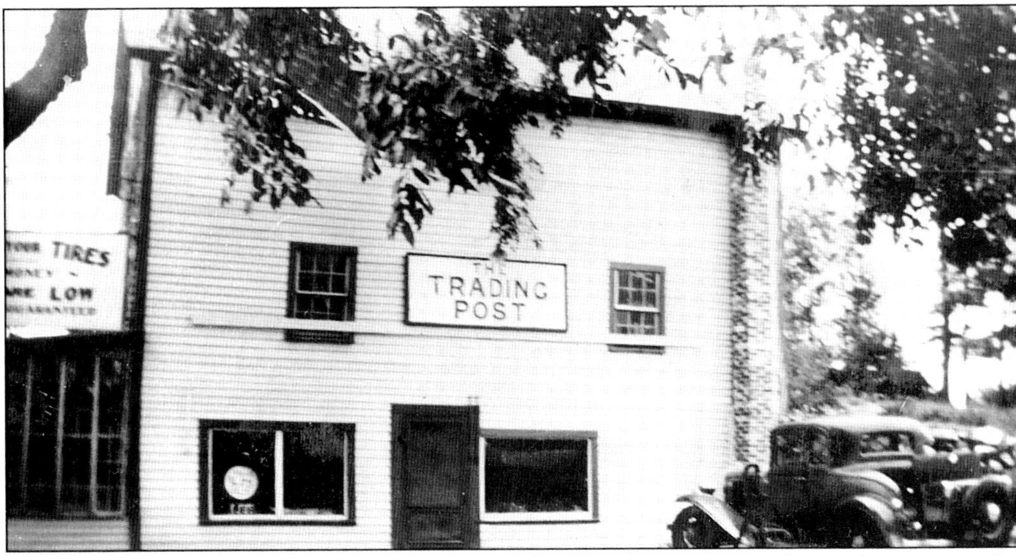

Loren H. Blenkhorn opened this store on Cambridge Street in 1932, located in a barn that belonged to Charles H. Foster and Henrietta "Nettie" Foster, not far from the common. The store was called the Trading Post and operated from 1932 to 1942. Loren Blenkhorn went to work as a carpenter at Fort Edwards during World War II, and his wife ran the store for a short time after that. Years later, the Value House opened on the site. (Courtesy of the Burlington Archives, No. 436.)

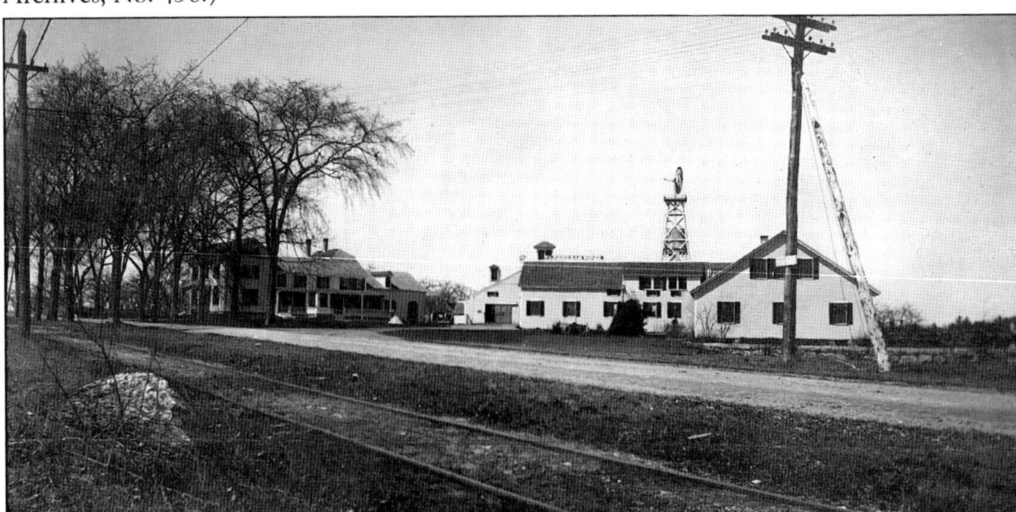

The Reed Ham Works was Burlington's biggest business and industry *c.* 1900. The barn is still standing at 328 Cambridge Street and the Thomas I. Reed house is still standing at 326 Cambridge Street. In this *c.* 1915 view, streetcar tracks and a windmill are clearly seen. In the late 19th and early 20th centuries, Burlington had several large pig farms, or "piggeries," and Reed was able to expand his family's business of smoking hams. Isaiah Reed (1816–1874) built the house at 326 Cambridge Street and started a ham-curing business *c.* 1846. The processing plant was large enough for 100 hams, with a floor area of 10,000 square feet, three large smokehouses, and a vault for 400,000 pounds of meat. By 1914, the ham works employed 15 to 17 men, but business declined by the Great Depression and, in 1953, the ham works stopped operations. (Courtesy of the Burlington Archives, Nos. 142 and 189.)

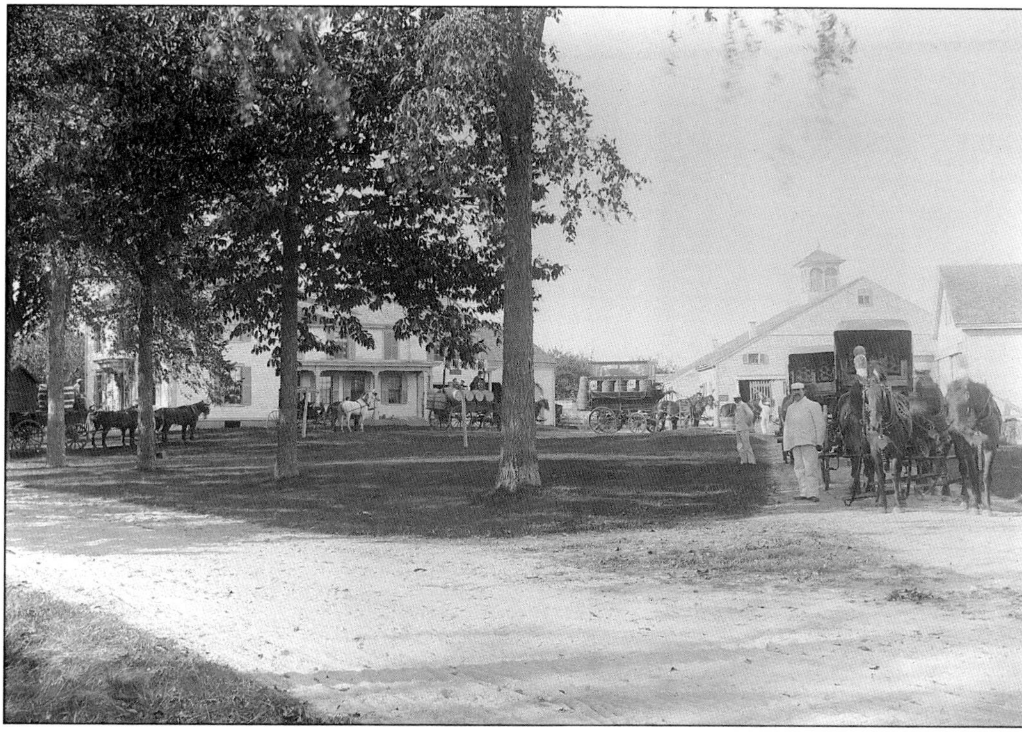

The Reed Ham Works produced smoked hams that were sold to markets as far away as the Robert College for the American Board of Foreign Missions in Constantinople in 1888. The works also developed a large retail business in Winchester, Medford, and Boston that operated until the 1950s. In this *c.* 1900 view, business appears to be booming. The carts may be part of an exhibit in the Burlington Agricultural Fair. (Courtesy of the Burlington Archives, No. 376.)

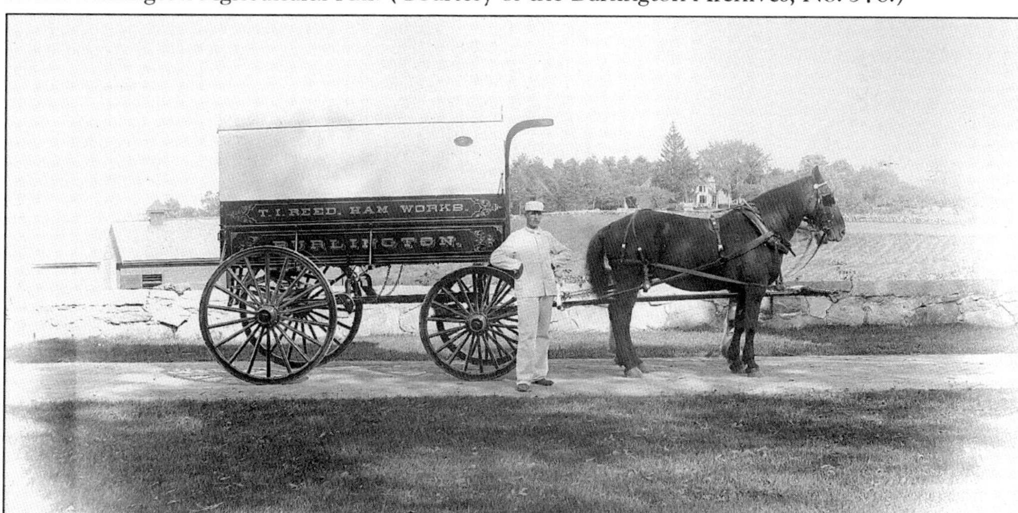

Burlington Archive sources identify this *c.* 1900 image of a driver and cart from the Reed Ham Works as one of a series produced for the first annual Burlington Cattle Show, which opened on September 29, 1889. The *Woburn Press* reported that T.I. Reed's ham-curing establishment had a fine exhibit at the first of many Burlington Agricultural Fairs. (Courtesy of the Burlington Archives, No. 375.)

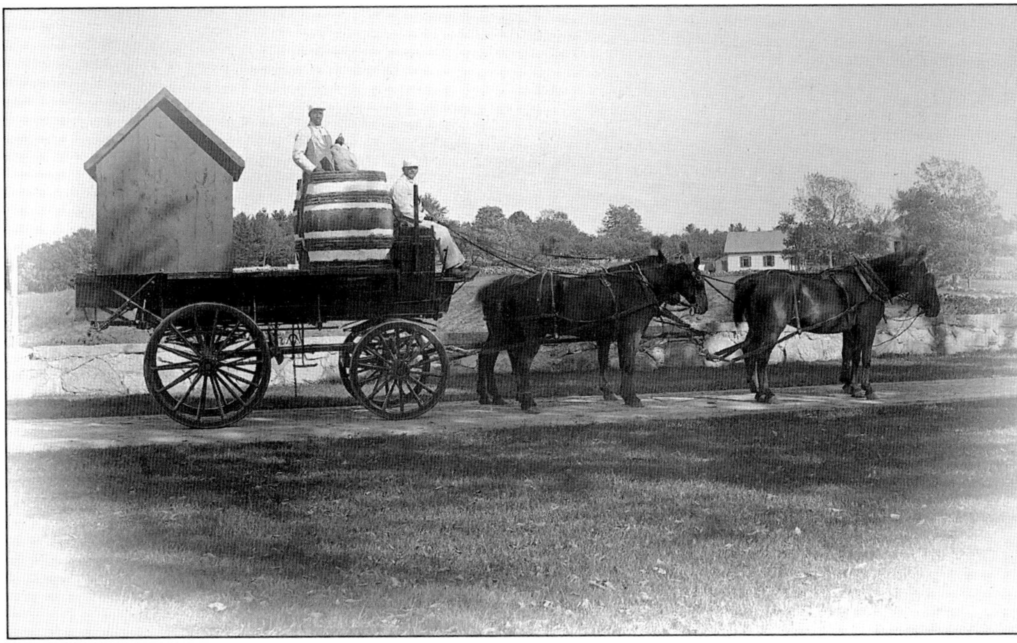

Workers of the Reed Ham Works are shown *c.* 1900 on a cart with barrels. Once a thriving industry, the smoked-ham business fell on hard times during the Great Depression and World War II. By the 1950s, the Reed Ham Works had stopped all operations. (Courtesy of the Burlington Archives, No. 377.)

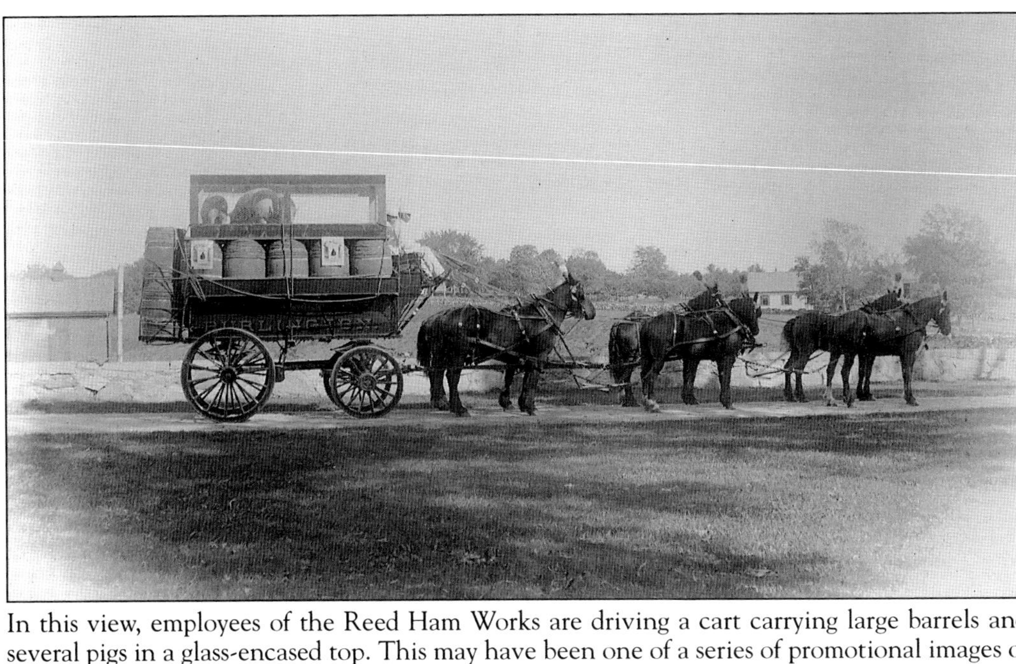

In this view, employees of the Reed Ham Works are driving a cart carrying large barrels and several pigs in a glass-encased top. This may have been one of a series of promotional images of the Reed Ham Works done for the 1889 Burlington Cattle Show. (Courtesy of the Burlington Archives, No. 378.)

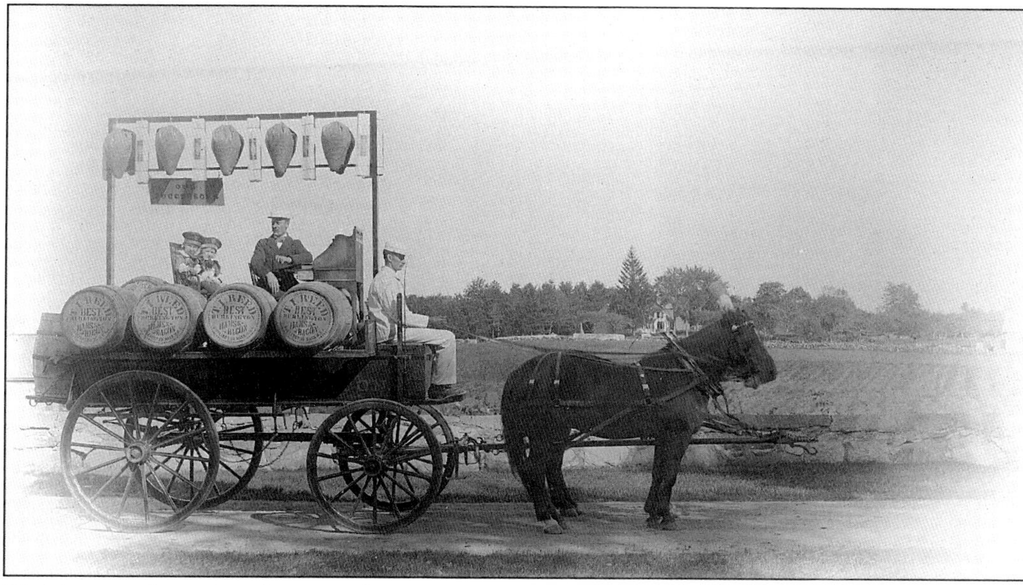

This is one of a series of images that were commissioned for the Burlington Cattle Show, held on September 29, 1889. The *Woburn City Press* wrote that the T.I. Reed Ham Works had a "pretty" design, which featured the children of T.I. Reed under a banner titled "Our Successors." Thomas Isaiah Reed expanded his father's ham-curing business and was a prominent citizen of Burlington by 1900. (Courtesy of the Burlington Archives, No. 381.)

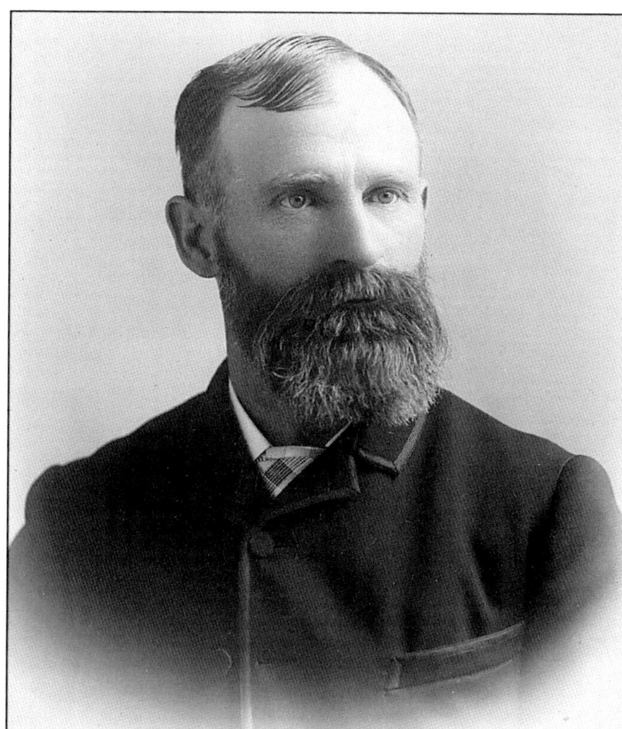

This late-19th-century portrait of Thomas Isaiah Reed was given to the Burlington Historical Commission by Guy Reed (Thomas's son) c. 1975. (Courtesy of the Burlington Archives, No. 382.)

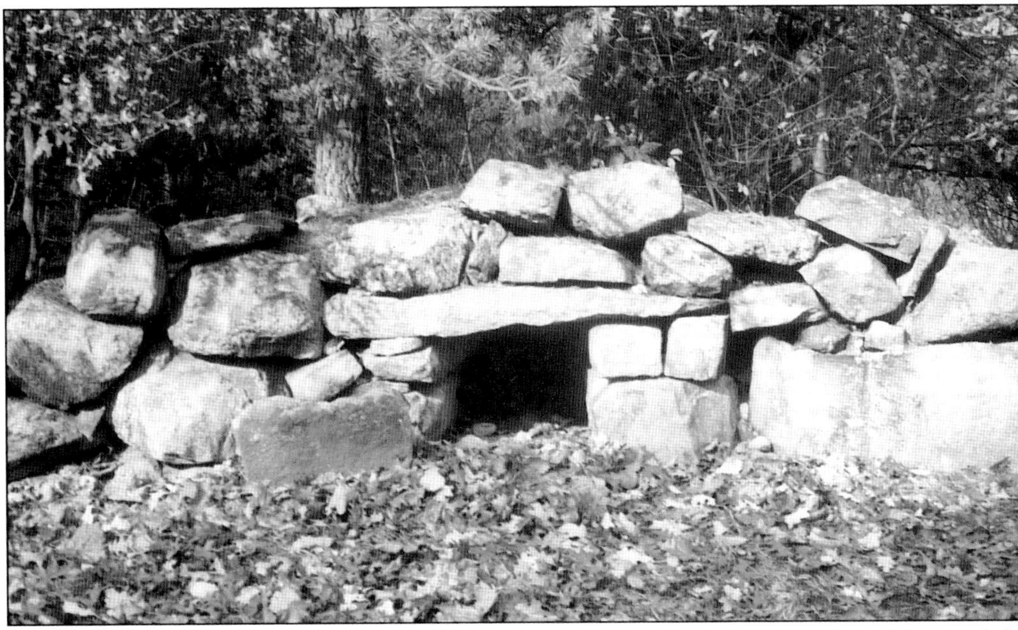

This unique structure is located south and west of the Francis Wyman House as part of the stone wall complex. Its original use is somewhat of a mystery. It is generally considered to be a Colonial farm feature, perhaps a pen to serve as protection for small animals from wolves. There is also a theory that argues the stone shelter is of Native American origin. (Courtesy of R.J. Costa.)

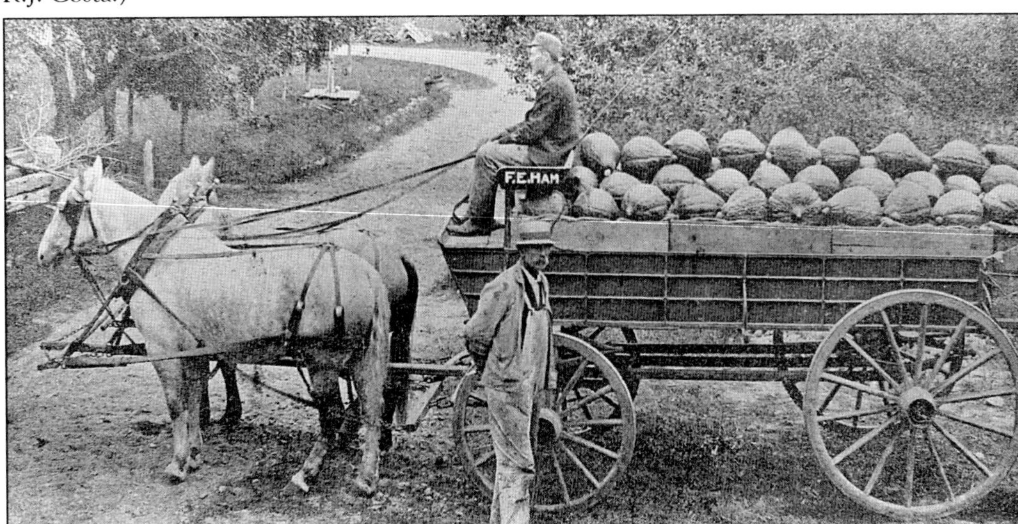

The corner of Adams Street and the Middlesex Turnpike was once the location of one of Burlington's finest farms. Fernald E. Ham bought the farm and house that was earlier used as the Richardson Tavern. The tavern served as a stage stop on the Middlesex Turnpike that opened in 1811. The stagecoach route went from Boston to Nashua, New Hampshire. Fernald E. Ham workers drive the squash cart in this scene from the late 19th century. During Prohibition, the tavern on the site was known as the Red Dog Inn, and some say it operated as a speakeasy. In 1938, the historic tavern burned to the ground. (Courtesy of the Burlington Archives, No. 157.)

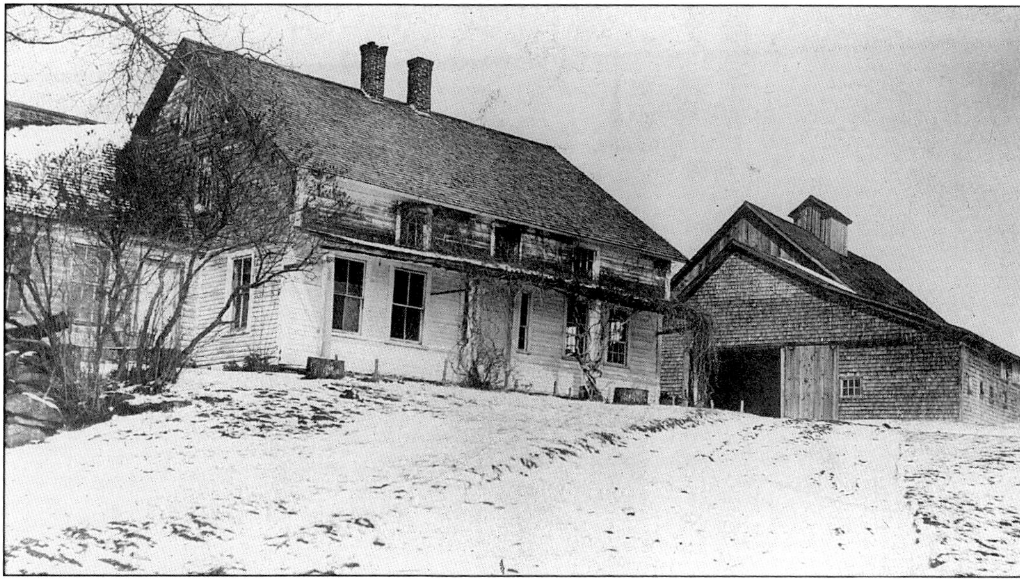

Shown c. the early 20th century, this connected farmhouse and barn complex is possibly the Charles G. Foster homestead, which was located at the first turn of the road on Chestnut Avenue. Charles G. Foster owned 71 acres in the area and cultivated 11 of them at the turn of the century. (Courtesy of the Burlington Archives, No. 166.)

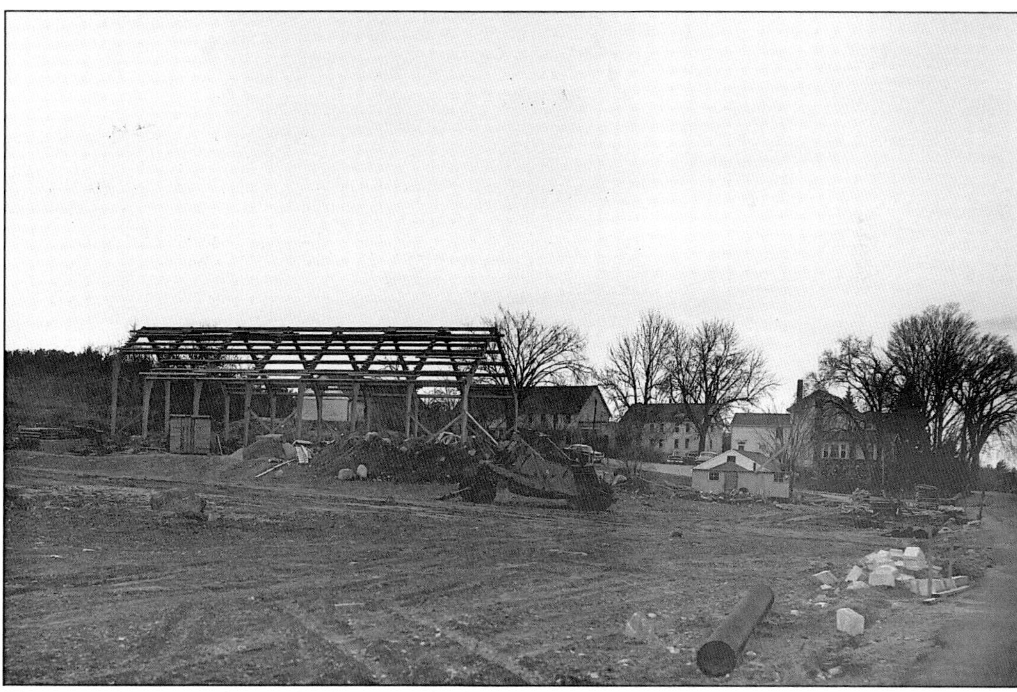

This c. 1957 image shows the framework of St. Margaret's Church, with the Walker farm in the background. The farmhouse was torn down, and the school of religion was built and dedicated in the fall of 1964. Another building on the site was moved back from the road and used as a squash house. Today, the building is still known as the squash house; it is the meeting place of the Burlington Historical Society. (Courtesy of the Burlington Archives, No. 169.)

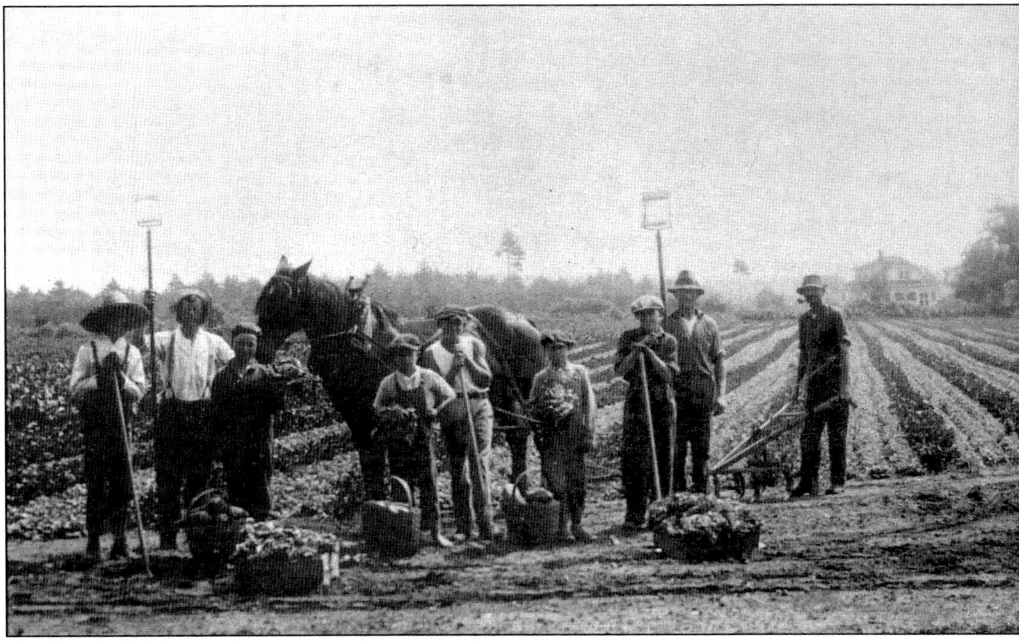

In this *c.* 1930s scene, workers at the Crawford farm pose for posterity. The Crawford farm was an extensive tract that occupied the area from Beacon Street to Newbridge Avenue. Prior to Crawford family ownership in the 20th century, the land was farmed by generations of Winns, Walkers, and Marions. In Colonial times, the area was known as Swamp Road. Today, it is where Route 128 is. (Courtesy of the Burlington Archives, No. 183.)

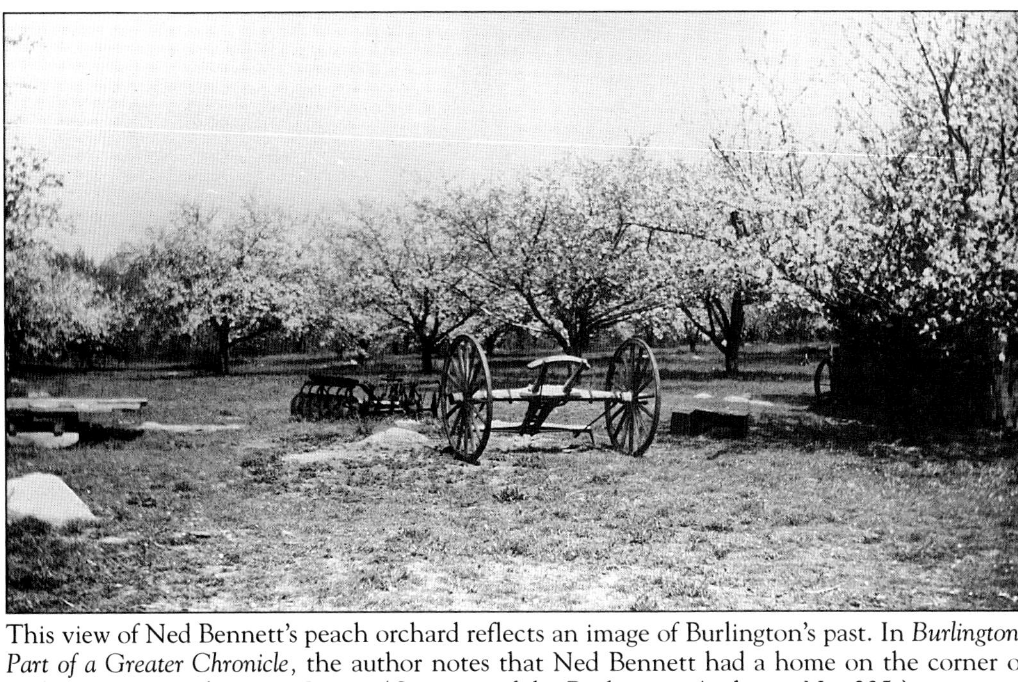

This view of Ned Bennett's peach orchard reflects an image of Burlington's past. In *Burlington: Part of a Greater Chronicle,* the author notes that Ned Bennett had a home on the corner of Forbes Avenue and Center Street. (Courtesy of the Burlington Archives, No. 335.)

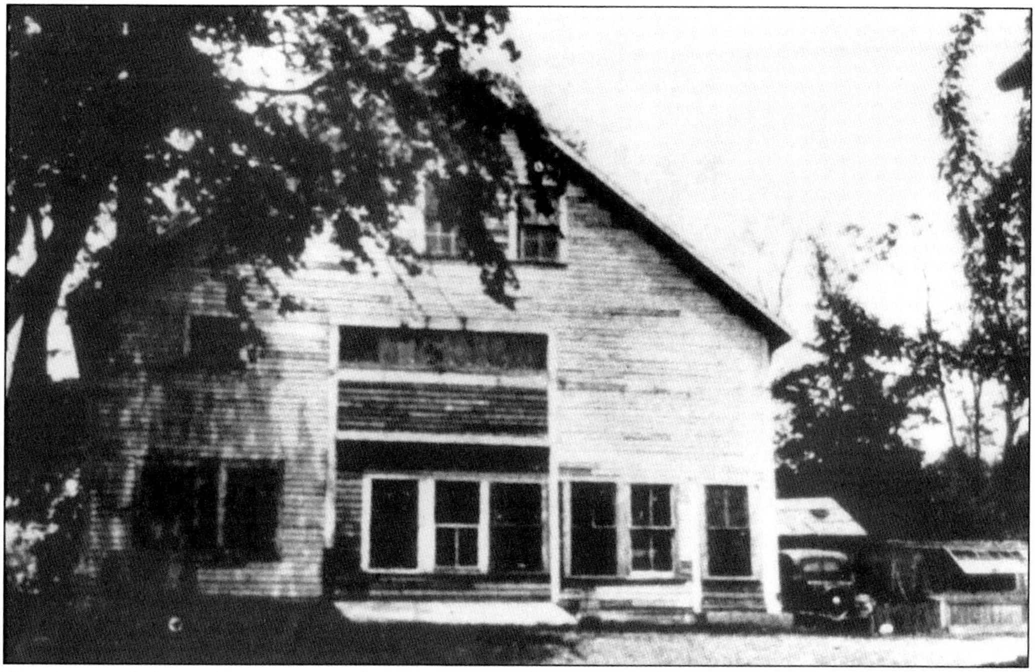

The Louis Columb barn was used as a meeting place for Burlington Catholics before there was a church building in Burlington. The barn had once been a speakeasy or nightclub known as the Winnmere Inn. The building was completely renovated, and the first service was held on October 31, 1937. By December 1938, the congregation moved to another farm on Peach Orchard Road. (Courtesy of the Burlington Archives, No. 484.)

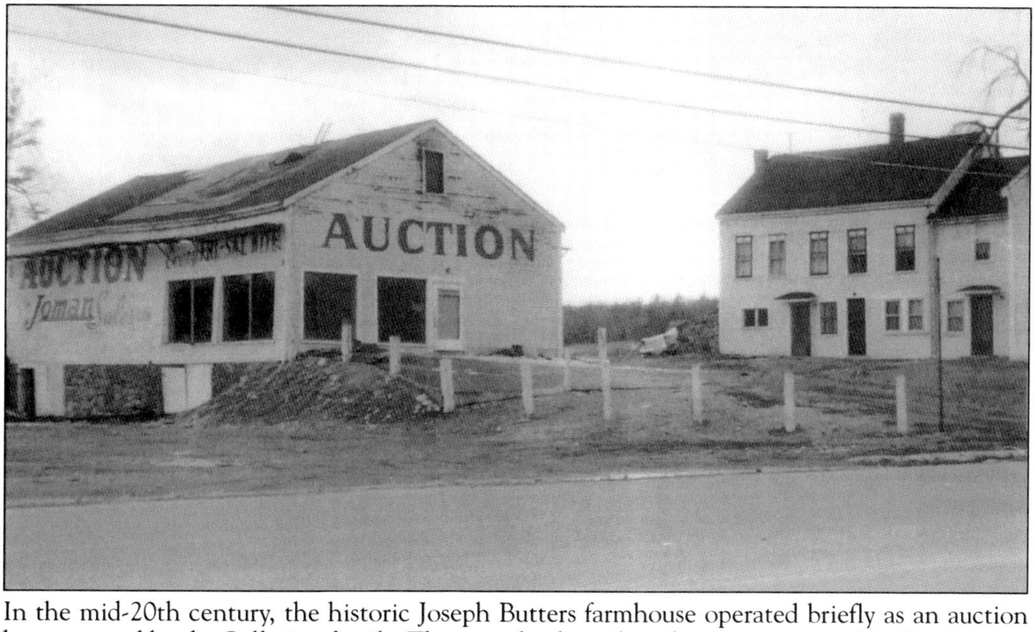

In the mid-20th century, the historic Joseph Butters farmhouse operated briefly as an auction house owned by the Sullujian family. The complex has a long history associated with it, serving as a home, a farm, a gas station, and an auction house until the site was demolished to make way for Terry Avenue in 1959. (Courtesy of the Burlington Archives, No. 366.)

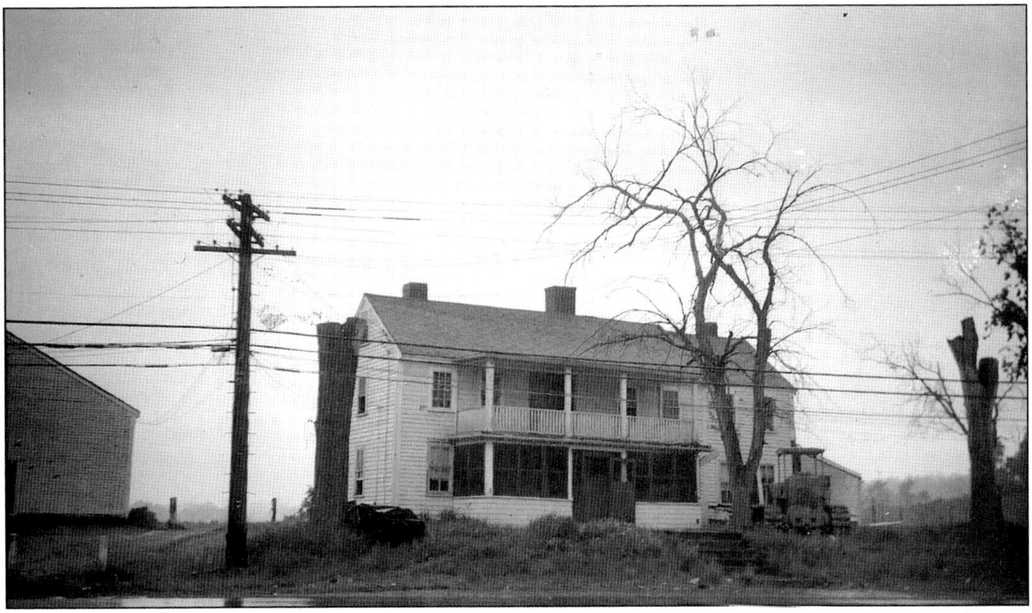

The Butters farmhouse stands alone before the machines of progress in this 1959 view, just before its demolition to create Terry Avenue. Two huge elm trees flanked either side of the farmhouse, which was purchased by Joseph Butters in 1812. The site was known as the Kendall farm and was later used for various businesses. A 1958 community map shows the Nu-Joman Auction and Discount Center at this location. (Courtesy of the Burlington Archives, No. 172)

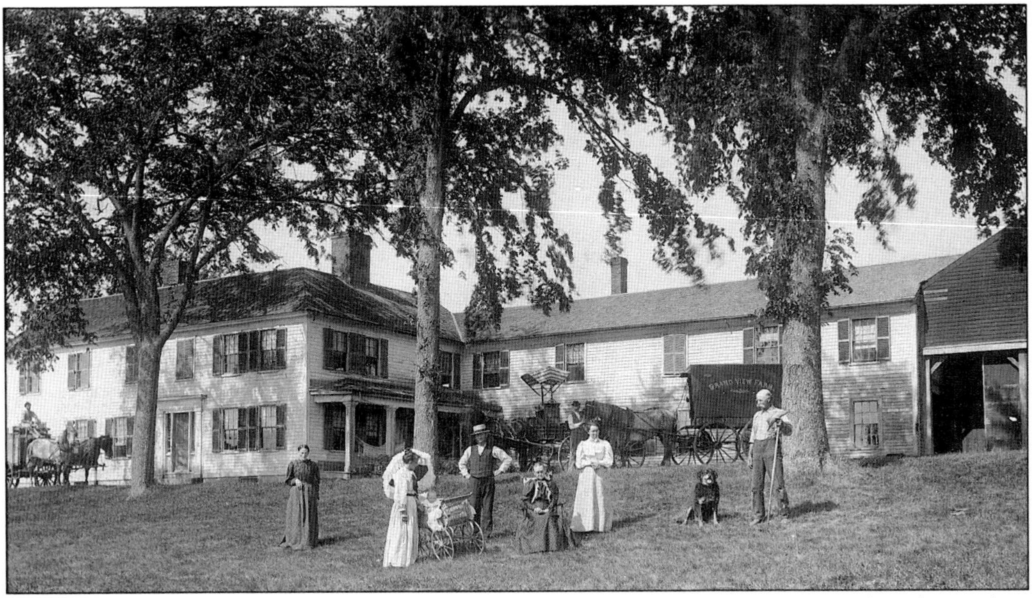

Grand View Farm (also known as the McIntire Farm or the Marion Tavern) is located at 59 Center Street. Grand View Farm is a major architectural landmark in the town of Burlington. It is considered Burlington's best example of a 19th-century connected farm complex. The property has seen use as a stagecoach halfway house on the Boston to Lowell and Concord, New Hampshire route as well as a large dairy farm and milk delivery business. (Courtesy of the Burlington Archives, No. 39.)

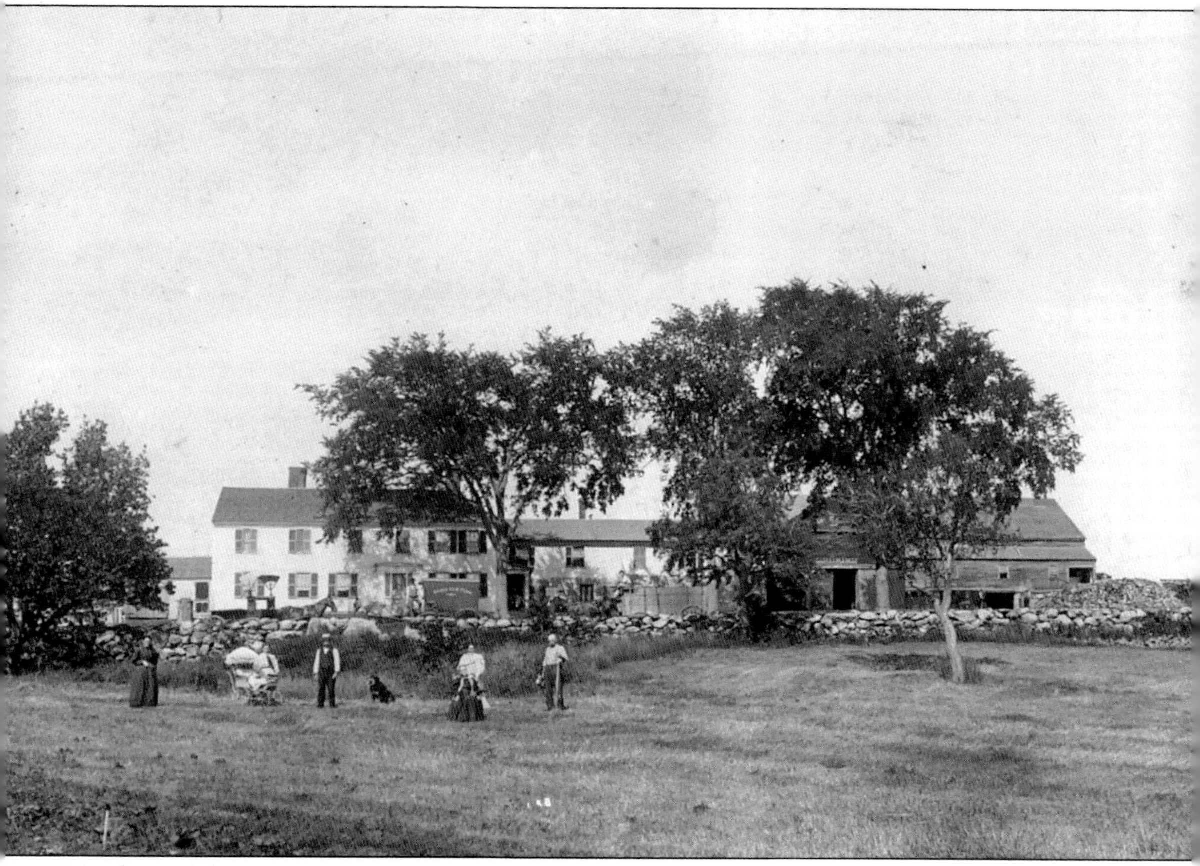

Members of the McIntire family pose in the field before their homestead, Grand View Farm, c. 1898. The farm consists of five principal structures, all linked together, in a concept of connected houses and barns conceived c. 1840. At that time, the complex was the Marion Tavern, a stagecoach stop run by Abner Marion. Charles McIntire bought the property in 1870 and ran a large dairy farm and milk route for many years. (Courtesy of the Burlington Archives, No. 40.)

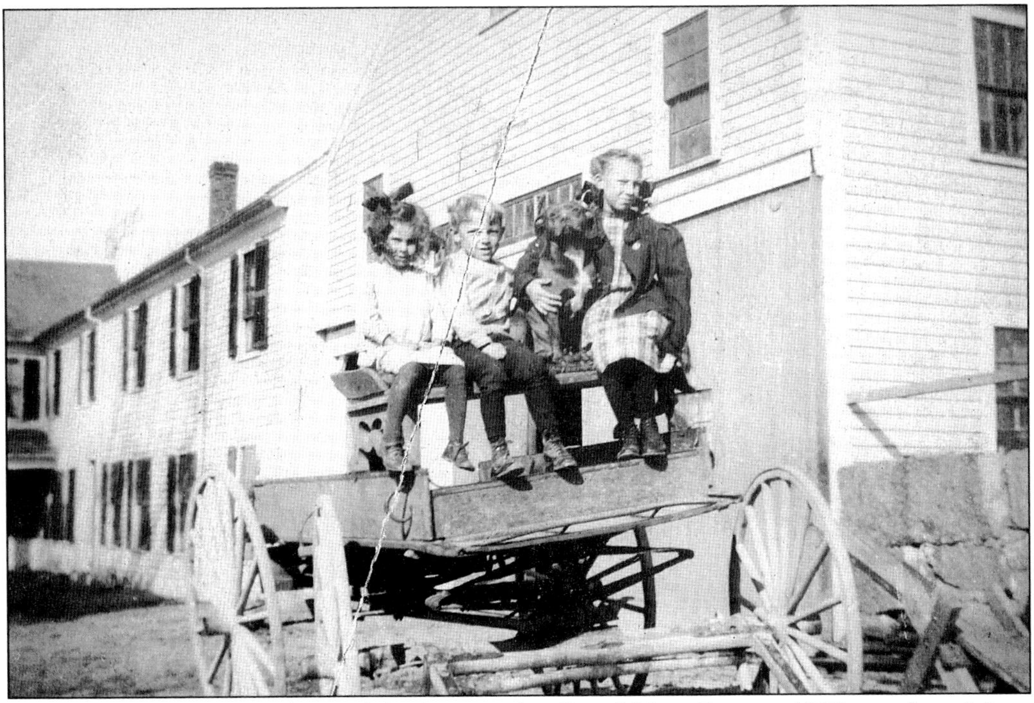

Pictured in this scene in front of the barn at the Grand View Farm c. 1908 are, from left to right, Mary Bernice, Clarence Julius, and Helen Wilburta McIntire, the children of Walter S. McIntire and Claribel Cobb and grandchildren of Charles McIntire. (Courtesy of the burlington Archives, No. 41.)

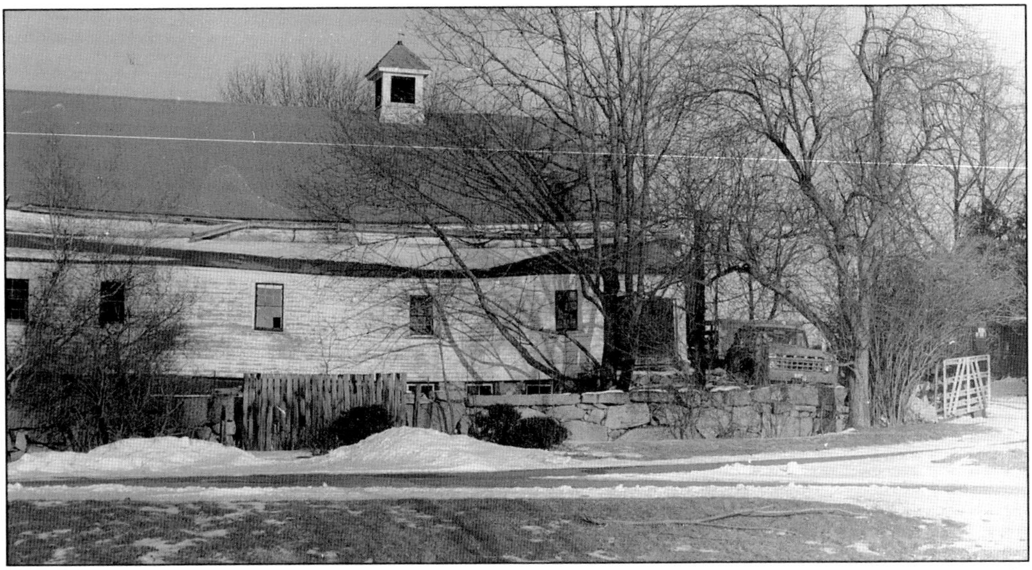

The Grand View Farm rear barn stands here in its original location. The barn is currently scheduled to be dismantled and moved to an early stone foundation of the Colonial barn on the Francis Wyman House property. A valuable addition to the emerging Francis Wyman Farm Museum project, the barn will be rebuilt to its pre-1850 appearance—a 30-by-40-foot English-style barn. (Courtesy of R. J. Costa.)

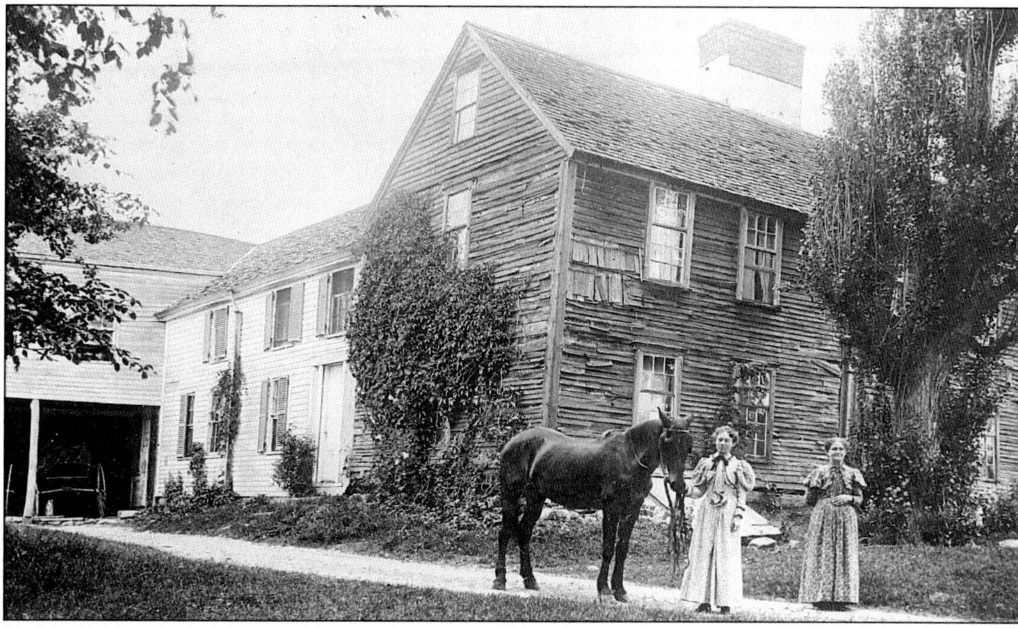

Cora and her sister Lizzie Lincoln McIntire, two Burlington teachers, pose in front of the family farm somewhere in the Bedford Street area near the Middlesex Turnpike in this late-19th-century view. The sisters were daughters of Daniel McIntire and Ellen Cahill. Capt. Daniel McIntire, the grandfather of the sisters, headed a local band of minutemen during the American Revolution and was very active in town politics. (Courtesy of the Burlington Archives, No. 66.)

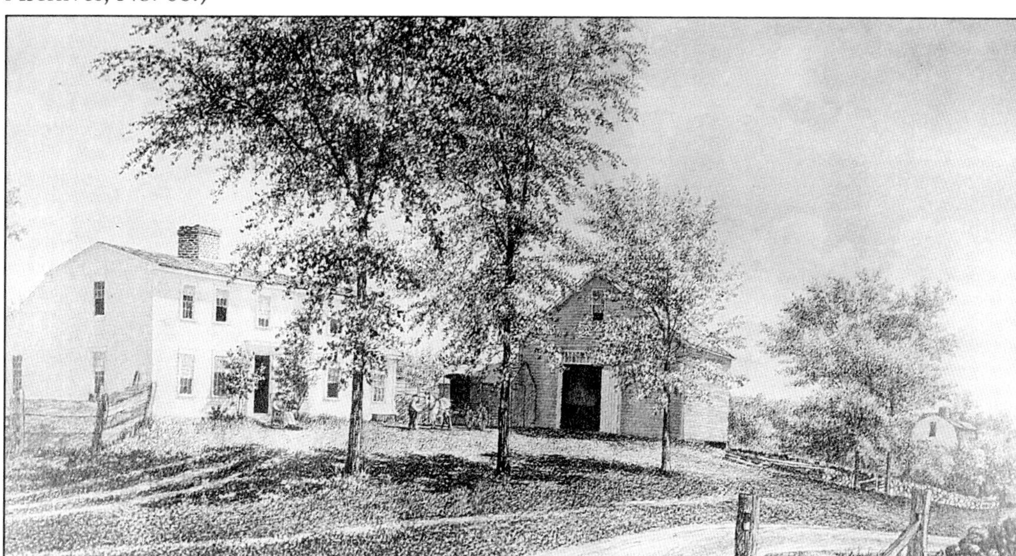

Roving Wilmington artist James Franklin Gilman painted this pastoral vision of the Isaiah Reed house sometime in the 1870s. The house, built *c.* 1770 by Nehemiah Hunt, is still standing at 23 Chestnut Street. The location was part of Colonial Cambridge Street (then called Up Street) in the 17th and 18th centuries. By 1851, the property was owned by Isaiah Reed, who started a smoked-ham farm nearby. The Reed family had a long association with the house, tracing ownership to John Reed, a weaver. (Courtesy of the Burlington Archives, No. 67.)

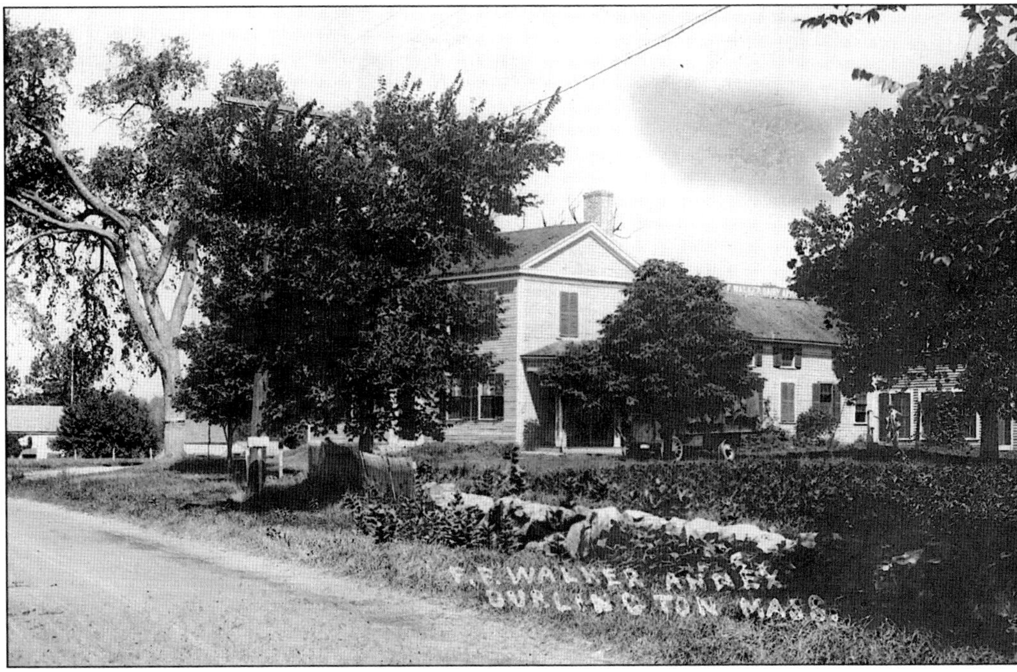

Housewright William Lawrence is said to have built this house for his neighbor Otis Cutler c. 1830. Called the Samuel Walker house and the Fred Freeland Walker annex, it stands at 128 Winn Street. Samuel Walker took over the property in 1874 and named it Oak View Farm. The cannon on the town common belonged to Samuel and for years was owned by Burlington's Republican Party. (Courtesy of the Burlington Archives, No. 140.)

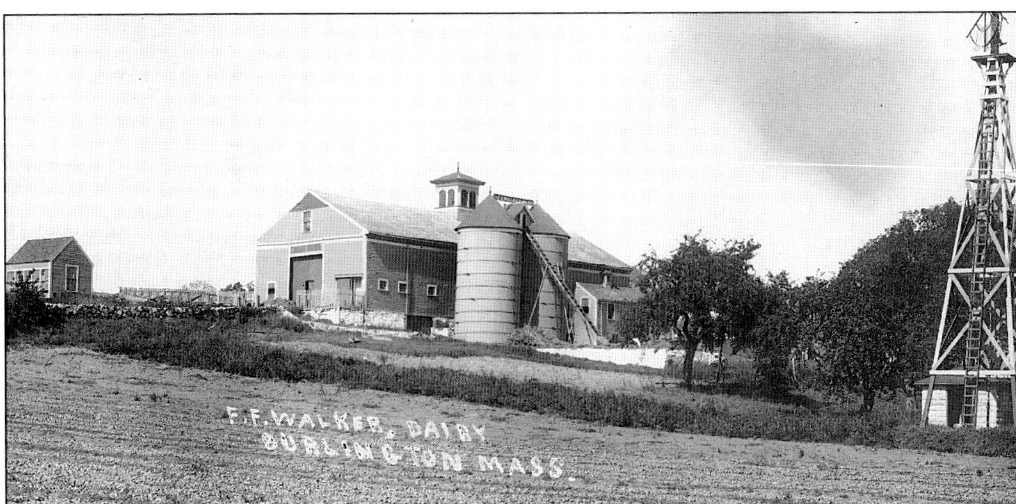

The Fred Freeland Walker farm was located where the St. Margaret's Church buildings and the Memorial School are situated today. Walker also owned the farmhouse across Winn Street known as the Samuel Walker house or the Kerrigan farm. This *c.* 1910 photograph shows the Walker farm barn, silos, and windmill. F.F. Walker sold the property to Thomas Dobbins, who operated a successful market garden on the site. (Courtesy of the Burlington Archives, No. 145.)

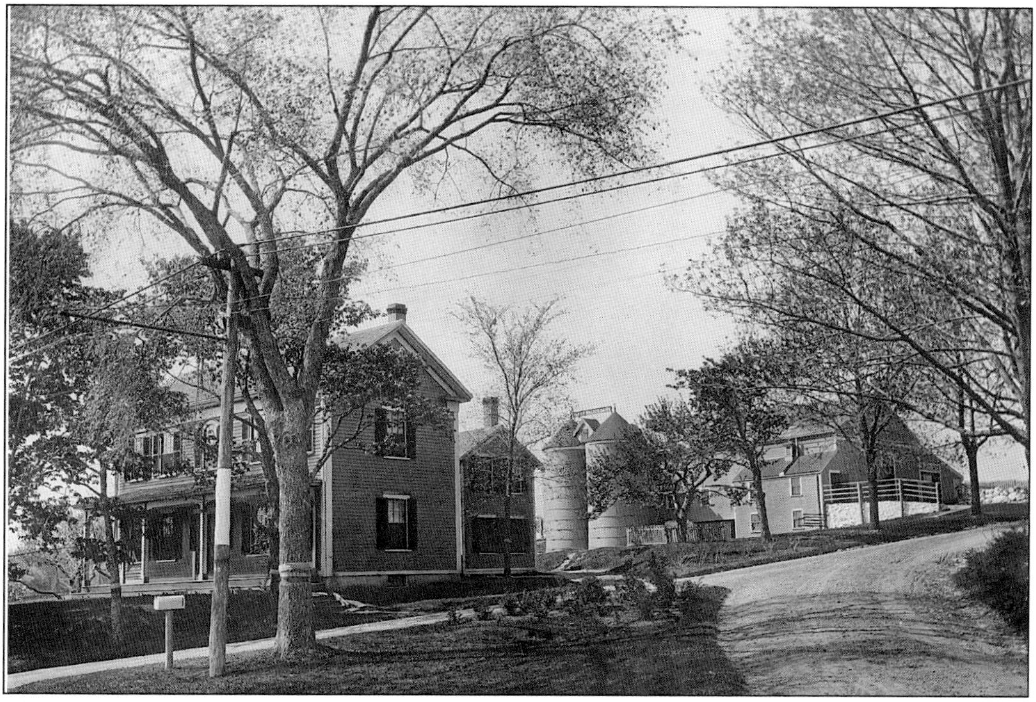

The Fred Walker farm, on Winn Street, is the now site of the St. Margaret Church buildings and the Memorial School. This image of the farm is believed to date from the 1910 era. The farm burned to the ground in 1930 according to sources from the town archives. St. Margaret's Church acquired the property in the late 1950s. (Courtesy of the Burlington Archives, No. 455.)

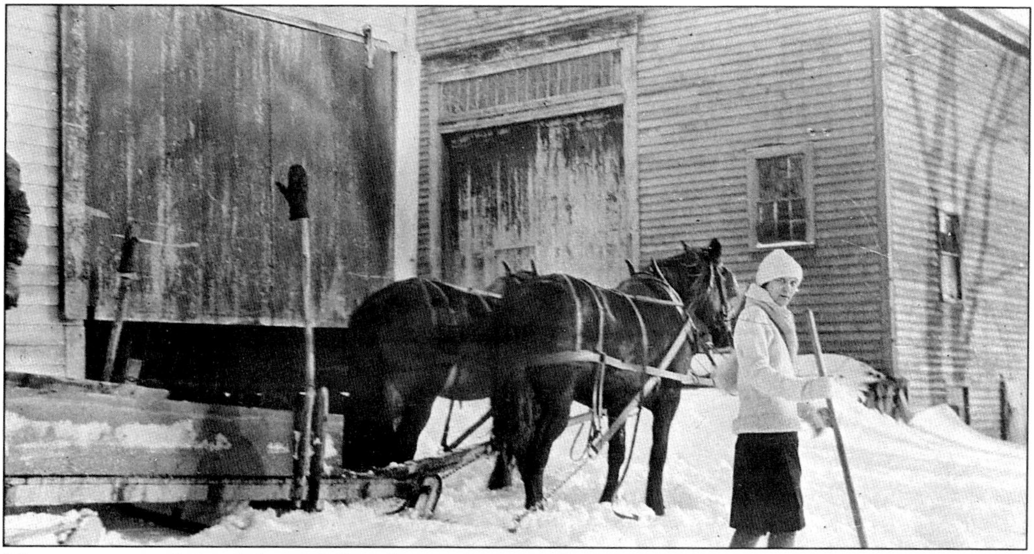

The exterior of the John Walker house barn is shown *c.* the 1930s, when Joshua Holden Bennett owned the property. The unidentified woman stands near a horse-drawn pung, a sleigh with a box-type body used when snow was on the ground to transport goods. The barn, although endangered, survives today at 138 Cambridge Street. (Courtesy of the Burlington Archives, No. 502.)

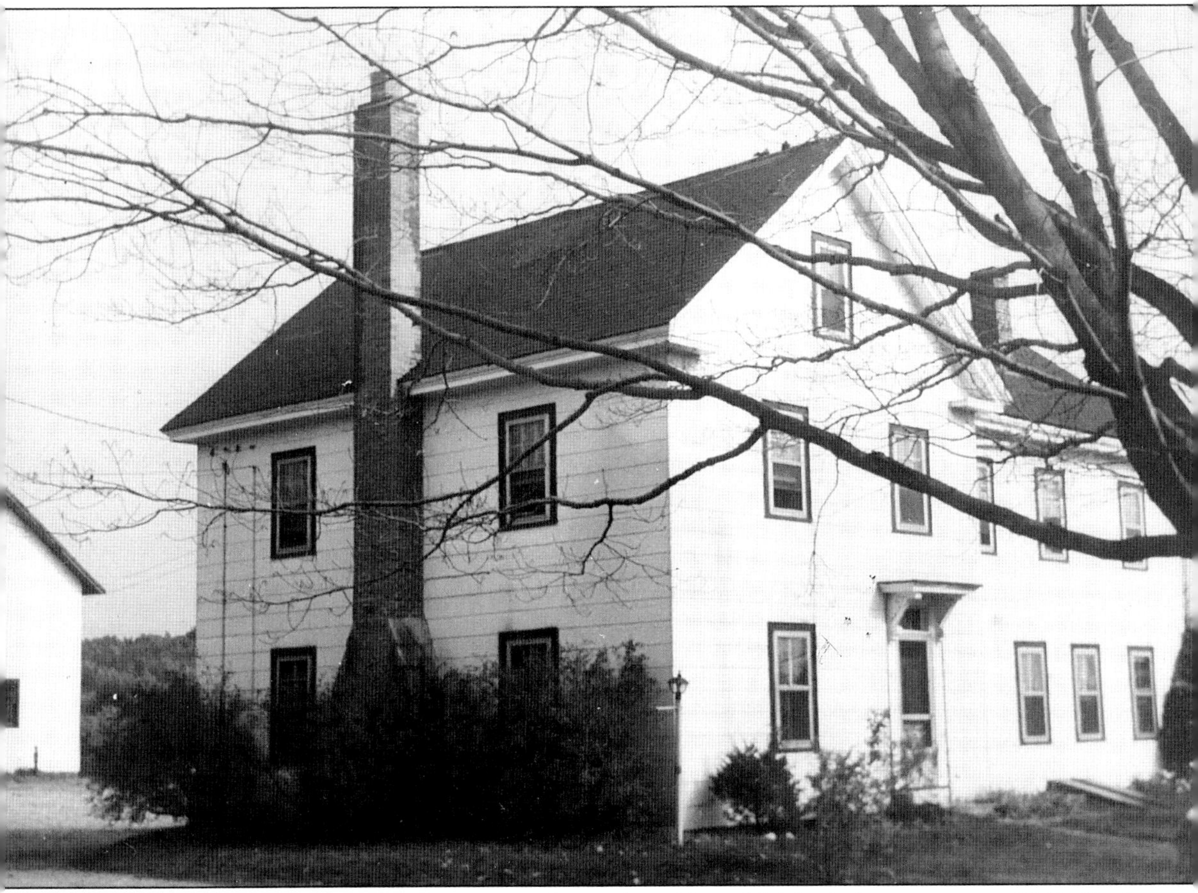

The almshouse, or poor farm, was once located on Daniel McIntire's property at 82 Bedford Street on the current site of the Pine Haven Cemetery. A McIntire house and barn had stood on the site since the 1750s. The photograph shows the property around the early 20th century. Daniel McIntire rebuilt the farmhouse and current barn *c.* 1847. The McIntires seem to have donated the property to the town for use as an almshouse sometime after the Civil War. The house burned in 1879 and was rebuilt by the town in 1880, and the *c.* 1847 barn was rebuilt using the same materials in 1890. The poor farm closed in 1906. The house was razed in 1990, and the barn has been developed as a multidenominational chapel. (Courtesy of the Burlington Archives, No. 506.)

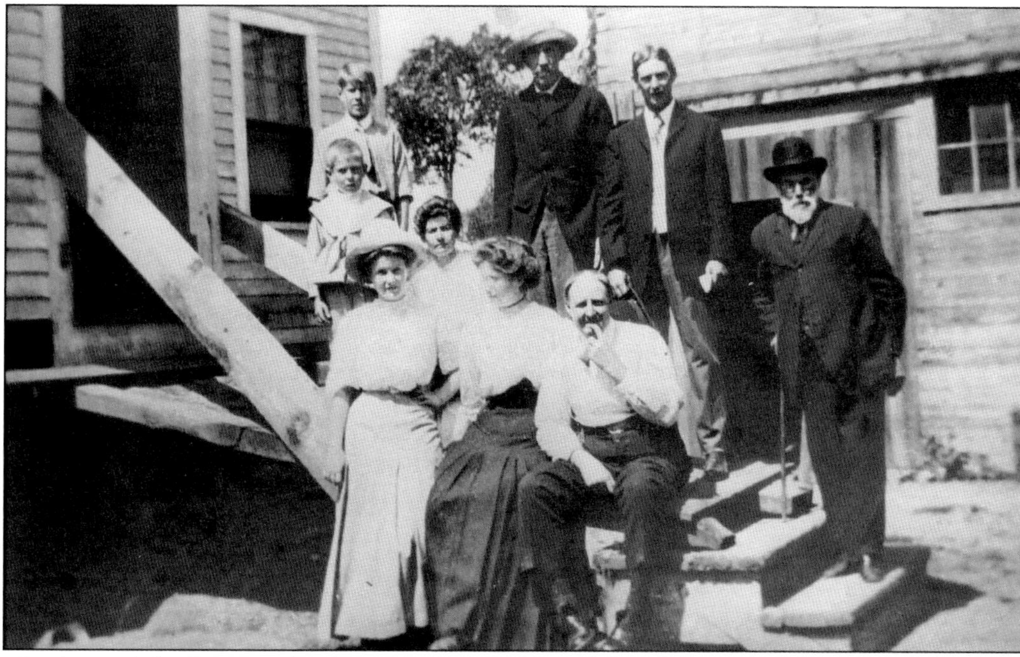

Members of the Pearson family pose on the steps of their homestead just prior to its move from its original location on the town common in 1908. The house stood on the corner of Cambridge and Bedford Streets. The Simonds Trustees acquired the Pearsons house, and it was sold to Joshua Bennett, who had it moved halfway down the hill toward Winn Street. In the early 1960s, the house was sold to Kemps, who tore it down and built a fast-food hamburger stand. (Courtesy of the Burlington Archives, No. 435.)

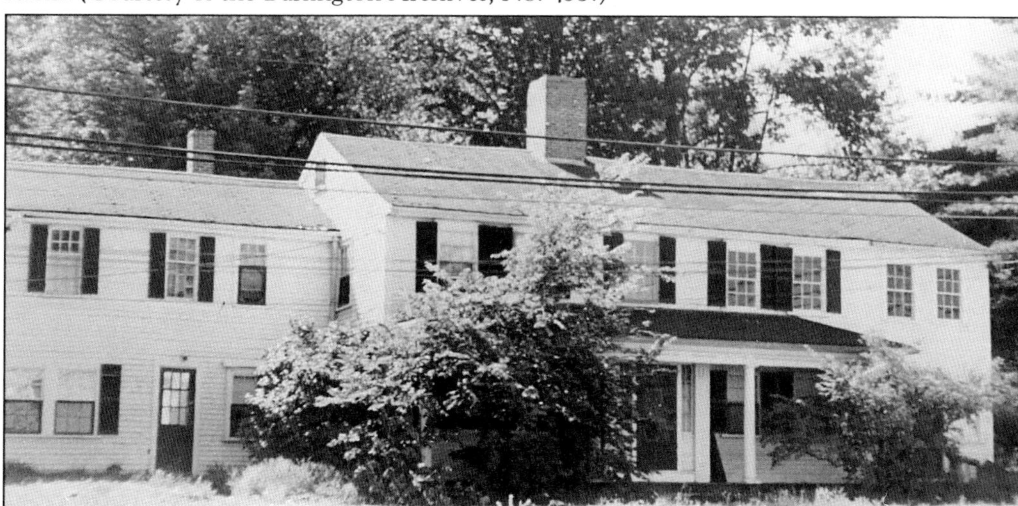

The Sylvanus Wood farm covered the area on either side of Cambridge Street near Skilton Lane. The barn was situated at the corner of Skilton Lane and Cambridge Street. The hill behind the house (now reached by Arthur Woods Avenue) was part of an extensive farm, which totaled 110 acres by 1900. Before the creation of the Burlington Water District, the Murray family operated a well in this area and sold water to neighboring residents. (Courtesy of the Burlington Archives, No. 439.)

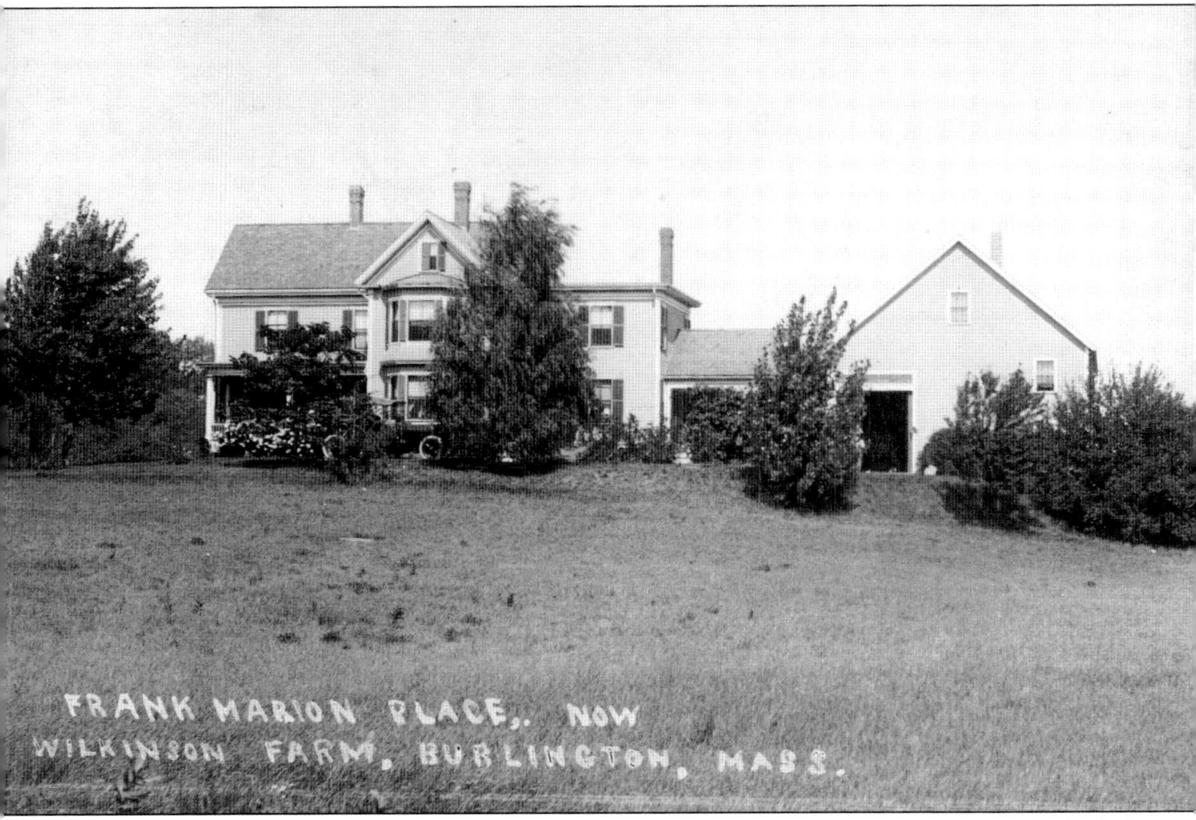

This Burlington farm is associated with the Winn, Marion, Wilkerson, Crawford, and Cummings families. It is usually known as the Frank Marion farm or the Crawford farm. The farm was located in the area between Beacon Street and Newbridge Avenue. The building of Route 128 in the 1950s split the farm in two, requiring a mile-and-a-half detour down Newbridge Avenue. The knoll where the house and barn were located was leveled to build the Beacon Village Apartments c. 1971. (Courtesy of the Burlington Archives, No. 332.)

Seven

HISTORIC BURLINGTON HOUSES

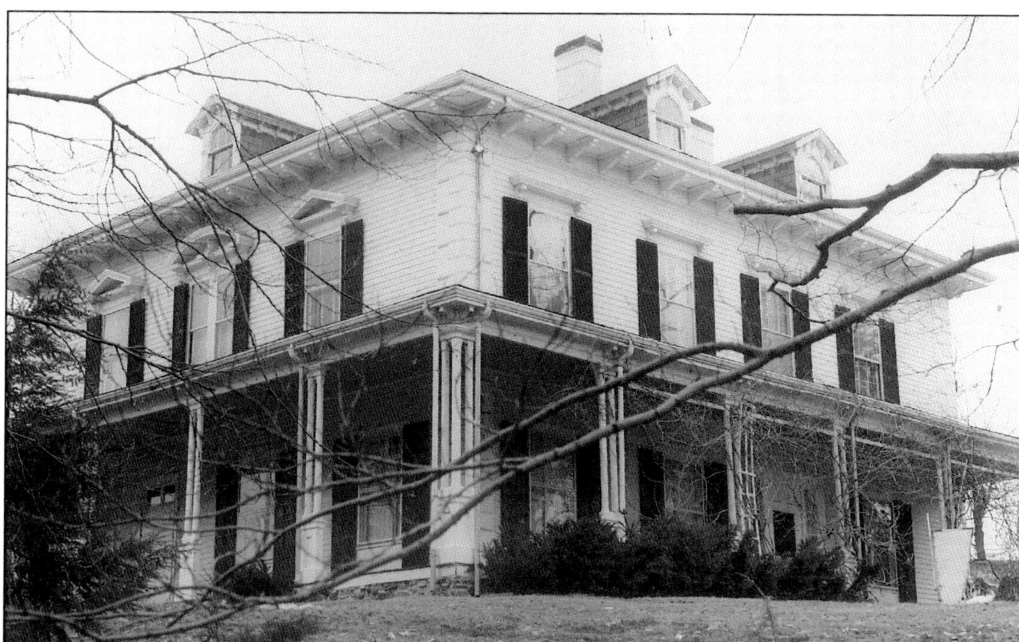

Once considered the finest mansion in Burlington, the Dr. Nathaniel L. Frothingham house still stands (although much altered) at 6 Spruce Hill Road. The house was built for one of Burlington's and Boston's leading citizens of the mid-19th century, Rev. Dr. Nathaniel L. Frothingham. Frothingham was best known as the pastor of the First Church, Boston. He and his wife, Ann Gorham Brooks, fell in love with Burlington's natural beauty. Their son Ward is credited with acquiring the land and having the house built in 1853. (Courtesy of the Burlington Archives, No. 167.)

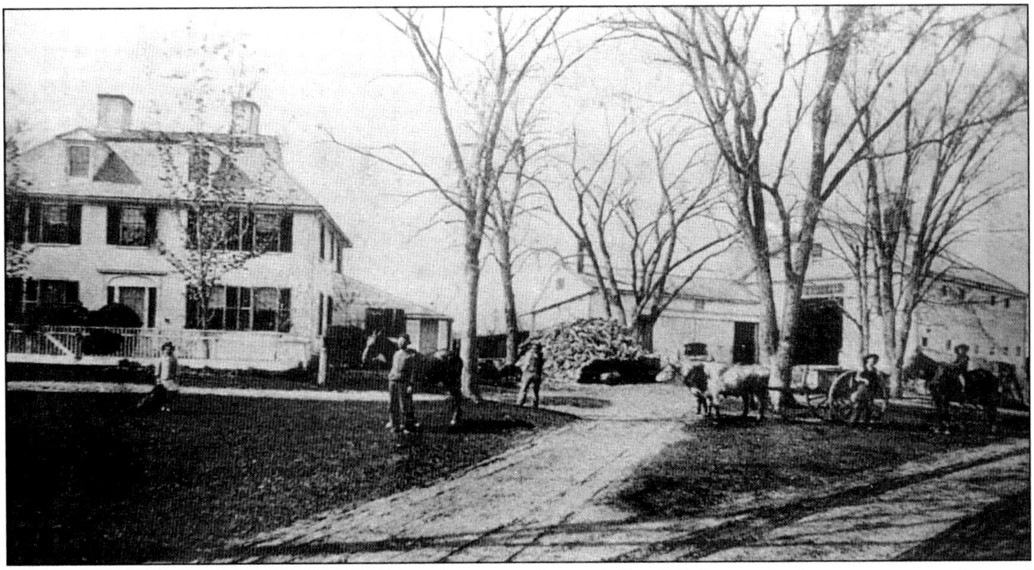

The Winn family were some of the earliest settlers of the Woburn-Burlington area. Edward Winn began the family line in America when he landed in 1640 and helped establish the town of Woburn in 1642. Several generations later, Timothy Winn built this house in 1732 on the corner of today's Winn Street and Newbridge Avenue. This photograph shows the farm in its original location in the 1930s before it was dismantled and moved to Wellesley, where it stands today. (Courtesy of the Burlington Archives, No. 57.)

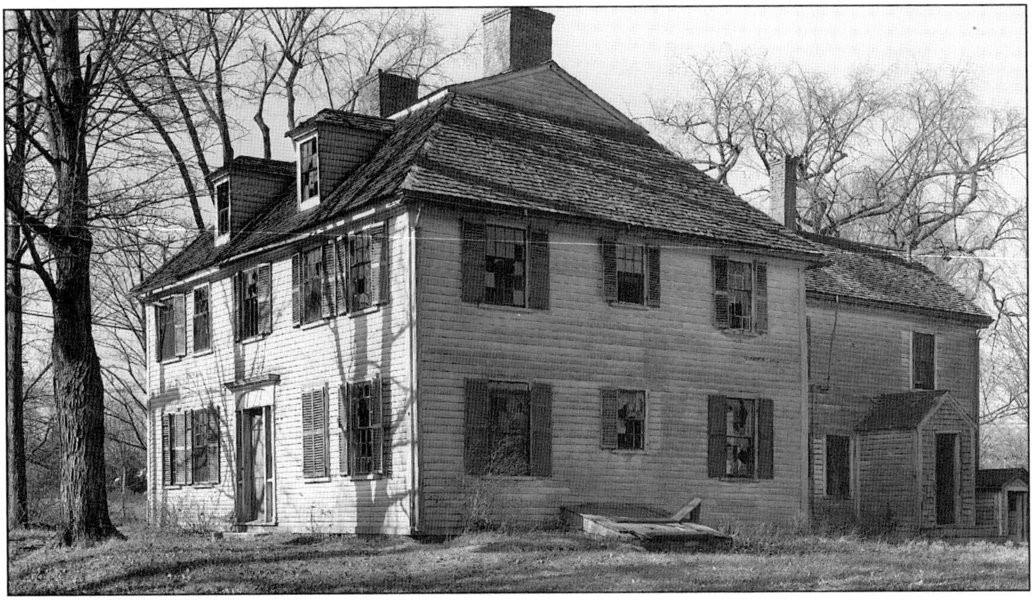

Timothy Winn (1712–1800)—town father, state representative, and notable Burlington citizen of the 18th century—built this house in 1732 on the corner of what is today Winn Street and Newbridge Avenue. The house remained in the Winn family until World War I, when it was sold and made into a multifamily unit with the addition of an ell. It was then purchased, dismantled, moved, and reconstructed in Wellesley in 1938. The house is now one of 61 properties that make up the Hunnewell Estates Historic District at Washington Street and Pond Road in Wellesley and Natick. (Courtesy of the Burlington Archives, No. 176.)

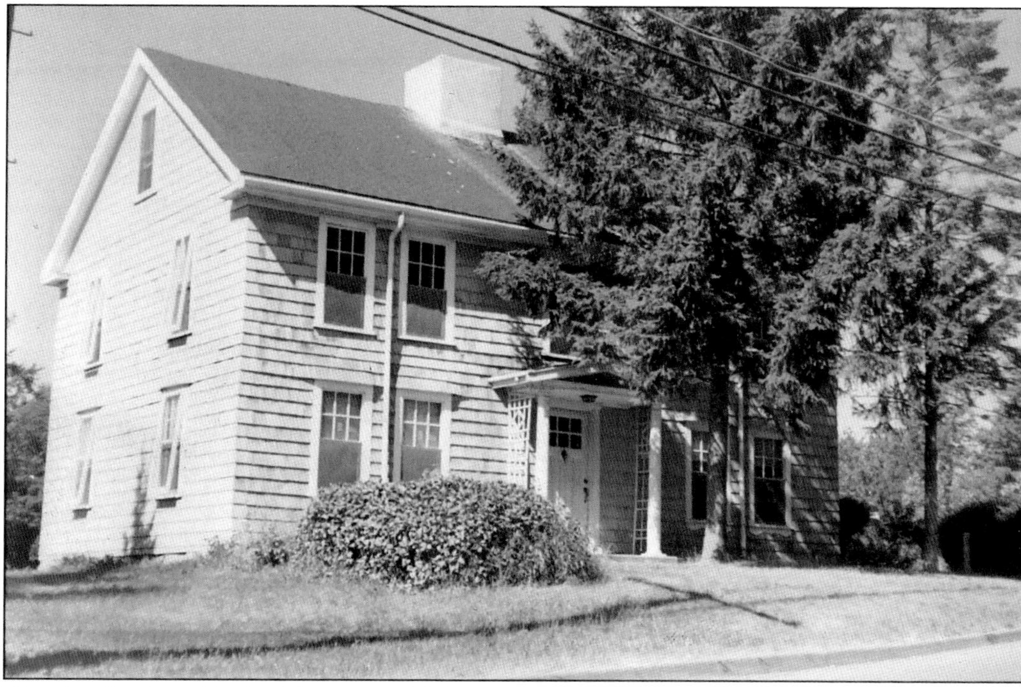

The Lt. Reuben Kimball homestead (also known as the Bell-Foster house), located at 28 Bedford Street, was probably built c. 1785 and was once part of a 95-acre farm. Reuben Kimball served in the Revolutionary War and was active in Burlington school affairs in the 1790s. The Bell family owned the property through much of the 19th century, and the hill was sometimes referred to as "Bell's Hill." (Courtesy of the Burlington Archives, No. 480.)

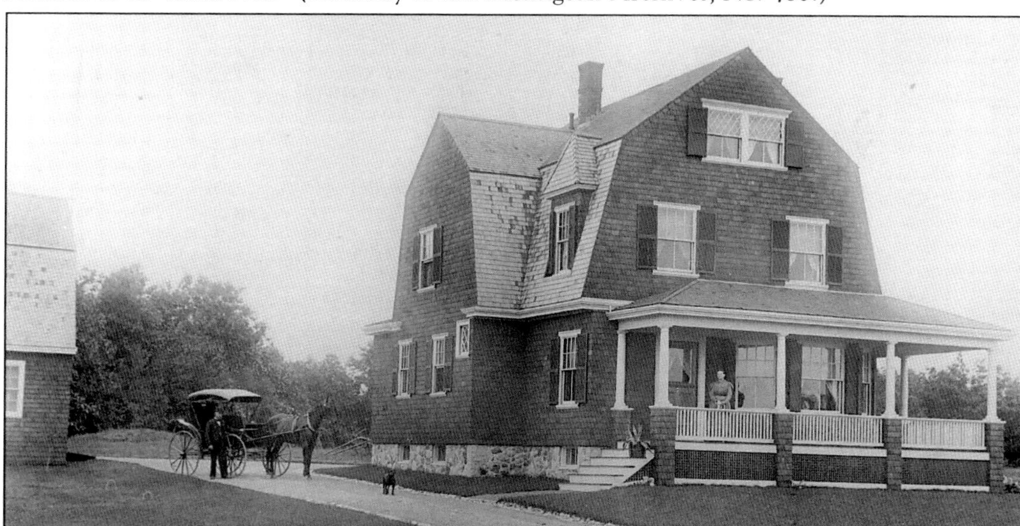

This imposing structure, currently located at 67 Center Street, was built by Hugh Stewart and was completed sometime in 1899. Hugh Stewart and his wife, Elizabeth, were born in Ireland. They moved from Cambridge to Burlington in the 1890s. Stewart became an active citizen and was on the first board of park commissioners. In 1909, this commission laid out the first baseball diamond at Simonds Park. Today, the Fellowship Bible Church uses this house as its parsonage. (Courtesy of the Burlington Archives, No. 516.)

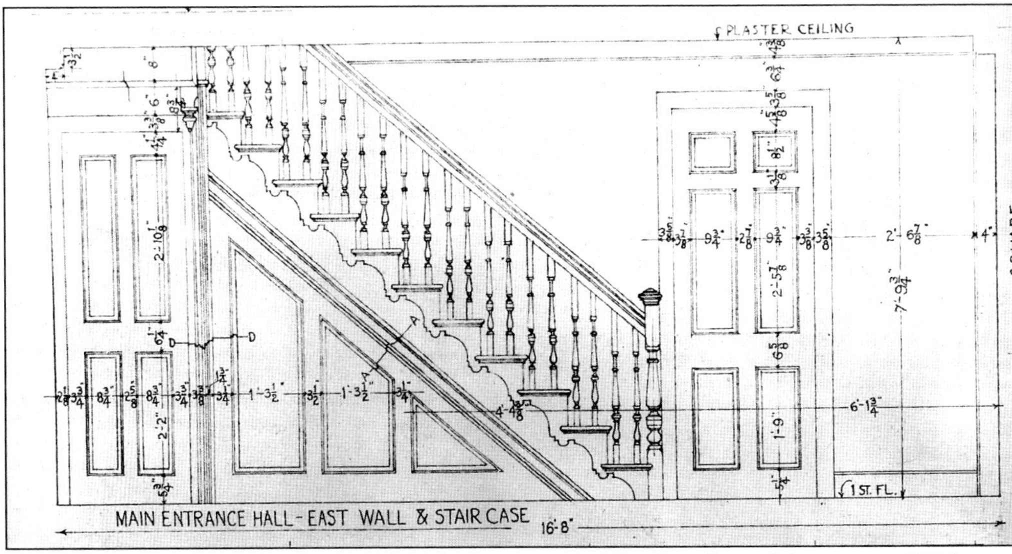

Timothy Winn—the grandson of Edward Winn, one of the founders of the town of Woburn—built in 1732 the largest and most beautiful farmhouse ever constructed in Burlington. This measured drawing was produced by Henry J. Welsh for the Works Progress Administration's Historical American Buildings Survey during the Great Depression. This drawing shows the classic design of the entrance hall, known for its fine Georgian-style paneling. (Courtesy of the Burlington Archives, No. 513.)

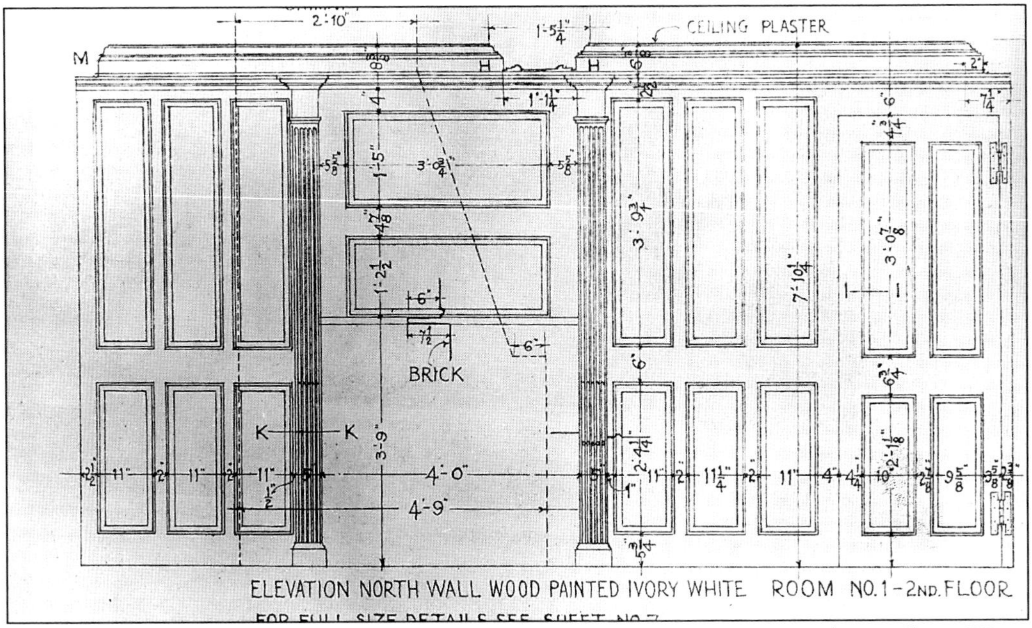

Once considered one of the finest Colonial-style buildings in Burlington, the William Winn mansion now proudly stands in Wellesley. This measured drawing shows the fireplace wall of one of the upstairs bedrooms. The house was well known for it beautiful wood paneling. The study was done during the Great Depression as part of the WPA program called the Historical American Buildings Survey. (Courtesy of the Burlington Archives, No. 60.)

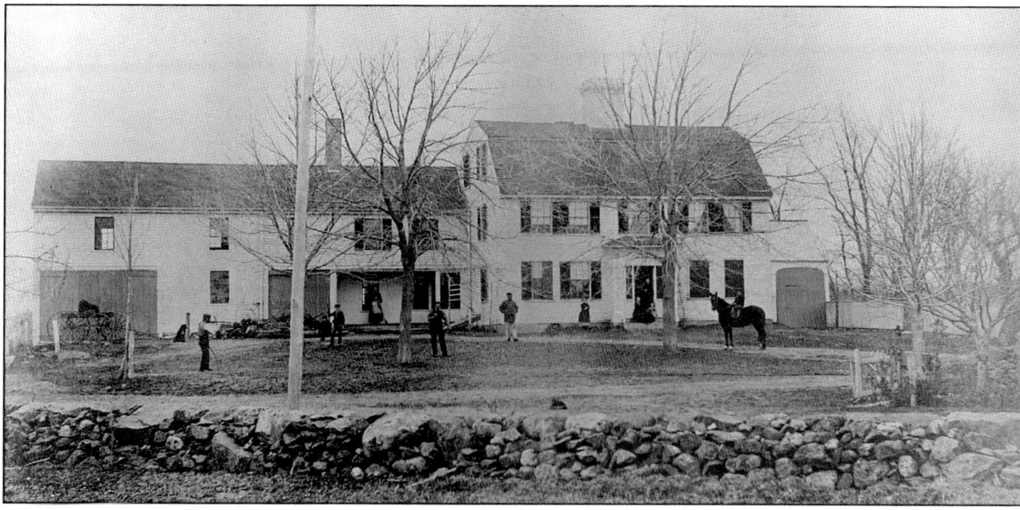

The John Winn house, at 13 Wyman Street, is one of Burlington's oldest and most remarkable historic structures. Known as the Hens and Chickens Tavern after Lt. Joseph Winn returned from the American Revolution, the house was probably built on the site of Edward Winn's 1640 homestead. The home derives its name from John Winn, a direct descendent of Edward, who was born in the house in 1828. John Winn became a successful businessman, running a thriving dairy business with his son in the 1890s. This view of the farm, *c.* 1890, shows the ell that housed the carriage shed on the lower level and a private social hall on most of the second floor. (Courtesy of the Burlington Archives, No. 69.)

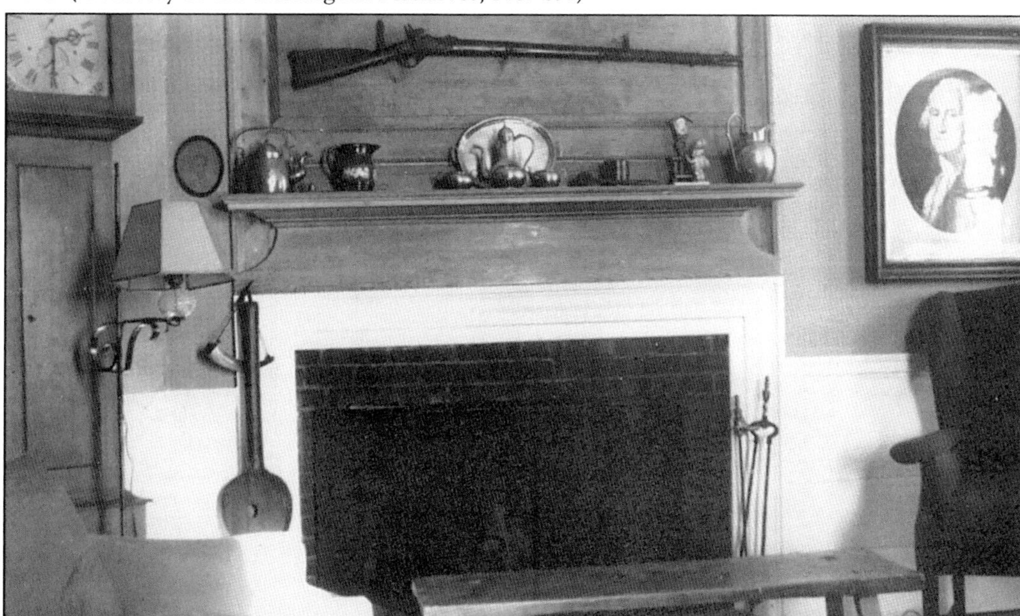

The front sitting room of the John Winn mansion is located to the left of the front entryway. The house is Burlington's only 18th-century Georgian gambrel mansion and surviving Colonial tavern according to *The Historic Preservation Survey of Burlington*. The house was built by Timothy Winn in 1734, and five generations of Winns (or Wynns) grew up in the 1730s homestead. The front sitting room features Winn heirlooms such as the grandfather clock and the musket said to belong to Lt. Joseph Wynn. (Courtesy of the Burlington Archives, No. 70.)

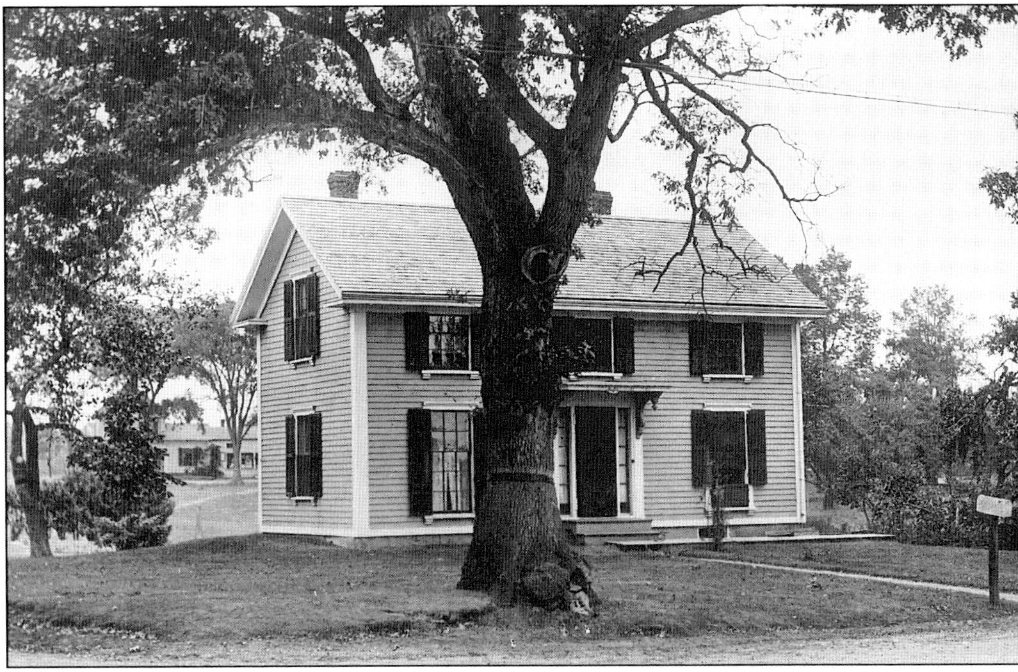

The Symmes house was located at the corner of Bedford and Cambridge Streets. According to sources from the Burlington Archives, the house was built by the grandfather of Florence Symmes, Horace Richardson Pearsons, c. 1860. Pearson died of typhoid fever at Fort McHenry in Baltimore, Maryland during the Civil War. The house was one of the last to be acquired by the Simonds trustees and was moved by the 1950s to help create today's town common. (Courtesy of the Burlington Archives, No. 188.)

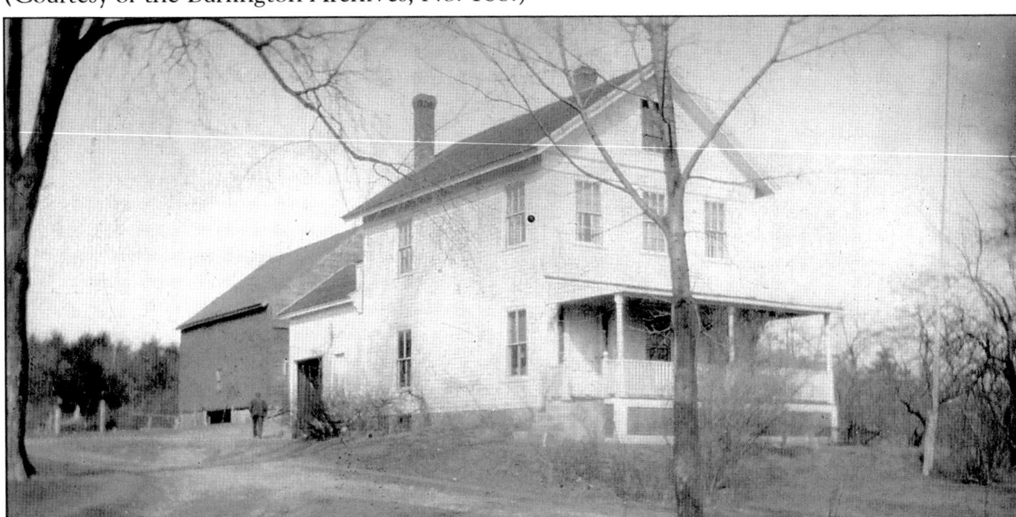

The house at 92 Francis Wyman Road was built by Bradford Skelton in 1864 shortly after he returned from the California gold fields. Skelton was only 21 when he left Burlington to find fame and riches during the California gold rush. He spent several years searching in vain but sent many colorful letters home describing the daily routine of a gold miner. Bradford married Almira Shedd, and the couple raised four sons, who were all prominent in town affairs through the middle of the 20th century. (Courtesy of the Burlington Archives, No. 508.)

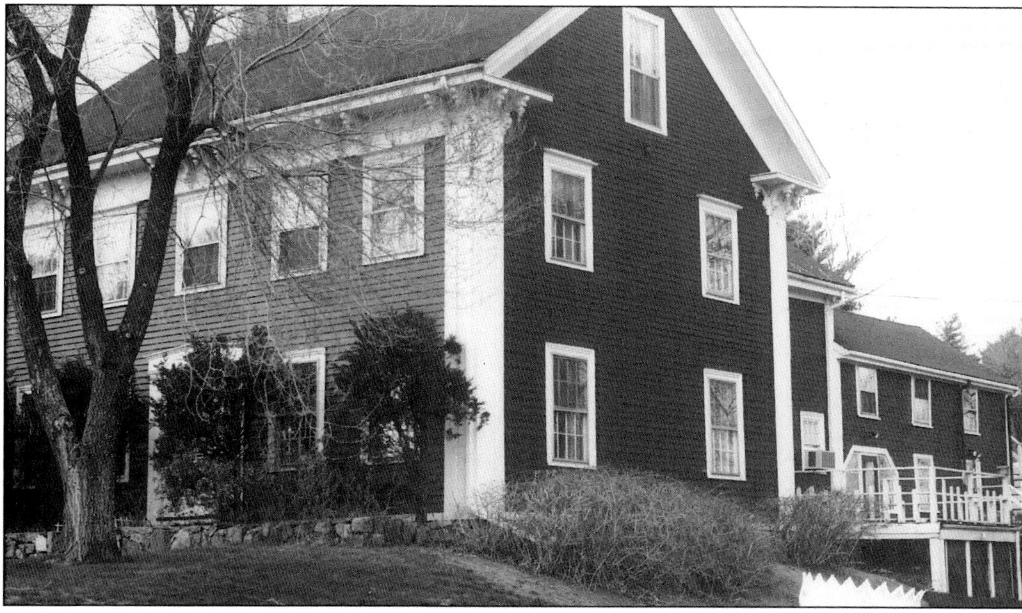

The Capt. Ishmael Munroe house, at 2 South Bedford Street, was built using the remnants of an early-18th-century structure built by Lt. James Simonds *c.* 1730. According to local historian Lotta Cavanaugh Rice Dunham, who was born and lived in the house, Capt. Ishmael Munroe bought the property in 1795. Around 1850, Ishmael and his son Jacob Munroe tore down the house, moved the ell, and built a new house. Ishmael Munroe was a noted housewright, or master carpenter, and his creation was a blend of the Greek Revival and Italianate styles. (Courtesy of the Burlington Archives, No. 162.)

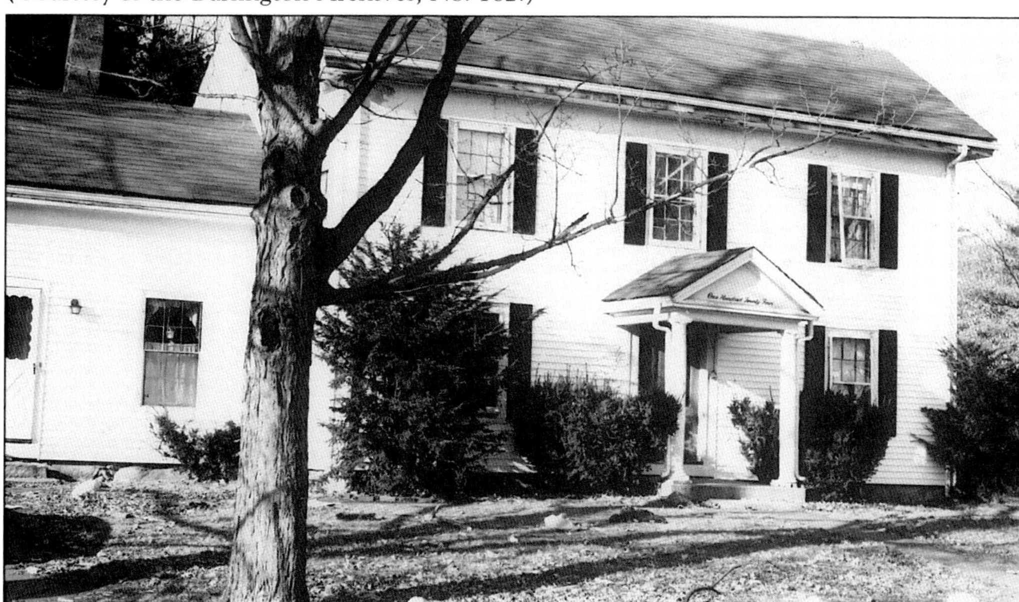

Once the home of Nathan and Rachel Crosby Simonds (the parents of Marshall Simonds), this house is still standing at 124 Bedford Street. The house was built for Nathan and Rachel Simonds between 1850 and 1860 on land inherited from Calvin Simonds (1752–1840), Nathan's father. (Courtesy of the Burlington Archives, No. 161.)

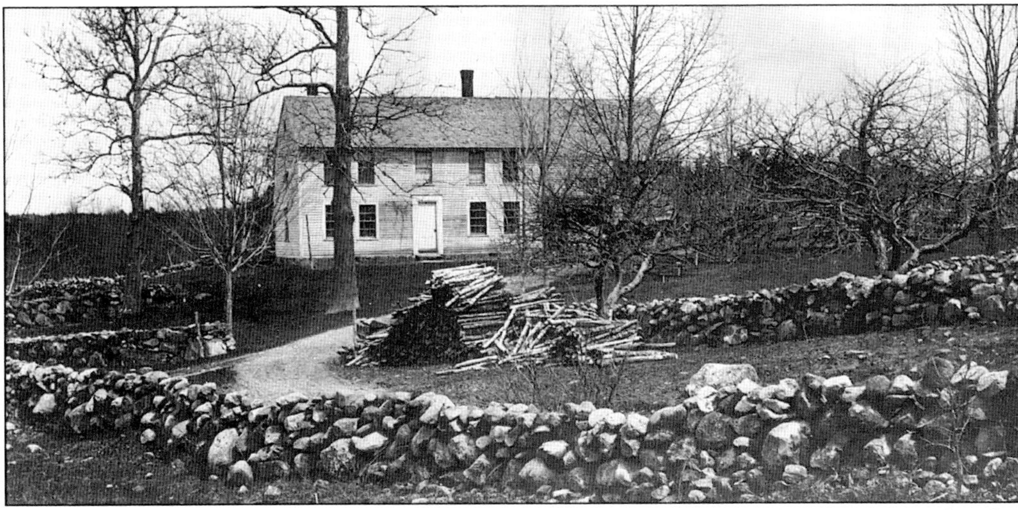

The Lt. Nathaniel Cutler house was built sometime in the 1720s and is now considered to be one of Burlington's earliest structures. It may be the oldest house standing in town today. Samuel Snow is on record as the first owner. Snow sold the property to Nathaniel Cutler in 1724. In that year, the property consisted of a house, a barn, and 34 acres of land. It is located in the "Wood Hill" part of Burlington at the corner of Mill Street and Chandler Road. (Courtesy of the Burlington Community Scholarship Foundation.)

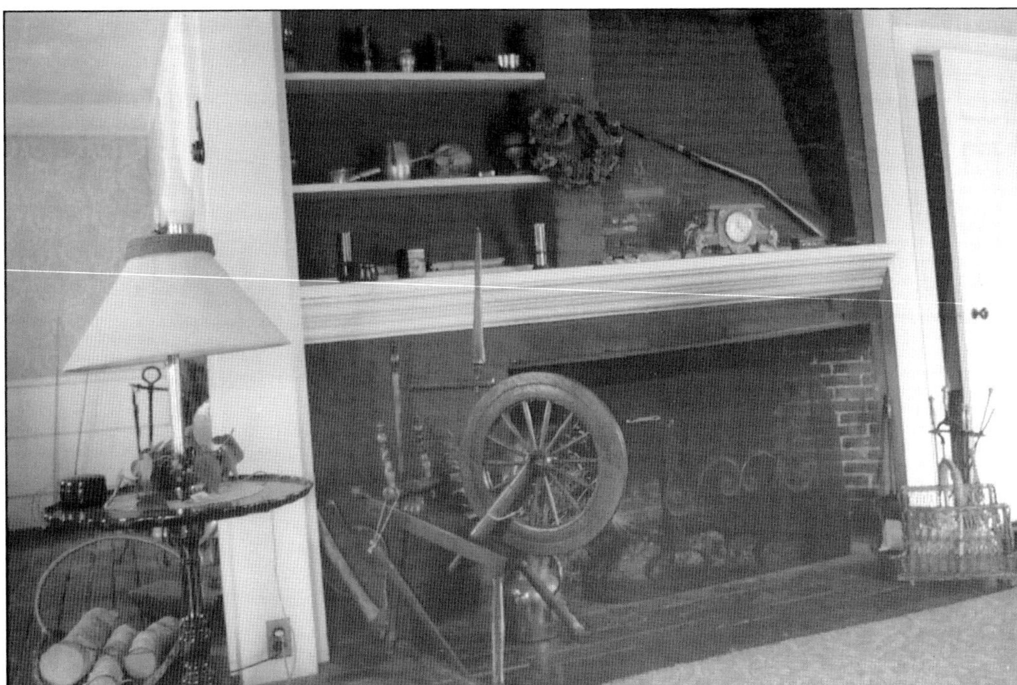

This photograph shows the fireplace wall in the Jotham Johnson house, which is still standing at 56 Lexington Street. The two most notable Burlington historians, Lotta Dunham and Ed Fogelberg, differ as to the building date of this house—1732 and 1770. Recent scholarship has shown errors in the early written history pertaining to the site, and further study is necessary. (Courtesy of the Burlington Archives, No. 154.)

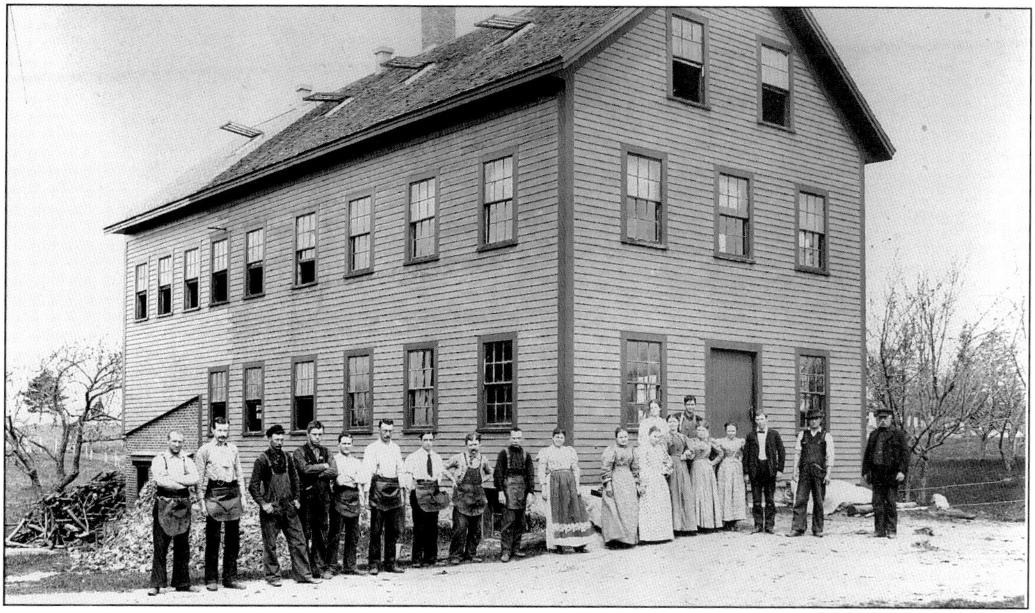

Workers line up in their work clothes outside the William Edward Carter heel shop c. 1900. William E. Carter ran a shoe heel and shoe stock factory on Cambridge Street near the intersection of Bedford Street from c. 1880 to 1904. The heel shop employees were from Woburn and Burlington; the Woburn girls boarded with Burlington families. The shop made the heels of shoes from scrap leather trimmings from the Woburn tanneries. The finished product was sent to a shoe shop in Brockton. (Courtesy of the Burlington Archives, No. 47.)

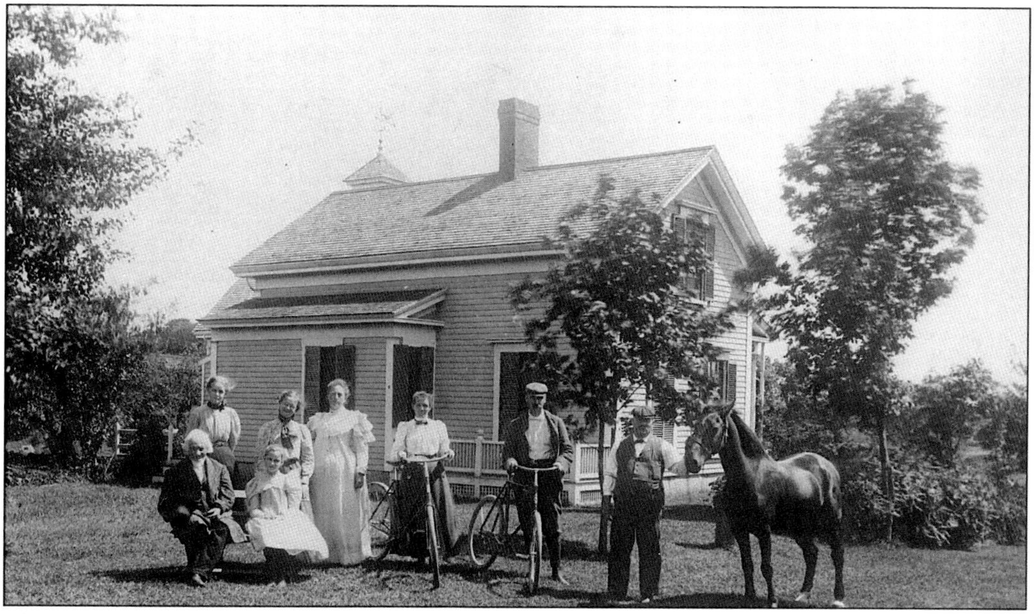

The Jonas Lawrence house is shown c. 1898 with members of the Brown family posing on the Peach Orchard roadside. Jonas Lawrence built a timber-framed, Federal-style structure on the site in 1799 and later modernized it in the Greek Revival style. Located at 110 Winn Street, this was the "second house" to master carpenter William Lawrence, who built several houses in Burlington during the Federal era (1790–1840).

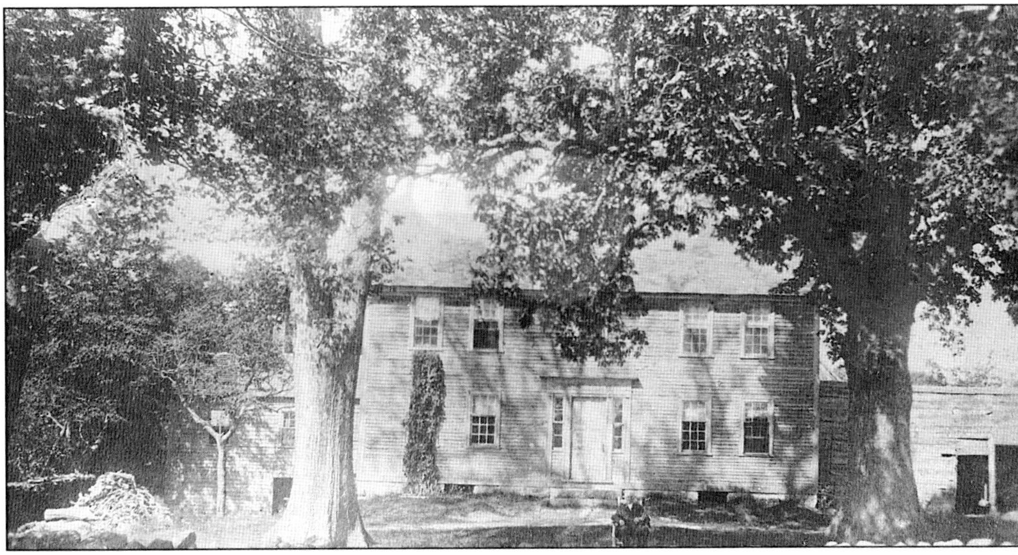

The Samuel Shedd house, still standing at 4 Francis Wyman Road, is fine example of an early Federal-style farmhouse. Samuel Shedd was 32 years old in 1798 when he came to Burlington from Tewksbury and built this house. In the same year, he married Lydia Clark, and they raised a family of six in that house. Samuel Shedd live there until his death in 1861. (Courtesy of the Burlington Archives, No. 427.)

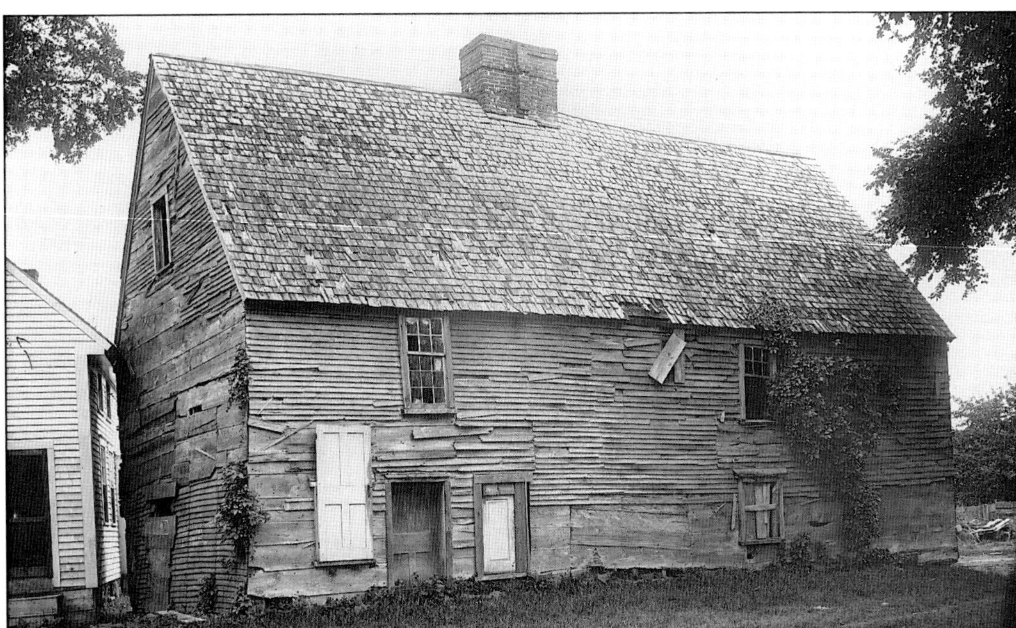

In the area where Winn Street meets Center Street, the first Cutler house was built *c.* 1650, very near the present-day Samuel Edward Walker house. This house was built 12 years after the founding of Woburn, the 10th town in Middlesex County, incorporated in 1642. At that time, Burlington was a remote section of the town of Woburn, but this location was on the road to another early settlement, Billerica. (Courtesy of the Burlington Archives, No. 62.)

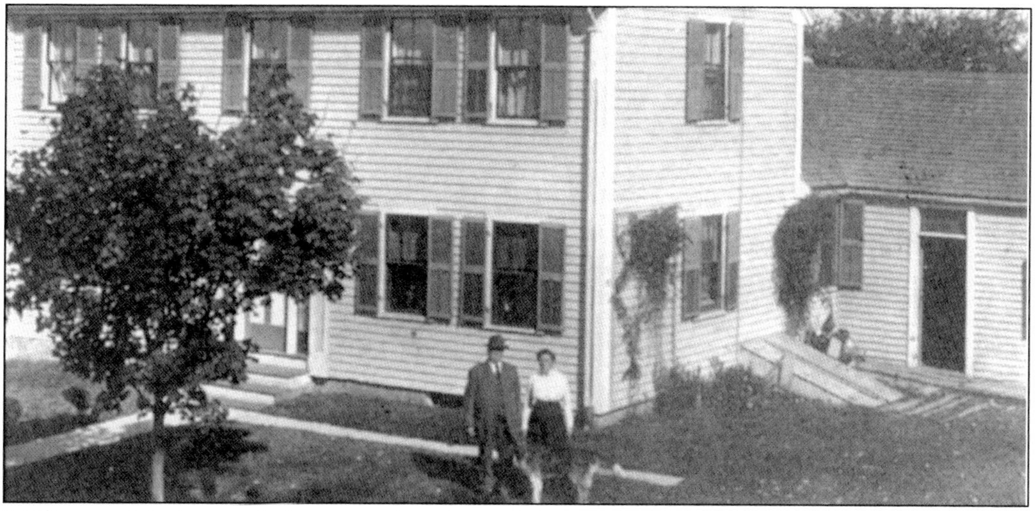

William and Rebecca Graham stand in front of their farm on Stony Brook Road *c*. 1910. The imposing structure at 28 Stony Brook Road was probably built in the latter part of the 18th century by Thomas Locke or Thomas Locke Jr., whose family operated a sawmill and gristmill on the Burlington-Lexington line. In 1799, this area of the newly created town of Burlington was "annexed" by Lexington. In the mid-20th century, it was the home of two prominent town servants and involved citizens, Selwyn Harrison Graham and his wife, Maud M. Smith Graham, town clerks for nearly 60 years. Drs. James and Mary Beaudry are the owners today. (Courtesy of the Burlington Archives, No. 73.)

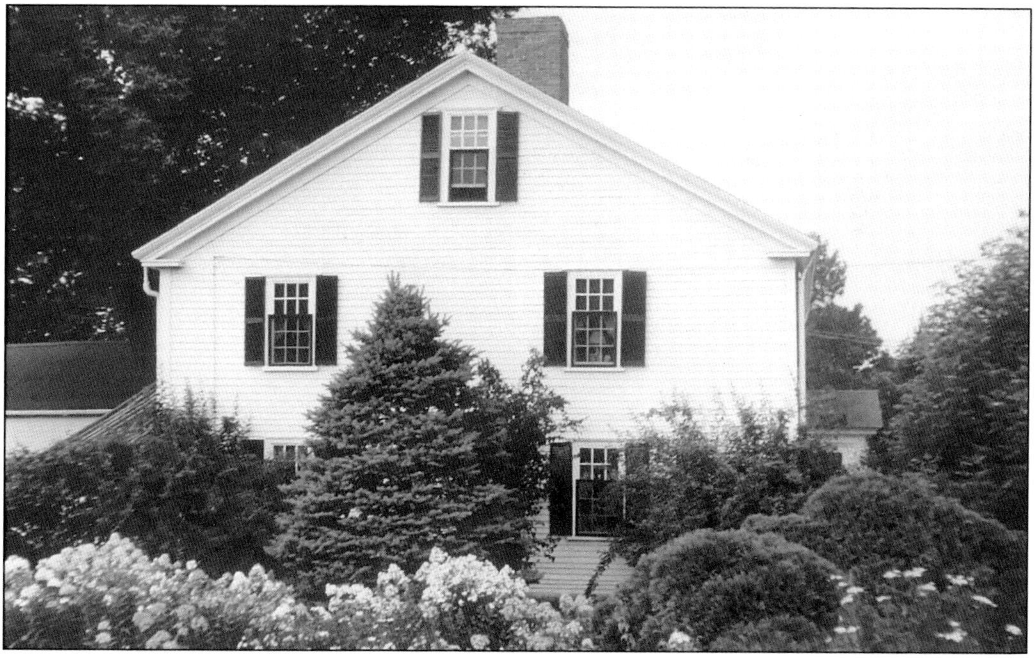

Located on the town common at 9 Bedford Street is the stately Maj. Gen. John Walker house, a typical New England Colonial-style house with an outbuilding and attached barn. This image of the New England Flower Garden from the 1960s shows the efforts of the professional gardener, James Tucker, related to the owners at that time. (Courtesy of the Burlington Archives No. 479.)

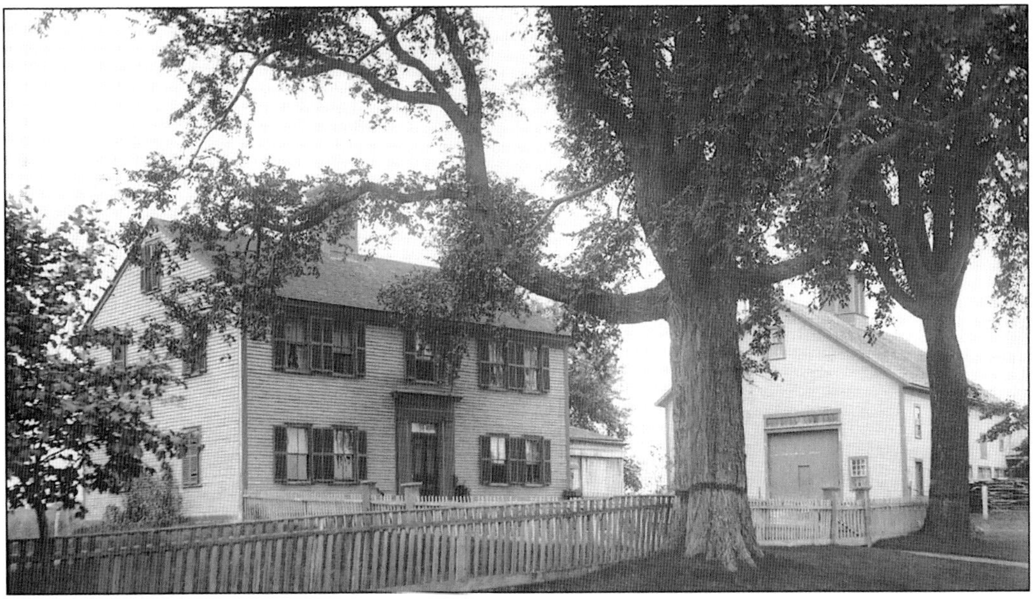

The Nathaniel Kendall house may have been built prior to the Revolution and is still standing at 25 Wyman Street. Research suggests that the house was built between 1742 and 1777, probably by Nathaniel Kendall. The property changed hands several times and was owned by John Winn between 1882 and 1910, influential farmer and member of the state legislature. After 1910, the land was developed as a successful market garden by the Given family. (Courtesy of the Burlington Archives, No. 72.)

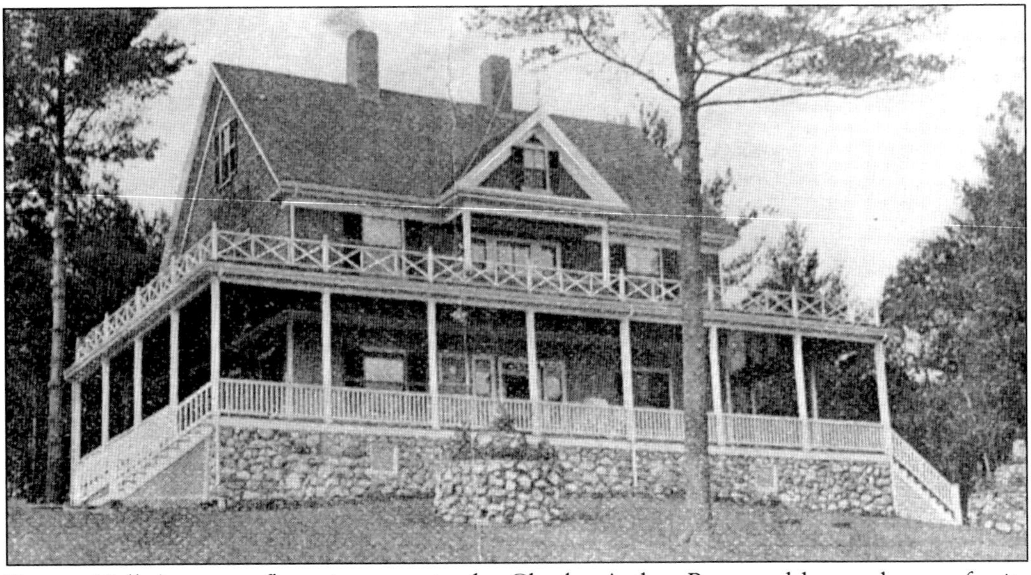

Terrace Hall Avenue reflects its name in the Charles Arthur Raymond house, known for its terraced lawns and gardens at the turn of the century. Raymond was a retired shoe merchant who built the house in 1895 on the north side of Terrace Hall Avenue. Charles A. Raymond was a large landowner in Burlington, with four houses and 524 acres of land in various parts of town. Included on the Terrace House property was a barn, horse stable, engine house, and tank house. Across the street was a duck pond with an island. (Courtesy of the Burlington Archives, No. 144.)

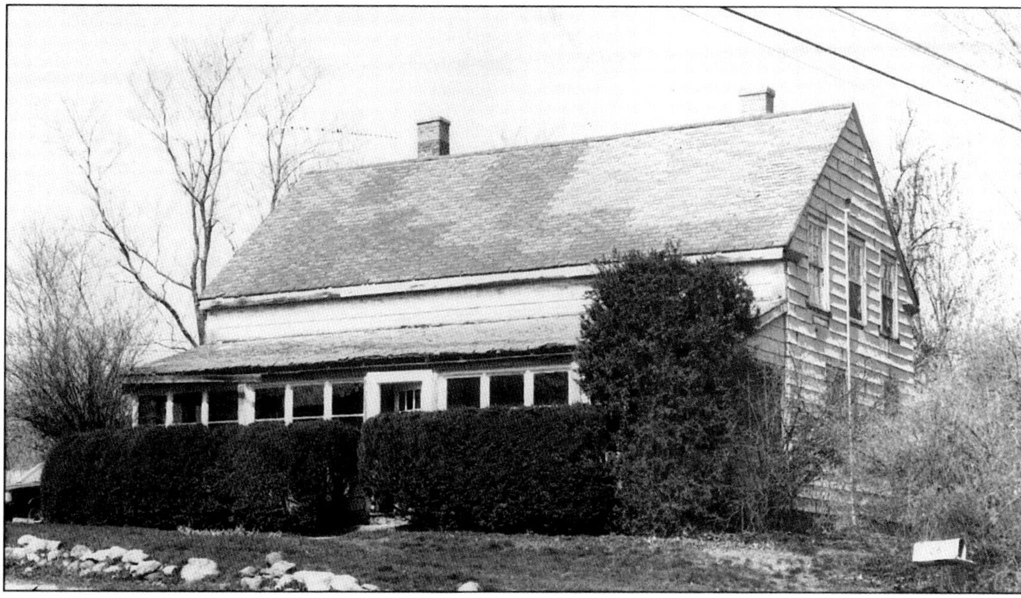

Augustus Prouty was born in Hampden, Maine, on March 28, 1828. With his wife, Rachel B. Keith, he moved to Burlington and became involved in town government, holding several elected positions. For years, his homestead was the only one located on Prouty Road. After Prouty's time, the area became known as Johnson's Grove, a social gathering place for Burlington's growing Scandinavian population during the 1920s. (Courtesy of the Burlington Archives, No. 151.)

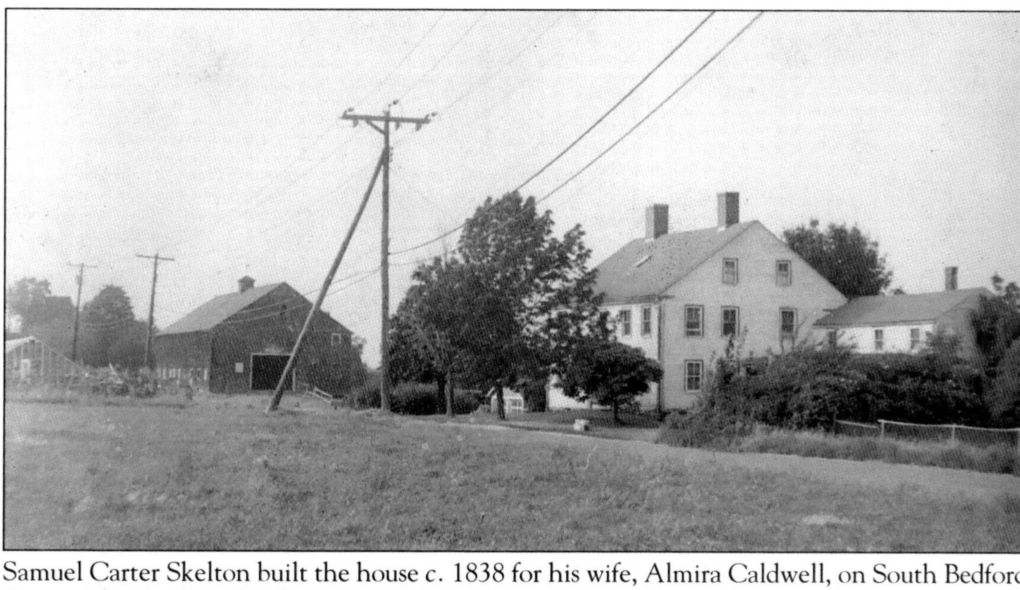

Samuel Carter Skelton built the house *c.* 1838 for his wife, Almira Caldwell, on South Bedford Street. The Graham brothers owned the property in the early 20th century, and it prospered as a market garden until the building of Route 128 split it apart in the late 1940s. A plan was hotly debated and narrowly defeated in the 1940s to develop the farm into a dog racing track. The land was sold to industrial firms, and the house was demolished *c.* 1974. (Courtesy of the Burlington Archives, No. 152.)

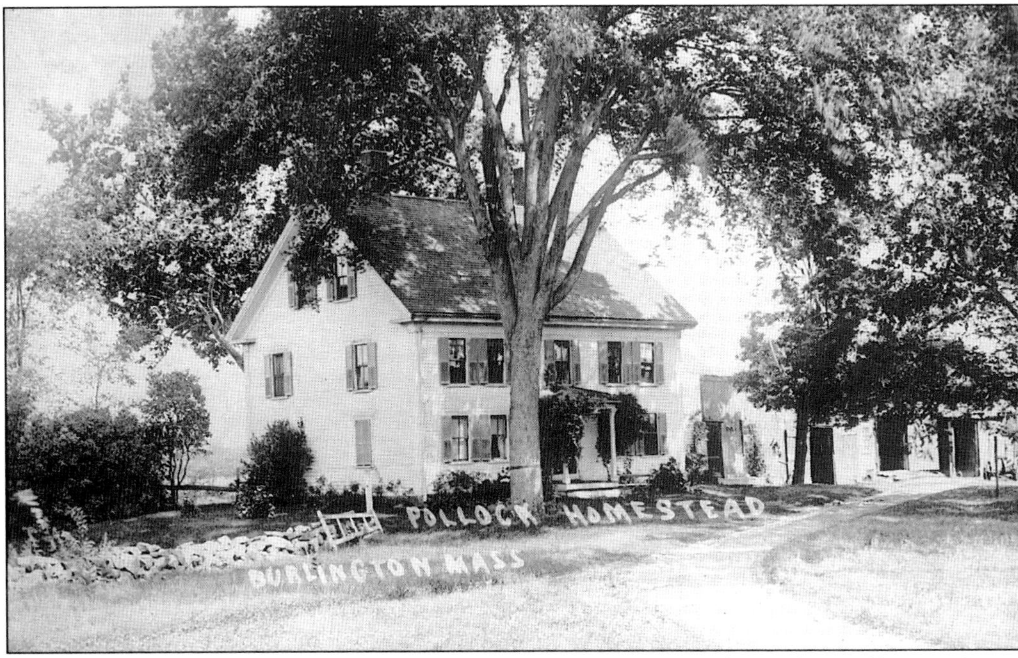

From c. 1885 to 1945, the homestead of John Pollack was located on a lane off Winn Street, as this c. 1915 photograph shows. The house was saved from demolition by Francis Sylvester, a former owner, when he had the house moved to 10½ Florence Street sometime after 1947. (Courtesy of the Burlington Archives, No. 174.)

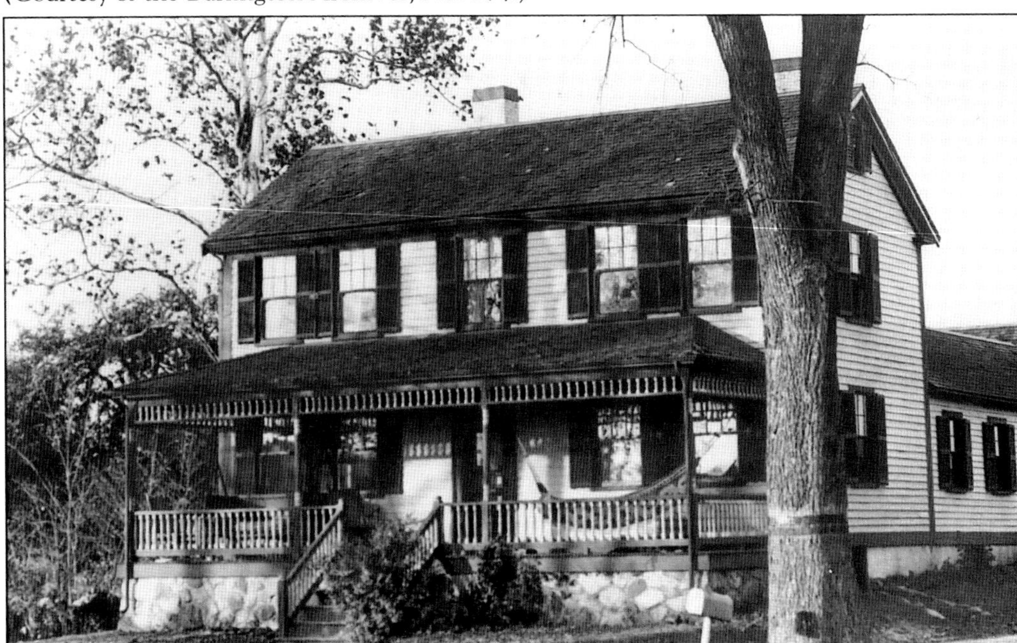

Once the home of William Edward Carter (who operated a heel factory on Cambridge Street), it was also the home of Addie Blodgett. The house was built prior to 1851 by Albert Wood. The Blodgett house was located on the corner of Sears and Center Streets where the Colonial Building now stands. (Courtesy of the Burlington Archives, No. 175.)

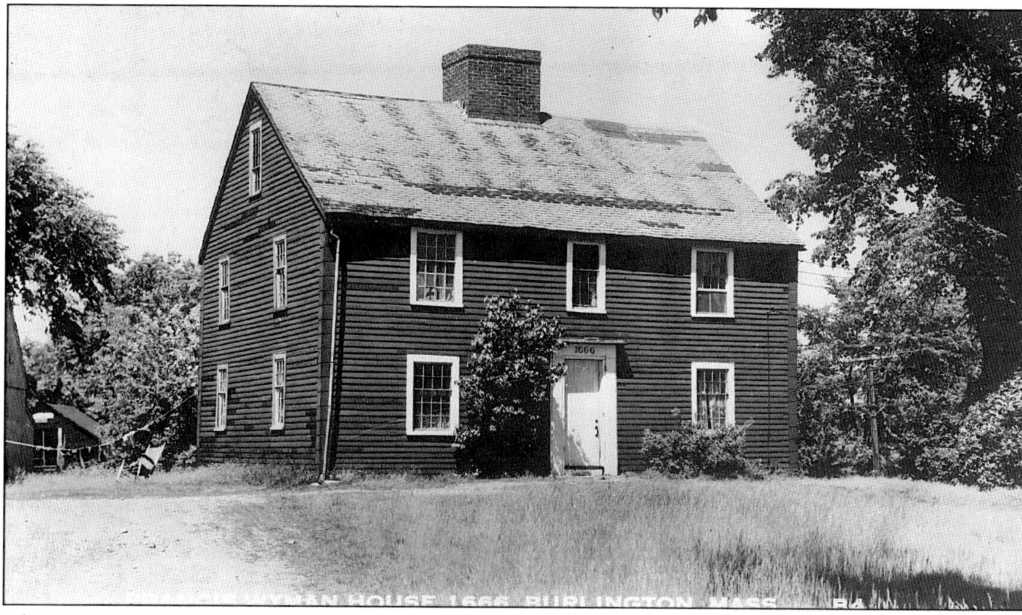

The Francis Wyman House, dating to 1666, has long been considered Burlington's oldest house. In November 1996, a tragic fire destroyed much of the interior, but the structural foundations remained intact. As a result of a professional architectural study, it was concluded that the structural evidence supports a building style more typical of 1730 than 1666. The current restoration is an early Georgian style built on a foundation that may date to 1666. (Courtesy of the Burlington Archives, No. 390.)

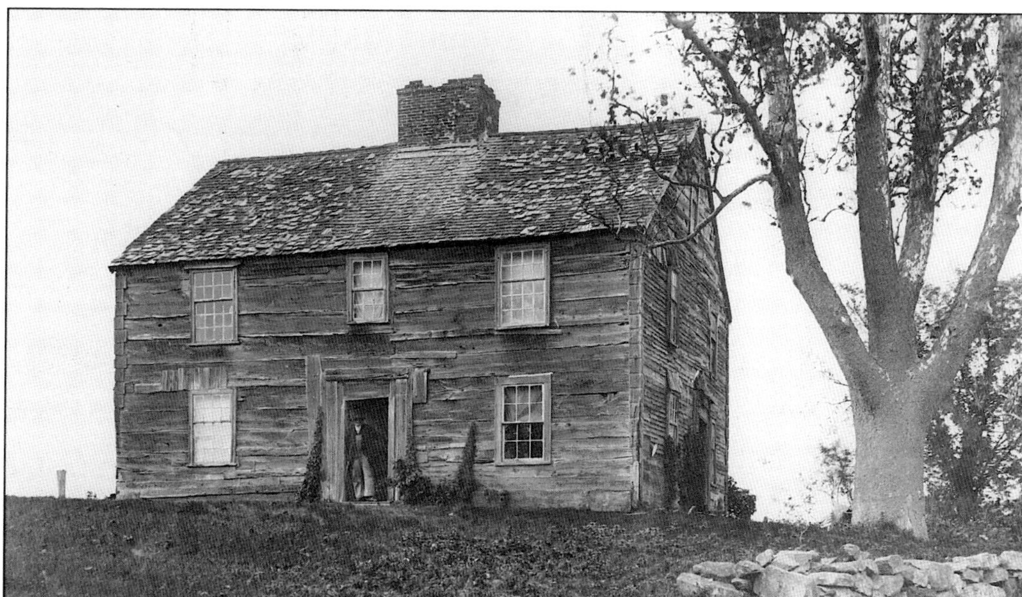

Joshua Reed stands in the doorway of the Francis Wyman House *c.* 1897. Joshua Reed and his family occupied the house from 1823 to 1899, when it was acquired by the Wyman descendants. Once thought to be built in 1665 and 1666, more recent evidence indicates that date to be *c.* 1730, still making it one of oldest houses in Burlington. (Courtesy of the Burlington Archives, No. 53.)

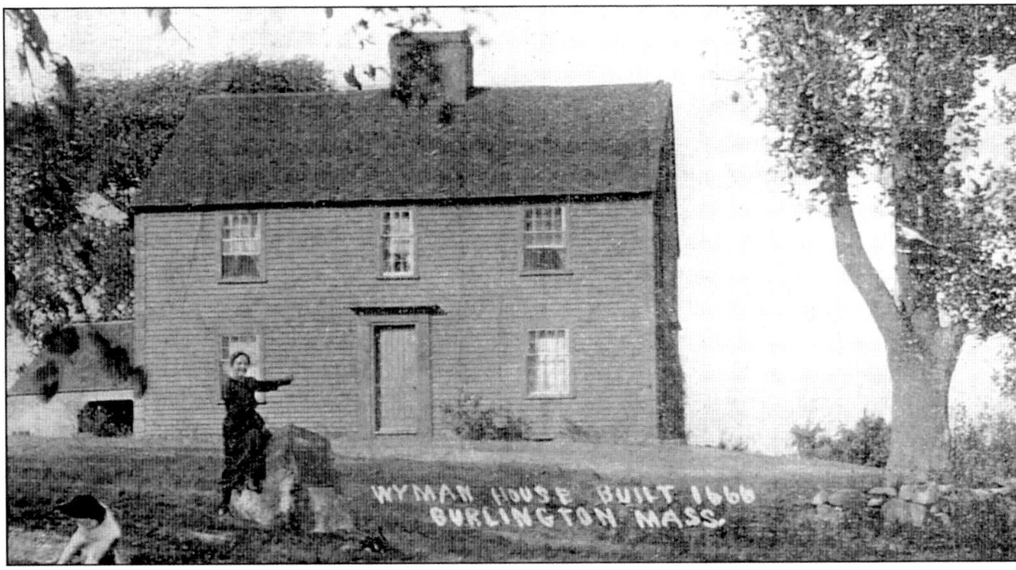

The Francis Wyman House is owned by the Francis Wyman Association, an organization of Wyman family members who trace their ancestry to brothers Francis and John Wyman, early settlers of Woburn. (Courtesy of the Burlington Archives, No. 362.)

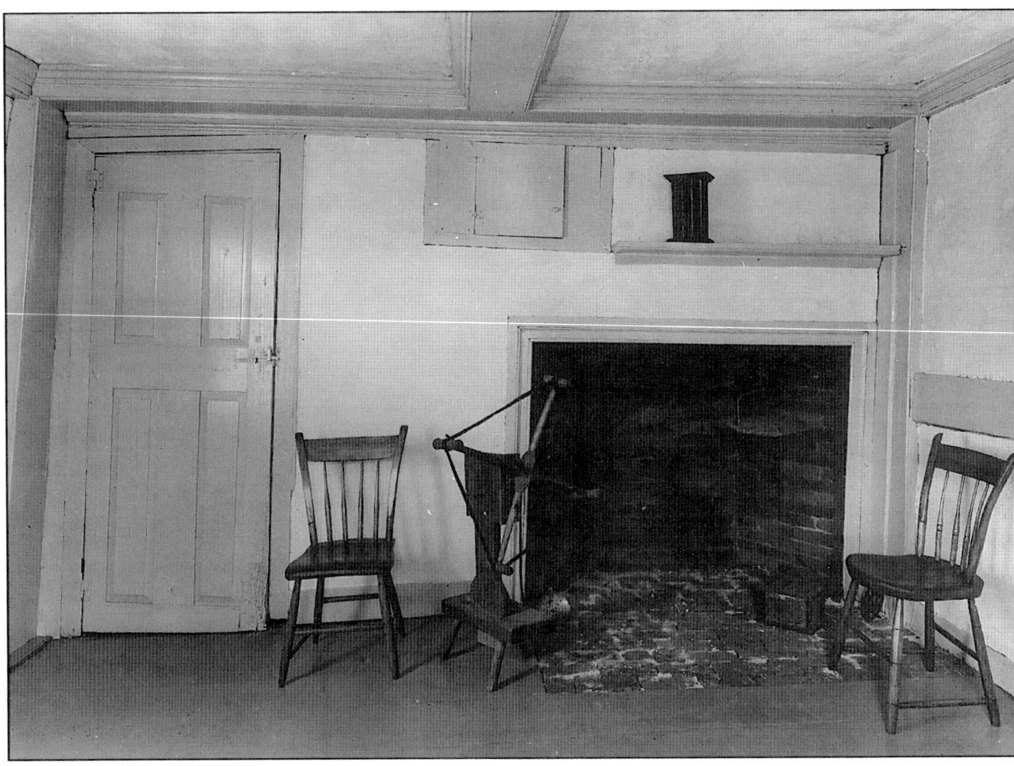

This 1936 view shows one of the eight fireplaces in the Francis Wyman House. The house was used by multiple generations of Wymans and Reeds as a solid farmhouse for rearing a family. The interior was upgraded and modernized *c.* 1795, when Federal-style features were added. (Courtesy of the Burlington Archives, No. 54.)

Shown is the early Georgian front stairway of the Francis Wyman House before the November 1996 fire, which gutted most of the interior original paneling. The first Francis Wyman House was built by brothers Francis and John Wyman in 1665 and 1666 on the foundation of the current 1730s structure. Francis and his brother John emigrated to America from West Mill, England, in 1640 and became farmers and tanners in the Colonial outpost known as Woburn. Both built farmhouses in the garrison style in the northern part of Woburn that would become the town of Burlington by 1799. (Courtesy of the Burlington Archives, No. 398.)

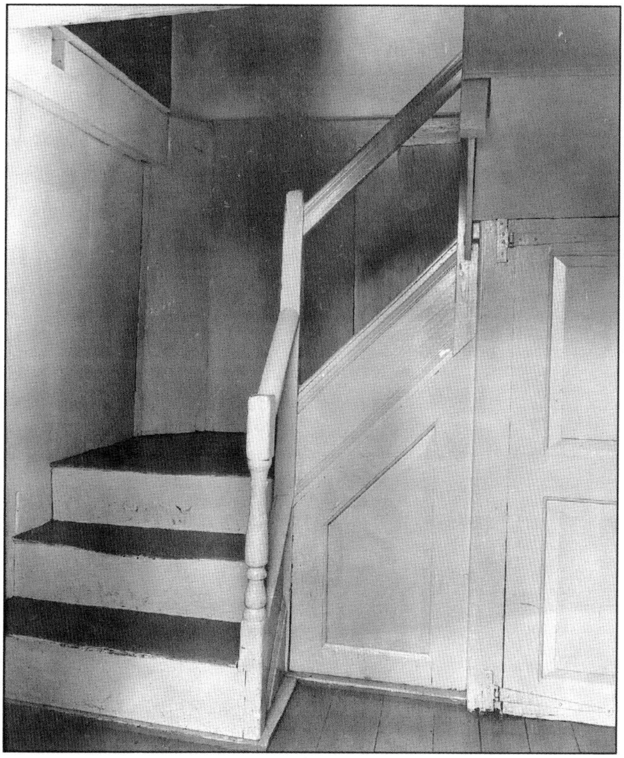

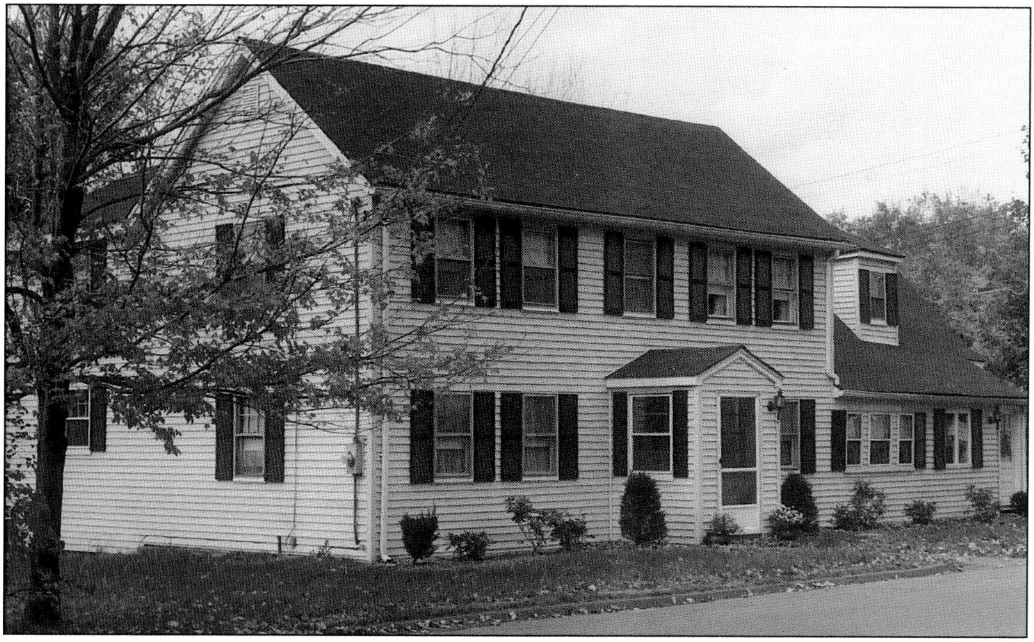

Local tradition maintains that the house at 114 Lexington Street was built for the Converse family and the house at 116 Lexington Street was built for the John Radford family. There is still much debate as to the exact building dates of the houses. Town historian Ed Fogelberg believes the two houses may have once been connected. (Courtesy of the Burlington Archives, No. 173.)

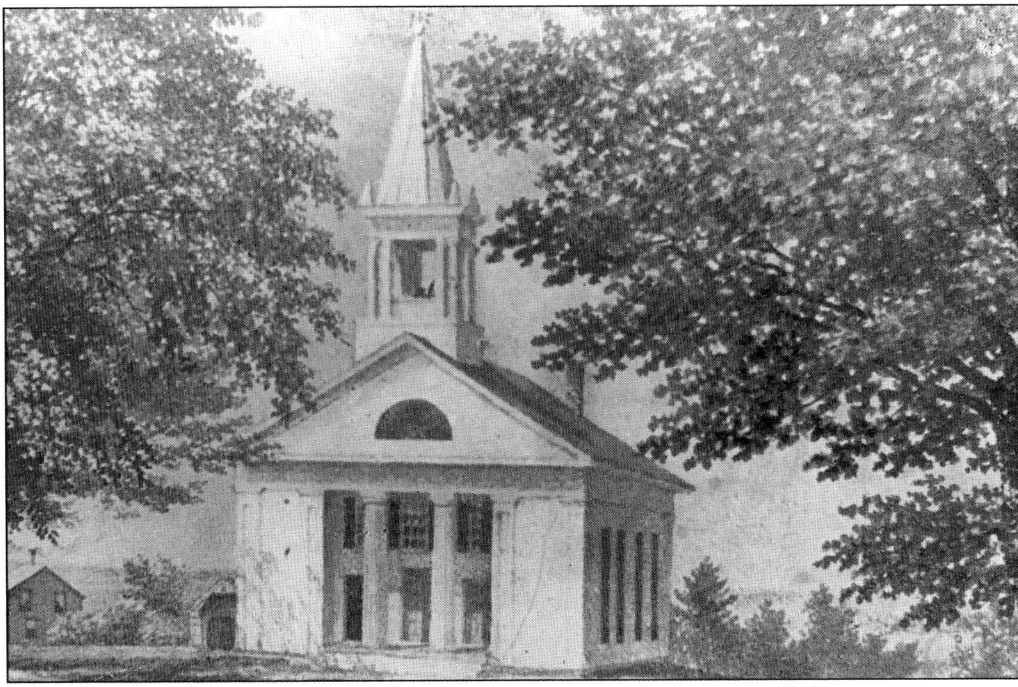

James Franklin Gilman was an itinerant Wilmington artist who painted this *c.* 1872 scene of the Church of Christ's Meeting House (today's United Church of Christ Congregational). This is how the Colonial meetinghouse looked in its Greek Revival phase (1846 to 1888). In 1888, major renovations were done—the steeple and columns were removed and a bell tower was added. This image reflects the building's stature as Burlington's best surviving example of an 1840s Greek Revival Colonial landmark. (Courtesy of the Burlington Archives, No. 432.)

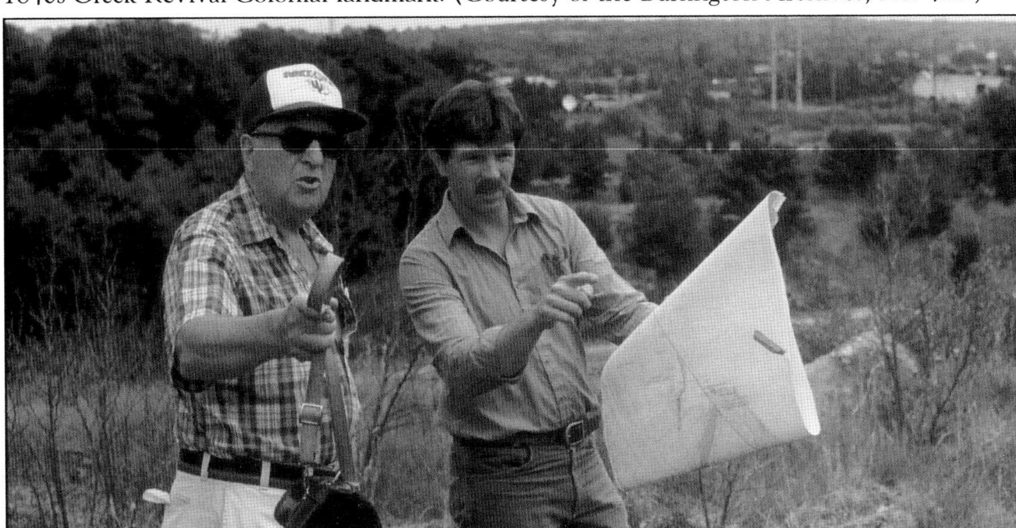

In this scene, town historian Ed Fogelberg (left) and town engineer Al Nelson map the Cummings property, a 99-acre tract near Northeastern University. Fogelberg was born in Boston on June 29, 1910, and moved to Burlington in 1923. For nearly 50 years, he served the town in many capacities, but one of his greatest contributions is recording the town's rich past in his book *Burlington: Part of a Greater Chronicle*. (Courtesy of the Burlington Archives.)